Proverbs

The command of faith given - now she
is a need for - other leaders to be Raised
3K People - only 11 leaders -

P - Prohib

THE CROSSWAY CLASSIC COMMENTARIES

Proverbs

by
Charles Bridges

Series Editors
Alister McGrath and J. I. Packer

CROSSWAY BOOKS
WHEATON, ILLINOIS • NOTTINGHAM, ENGLAND

Proverbs

Copyright © 2001 by Watermark

Published by Crossway Books
        a publishing ministry of Good News Publishers
        1300 Crescent Street
        Wheaton, Illinois 60187

First printing, 2001

Printed in the United States of America

Library of Congress Cataloging-in-Publication Data
Bridges, Charles, 1794-1869.
    Proverbs / by Charles Bridges.
        p.   cm. — (The Crossway classic commentaries)
    ISBN 13: 978-1-58134-300-7 (trade pbk. : alk. paper)
    ISBN 10: 1-58134-300-0
    1. Bible. O.T. Proverbs—Commentaries. I. Title. II. Series.
BS1465.53 .B75   2001
223'.7077—dc21   2001003931

VP		18	17	16	15	14	13	12	11	10	09	08
17	16	15	14	13	12	11	10	9	8	7	6	5	4

First British edition 2001

Production and Printing in the United States of America for
CROSSWAY BOOKS
Norton Street, Nottingham, England NG7 3HR

ISBN 1-85684-210-X

Contents

Series Preface

The purpose of the Crossway Classic Commentaries is to make some of the most valuable commentaries on the books of the Bible, by some of the greatest Bible teachers and theologians in the last 500 years, available to a new generation. These books will help today's readers learn truth, wisdom, and devotion from such authors as J. C. Ryle, Martin Luther, John Calvin, J. B. Lightfoot, John Owen, Charles Spurgeon, Charles Hodge, and Matthew Henry.

We do not apologize for the age of some of the items chosen. In the realm of practical exposition promoting godliness, the old is often better than the new. Spiritual vision and authority, based on an accurate handling of the biblical text, are the qualities that have been primarily sought in deciding what to include.

So far as is possible, everything is tailored to the needs and enrichment of thoughtful readers—lay Christians, students, and those in the ministry. The originals, some of which were written at a high technical level, have been abridged as needed, simplified stylistically, and unburdened of foreign words. However, the intention of this series is never to change any thoughts of the original authors, but to faithfully convey them in an understandable fashion.

The publishers are grateful to Dr. Alister McGrath of Wycliffe Hall, Oxford, Dr. J. I. Packer of Regent College, Vancouver, and Watermark of Norfolk, England, for the work of selecting and editing that now brings this project to fruition.

THE PUBLISHERS
Crossway Books
Wheaton, Illinois

Introduction

Thomas Scott, the brilliant ex-unitarian brought to evangelical faith by John Newton, wrote a multivolume exposition of the whole Bible that achieved great popularity in the early years of the nineteenth century. In the preface to his treatment of Proverbs he declared: "It would be very useful for those who can command their time at some stated season every day to read and deliberately consider a few of those maxims, with reference to their own conduct in the various affairs in which they are concerned." Billy Graham, whose habit has been to read a chapter from Proverbs daily, would no doubt agree; as did Charles Bridges, who quoted Scott's words with approval toward the close of his own preface to the present exposition. In our day, as in his, many professed Christians never look at Proverbs, and many more find reading the book a dreary duty, boring them to tears and, as far as they can see, not benefiting them at all. But that is something that this classic commentary can help change.

Who was Charles Bridges? The nephew of Nathaniel Bridges, who in his day was known as the most learned and influential evangelical minister in the Oxford area, Charles spent his working life as a country clergyman of the Church of England. Born in 1794 and ordained in 1817, he died in 1869. As vicar of Melcombe Regis and Hinton Martell, where he served for the last twenty years of his life, he was an influential member of the Dorset Clerical Society who greatly impressed the young Handley Moule, later a Cambridge don, principal of Ridley Hall, and Bishop of Durham. Like his uncle, Charles was a scholar, and like Scott he was a clear, easy-flowing writer. His 1829 treatise *The Christian Ministry* became a standard work, going through eight editions in twenty-five years, and this major exposition of Proverbs, published in 1846, reached its fourth edition in 1859.

Bridges lived at a time when learned evangelical clergy, self-taught in theology for the most part, were constantly expounding from the Bible the roots and fruits of true piety; his work on Proverbs should be seen as a contribution to this endeavor. Of himself he says that, having in a major exposition of Psalm 119 "shown at large Christian experience to be built upon the doctrines of the Gospel," he wished to exhibit Christian practice as resting on this same foundation. He interprets Proverbs *canonically*—that is, as an organic part of the Bible as a whole, the "word of Christ" as he calls it—and *evangelically*—that is, as assuming the change of heart through the Holy Spirit's regenerating action about which evangelical theology is explicit—and *practically*—that is, as a guide to wise and godly behavior in all human relationships. And he sees Proverbs as enforcing the truth that "Holiness is happiness. It is not indeed the mirth of the fool or the gaiety of the thoughtless. But it is the only thing that deserves the name of happiness; the only solid, permanent principle of enjoyment." These are the perspectives that give his exposition its special flavor.

I commend it enthusiastically.

J. I. PACKER

Preface
By Charles Bridges

Proverbial teaching is one of the most ancient methods of instruction. It was well suited to the time when books were scarce and philosophy was little understood. The mind, not used to the slow process of reasoning, was more easily engaged by terse sentences that expressed a striking thought in a few words. The wise man himself has given the best definition of these aphoristic maxims. He describes them as "apples of gold in settings of silver" (Proverbs 25:11).

The Book of Proverbs is a mine of divine wisdom. The descriptions of God are holy and reverential. Human nature is observed accurately and in great detail. It commends a way of life that equips people to live a life of good deeds. As Mr. Scott has well remarked, "We will understand the meaning and usefulness of the Book of Proverbs in proportion to our experience of true religion, our acquaintance with our own hearts and with human nature, and the extent and accuracy of our observation of the character and deeds of men." Eusebius states that in the Book of Proverbs is found "wisdom fraught with every kind of virtue."

I have divided the Book of Proverbs into three sections. The first part is 1:1—9:18. It is, as Dr. Good observes, "chiefly confined to the conduct of early life." Wisdom is likened to a tree of life, yielding refreshing shade and delicious fruit.

The second part is 10:1—24:34. The style and content of part 2 is quite different from that of part 1. It is clearly meant for those who are now mature in years. These proverbs enforce a moral principle in a few words that can be easily learned and so remembered. They use a variety of styles. Sometimes the style is very straightforward (10:19; 16:3; 22:2). Sometimes the style is very lofty (15:11; 21:16, 22). Sometimes the style is enigmatic (16:24; 17:8; 18:20). Sometimes the proverbs contain an antithesis (14:10; 16:16; 17:10; 18:4; 19:12; 20:14).

The third part is 25:1—31:31. Chapters 25—29 were written by

Solomon and edited some centuries later by the royal scribes in the reign of Hezekiah. The last two chapters were written by different people and preserved by divine care and are most worthy of being part of the inspired canon of Scripture.

The date of the writing of this book is uncertain. We cannot doubt that part of it is from the 3,000 proverbs of Solomon (1 Kings 4:32) before his most lamentable fall. Christian ministers should note that Solomon, no less than St. Paul, teaches us that preaching to others will not save our own souls.

The book should be interpreted with great care. As the principles set out in the Old Testament and the New Testament are essentially the same, it seems reasonable to expound the more obscure by the more clear. The primary duty of the expositor is to attach to each proverb its own literal and precise meaning. This is undoubtedly its spiritual meaning—that is, the mind of the Spirit. Judgment, and not imagination, must then be used to interpret the proverb. Where just the literal meaning is meant, it is not right to search out some new spiritual meaning, but rather to draw practical instruction from its obvious sense.

There is, however, a distinction to be made between exposition and illustration. The figures of speech used in the Book of Proverbs, *after their literal meaning has been stated*, may fairly be used to illustrate other truths that are not specifically mentioned. The sacred writers appear to endorse this, although it requires careful thought so that it does not twist the meaning of Scripture or identify us with those people whom Dr. South says "can draw anything out of anything."

Even with taking great care to give a sound interpretation, we must not forget that the Book of Proverbs is part of the book that is entitled "the word of Christ" (Colossians 3:16). This title is such an accurate description of the Book of Proverbs that its study brings the whole subject of the book before us. It encourages us to search the Old Testament (John 5:39), which is the key to open the divine treasure-house. As Mr. Cecil has observed, "If we do not see the golden thread through all the Bible, marking out Christ, we read the Scripture without the Key." As Augustine said, "The Old Testament has no true relish if Christ is not understood in it." These remarks, however, do not undervalue its large amount of historical and practical instruction. But, unquestionably, Christ is the Sun of the whole Scripture, and in his light we see light (Psalm 36:9). This light gives life throughout the Christian's experience. There is, therefore, as Professor Franke reminds us, "much joy, comfort, and delight to be found in the Old Testament (especially in reading those places that before were wearisome and almost irksome) when we perceive Christ is so sweetly pictured there."

It has been recorded of Mary Jane Graham, "She was delighted in the course of her study of the Book of Proverbs to have Christ so much and so frequently before her mind." We cannot but fear, however, that this part of the sacred book is not generally appreciated as it should be. The question has often been asked, "How can I read the book profitably?" It might seem that the instruction given in 2:1-4 was intended to answer such a question. The first thing to do, which should be done as any page or verse of the Bible is read, is to pray. Begin with prayer. Then link an enquiring mind to a praying heart. Actively seek and search for hidden treasure. The riches do not lie on the surface. You need to search the Scriptures (John 5:39). But how are we to apply the heart so that we understand the Book of Proverbs? We should use whatever study helps we may have at hand. Then when we discover God's words to be our treasure, we are to "eat" this invigorating food, so that it becomes the joy of our hearts (see Jeremiah 15:16).

An accurate apprehension of the main purpose and scope of this book will greatly facilitate its understanding. The purpose of the Book of Proverbs appears to be to give teaching about practical life. The true man of God will honor practical inculcation no less than doctrinal teaching. The truth that is in Jesus, in which we are taught by him, is practical truth (Ephesians 4:20-24). While other parts of Scripture show us the glory of our high calling, the Book of Proverbs instructs us in detail how we should walk so that we are worthy of this calling. We look into the Book of Proverbs as if we were using a microscope and view all the minute details of our Christian walk. There is not a mood, a look, a word, a movement, the tiniest duty in which we do not either deface or adorn the image of our Lord and witness to him. Even if the book served no other purpose, it would humble even the most consistent servant of God, making him aware of countless failures. Not only is the last chapter, as Matthew Henry says, "a looking-glass for ladies," but the whole book is a mirror for us all.

It is not just a mirror that reveals our defects. It is also a guidebook for godly living. The details about how to behave in many diverse spheres are given or implied most accurately and with a profound knowledge of the human heart. As Lord Bacon has commented, "Beside a code of laws directly religious, a variety of admirable rules streams forth from the deep recesses of wisdom and spreads over the whole field." All types and classes of people are spoken to here. The monarch is given divine wisdom (8:15-16). The principles of national prosperity and decay are set out (11:14; 14:34). The rich are warned about their besetting temptations (18:11; 23:4-5; 28:20, 22). The poor are comforted in their worldly humiliation (15:16-17; 17:1; 19:1, 22). Wise rules are given about self-discipline (4:23-37; 16:32). All this varied instruction is based on the principles of true godliness (31:10, 30). So, if the Psalms bring a glow to the heart, the Book of Proverbs makes the face shine. This book should be considered as a valuable Rule of Faith. As Mr. Scott observes, "It would be very useful for those who can command their time at some stated season every day to read and deliberately consider a few of those maxims, with reference to their own conduct in the various affairs in which they are concerned." Without doubt, if the world was governed by all of the wisdom of this one book, it would be a new earth in which righteousness lives.

The distinctive characteristic of the Book of Proverbs is that it is *a book for the young*. The answer to the question, "How can a young man keep his way pure?" is fully answered in the Book of Proverbs—"By living according to your [God's] word" (Psalm 119:9). The Book of Proverbs specifically states that it was written so that young people would learn from it (Proverbs 1:4; 4:1). It takes them, as it were, by the hand and warns them of impending dangers and imminent temptations and points them to God's ways through the most engaging motives. It was never more relevant than it is today. Our young people are growing up during a time when the foundations of the earth are being shaken, and when their hearts are being poisoned and perverted. Nothing is more important than to provide them with sound principles. What this priceless book impresses on their minds is the importance of basic principles in the heart—the value of self-discipline and the habit of bringing everything under the Word of God. It also teaches its readers to compare worldly and heavenly advice and to opt for the everlasting good in preference to the toys of earth. This practical godliness sheds a smile over a world of sorrow, is comforting sunlight in suffering, and always points to the principles of peace and perseverance (Psalm 119:165).

I conclude with the words of Geier, one of the most helpful expositors: "If there should be anything here to please the reader, ascribe not the writing to the pen, but to the writer; not the light to the lamp, but to the fountain [containing the oil]; not the picture to the pencil, but to the painter; not the gift to the unfaithful dispenser, but to God the bountiful Giver."

Charles Bridges
Old Newton Vicarage
October 7, 1846

Proverbs
Chapter 1

1-4. The proverbs of Solomon son of David, king of Israel. The book opens with a brief account about its author. **Solomon** is said to be the wisest of men. He is a wise man because he is a man of prayer (1 Kings 3:12; compare Proverbs 2:1-9). His exceptional wisdom was admired throughout the world (1 Kings 3:28; 4:34). He would have been respected if he had been the son of Jeroboam, but he was held in much higher honor because he was the **son of David,** whose godly prayers (Psalm 72:1) and counsels (Proverbs 4:1-4; 1 Kings 2:1-4; 1 Chronicles 28:9) would have shaped him. If the sayings of a king are kept, even if they have no intrinsic value, the wise sayings of the **king of Israel** (Ecclesiastes 1:1; 12:9-10) should attract our special interest.

As valuable as Solomon's proverbs were for their own wisdom, as they excelled the wisdom of the sages of his day or any other time (1 Kings 4:29-31), they claim our attention for a much greater reason. For a greater than Solomon is here (Matthew 12:42). Often wisdom is personified (Proverbs 1:20; 8:1-36; 9:1-18), and it is always inspired (2 Timothy 3:16) by God's wisdom; so it is true that the lips of this king **speak as an oracle** (Proverbs 16:10).

2. For attaining wisdom and discipline; for understanding words of insight. The purpose of this priceless book is not to teach secular or political wisdom, although many examples of each are included (6:1-11; 27:23-27), but the knowledge of God (1:7) that makes us wise about salvation and enables us to live godly lives (2 Timothy 3:15-17; Titus 2:11-12). Wisdom's stunning privileges are set out (3:13-18). It is emphasized strongly that this is the principal thing; it is our very life (4:5-9, 13).

3. We are directed to acquire **a disciplined and prudent life,** as a complete rule of **doing what is right and just and fair.** These include sound principles and their practical application in our lives.

4. Here also **the simple,** so readily deluded (14:15; Ezekiel 14:20), learn

15

about **prudence,** which is so necessary in order to discriminate between truth and error (1 Thessalonians 5:21) and to guard against false teachers (Psalm 17:4; 1 John 4:1). It is especially **the young** who are directed to this book, as their undisciplined ardor is wasted, and their minds are at the mercy of the opinions of the world all around them. They are in great need of some settled guiding principles for their lives. Here they find **knowledge and discretion,** which is a religion not of imagination, impulse, or sentiment, but the sound practical energy of scriptural truth.

5. Let the wise listen and add to their learning, and let the discerning get guidance. As well as the **simple** and the **young, the wise** gain instruction here. For a truly **wise** man is not a person who has attained everything, but one who knows that he has not attained and is pressing on to perfection (Philippians 3:12). David, while aware of many attainments, always sought after higher light (Psalm 119:98-100). Indeed, the most abundant stores would soon run down if they were not constantly replenished.

Listening is the way to acquire knowledge. **Let the wise listen.** Jethro instructed Moses (Exodus 18:17-26), our Lord his disciples (Matthew 13:11-16; John 16:12-13). Peter instructed his fellow apostles (Acts 11:2-18). Priscilla and Aquila explained to Apollos "the way of God more accurately" (Acts 18:24-26). Indeed, we must be listeners if we want to be teachers. As Bishop Hall once wrote, "He gathers who listens; he spends who teaches. If we spend before we gather, we will soon become bankrupt." The more we learn, the more we feel we need to learn, and the more willing we are to **listen and add to [our] learning** (compare 9:9; 18:15). ℞' ℞

6. The wise man himself expounded his **sayings and riddles of the wise** to the delight and instruction of his royal pupil (1 Kings 10:1-5). So to the teachable listener the deep things of God will be revealed (1 Corinthians 2:9-10). Hence the value of the minister of God who is the divinely appointed means to build up our faith (Ephesians 4:11-15; 1 Thessalonians 3:10). The church might have been spared many heresies if men had not followed unsound judgments but instead had honored God's messengers and humbly sought instruction from him (Malachi 2:7).

7. But fools despise wisdom and discipline. Solomon's preface has stated the purpose of this book of wisdom. The book itself now opens with a noble sentence. "There is not," as Bishop Patrick observes, "such a wise instruction to be found in all their books [speaking of books of non-Christians] as the very first of all in Solomon's, which he lays as the ground of all wisdom."

The fear of the LORD is the beginning of knowledge. Job had said this previously (Job 28:28). So had the wise man's father (Psalm 111:10). This saying is so weighty that Solomon repeats it (9:10). All man's happiness, all his duty, is dependent on his having reverence for God (Ecclesiastes 12:13). So as Solomon starts to instruct us from God's mouth he begins at the **beginning,** with the principal matter. All heathen wisdom is but foolishness. Of all **knowledge**, knowledge of God is the basic principle. There is no genuine knowledge without godliness.

But what is **the fear of the LORD**? It is that affectionate reverence by which the child of God bends himself humbly and carefully to his Father's law. God's wrath is so bitter and his love so sweet that we have this earnest desire to please him and to fear him, so that we will not sin against him (Hebrews 12:28-29).

Why do so many despise **wisdom** and instruction? Because **the beginning of wisdom, the fear of the LORD,** is not set before them (Psalm 36:1). They are unaware of its value. They scorn its directions. They are only wise in their own eyes. They are rightly called fools who despise such blessings. *Good Lord, may childlike fear of you be my wisdom, my security, my happiness!*

8. Listen, my son, to your father's instruction and do not forsake your mother's teaching. The young must note that **the fear of the LORD** is linked with respecting parents. God speaks here through the mouth of a parent or teacher, blending paternal tenderness with his divine authority—**my son**. The command supposes the godly character of parents and recognizes the responsibility of *both* parents. Children are rational creatures. **Instruction**, not blind submission, must be inculcated. **Listen . . . do not forsake.** Timothy was brought up to respect his mother's teaching (2 Timothy 1:5; 3:14-15).

The same reciprocal obligation binds the spiritual father to his children. Such was the apostolic ministry to the churches of Philippi and Thessalonica. Humility, tenderness, fellowship, and willing submission formed the basis of Christian love and happiness (Philippians 4:9-19; 1 Thessalonians 2:7-13).

10. Almost as soon as Satan became an apostate, he became a tempter. And he is very successful in training his servants in this work (16:29; Genesis 11:4; Numbers 31:16; Isaiah 56:12). **If sinners entice you.** This is no uncertain contingency. **Do not give in to them.** Giving in constitutes the sin. Eve consented before she picked the fruit. David gave in before he sinned (2 Samuel 11:2-4). But Joseph resisted and was saved. When you are tempted, do not blame God, or even the devil. The worst the devil can do is to tempt us; he cannot force us to sin. When he has presented his most subtle arguments, we choose to **give in** or to resist.

11. The invitation seemed harmless enough: **"Come along with us."**

14. But the demand to engage in action soon follows: **"Throw in your lot with us."** The sensitive conscience becomes more compliant every time it gives in. Who can stop himself once he starts on this downhill path? One sin makes way for another. David committed murder to hide his adultery (2 Samuel 11:4, 17, 25). The only safe course of action is to flee temptation. There is not one sin that the best of God's saints will not commit if they trust in themselves (Romans 11:20).

18-19. The sight of danger leads to the avoidance of danger. Instinct directs the bird, reason the man. Yet man is so infatuated with sin that in his pride he will not do what the bird does by instinct. She flies away from the net that she has seen being spread out, but man rushes into it. **These men** sought to kill others but ended up **waylay[ing] only themselves**.

20-21. A father's instruction has warned us against the enticement of Satan. **Wisdom**, the Son of God himself, now appeals to us in all the fullness of his divine authority and grace. Full of deep love for sinners, he **calls aloud**. Not in the temple, but **in the street, she raises her voice in the public squares; at the head of the noisy streets she cries out, in the gateways of the city she makes her speech.**

22. A **simple** person is another name for a foolish person. It describes those who do not fear God. They do not weigh what they say or do. They live as if there is no God and no eternity. Their minds are blinded by their love for sin. In other instances man delights not in his ignorance, but in its removal. But these **simple ones**, ignorant of the value and danger of their souls, **love [their] simple ways**. They think of all attempts to enlighten them as an intrusion on their indulgent rest. While they live wild, profligate, and lazy lives, they forget that God remembers their wickedness and that they will be judged (Hosea 7:2; Ecclesiastes 11:9).

They are encouraged by some who are even worse than themselves, **mockers**. Such people are shameless and take an active **delight in mockery**. They aim their poisoned arrows at godliness (Psalm 64:3-4). They regard any serious interest in religion as a weakness that is not worthy of any sensible person. They hate the words of Scripture. A saint in Scripture means one who is sanctified by God's Spirit. But to them it means a foolish person and a hypocrite. They are too proud to stoop to the thoughts of the Gospel of Christ. In this way the **simple ones** and those who mock show that they **hate knowledge**. In their attempt to protect themselves from anything that might alarm them, these people shut out everything that would make them wise and happy. In their lost condition they **hate knowledge** and so exclude anything that would teach them about salvation. Their minds are so preoccupied with other things that they hate the light and will not come to the light (John 3:19-20).

23. We are often told that all the illumination that is to be expected in our day is the written Word, interpreted, like any other book, by our own reason, and that the teaching of the Spirit is an enthusiastic delusion. This may be true of the simple ones and those who mock, as they are ignorant of the blindness of their own hearts and the power of natural prejudice, which divine grace alone can conquer. But the person who is aware of his own darkness and knows that nothing other than God's power can teach him must turn his ear to wisdom (2:3). This is not because the Word is dark, since it is light itself, but because *he* is dark and thus totally unable to receive instructions (1 Corinthians 2:9-14). Such people do not respond to

God's **rebuke** and so fail to benefit from all he offers them. They refuse to listen, and that is why God says, **I would have poured out my heart to you and made my thoughts known to you.**

24. When I called. The Savior calls by his Word, his providence, his ministers, and through the conscience. But they **rejected** God. God does not issue his warnings until his calls have been rejected. As such rich and free grace is rejected, who can calculate the guilt? In addition to this, all creatures are God's servants (Psalm 119:91). Man alone resists God's yoke. God **stretched** his **hand** (Isaiah 55:2) to offer his help, to confer his blessing, and even to draw our attention to his call. But we **rejected** him.

25. God's wisest **advice** was **ignored.** But, sinner, the day will come when the one who yearned and prayed and wept and died will have no pity on you (Ezekiel 5:11; 8:18).

26. On that day it will be as if he laughed **at your disaster.** He says, **I will mock when calamity overtakes you.** God will then delight in exercising his sovereign justice over you.

27. Then **calamity overtakes you like a storm.** You will be in utter despair **when disaster sweeps over you like a whirlwind, when distress and trouble overwhelm you.**

28. This is God's solemn declaration. As if he could tolerate these people who mock no longer, he says that when he called they ignored him, and now **"they will call to me but I will not answer."** That is, "They would not listen to my voice; now I will not listen to their cries." As Bishop Reynolds has put it, "The last judgment before the very last of all is come—the very outward court or portal of hell." This is the misery of deserted souls. It is dreadful to be deserted by God at any time (Hosea 9:12), but how much more in the day of trouble (1 Samuel 28:15). To have his face not only turned from us but turned against us, to have his eternal frown instead of his smile—this will be hell instead of heaven.

29. Does this measureless wrath seem to be inconsistent with a God of love? But God is a consuming fire (Deuteronomy 4:24). Think about God's **knowledge.** Instead of it being a delight, they **hated** it **and did not choose to fear the LORD.**

30. None of God's **advice** was accepted. All his rebukes were **spurned.**

31. Is it not just that sinners following their own choices should **eat the fruit of their ways and be filled with the fruit of their schemes?** The moral elements of sin constitute a hell in themselves, apart from the material fire. As Chambers has remarked, "The fruit of sin in time, when arrived at full and finished maturity, is justly the fruit of sin through eternity. It is merely the sinner reaping what he has sown. It makes no violent or desultory step from the other, as does the fruit from the flower. It is simply that the sinners 'will eat the fruit of their ways and be filled with the fruit of their schemes.'"

This picture may seem to speak of despair. But we have experienced miracles of divine grace, so that we do not need to despair. We must not, however, water down God's own words. Have we never seen this demonstrated as a sinner dies? He neglected and scoffed at the Gospel, and as he dies, he does not offer up one cry for God to have mercy on his soul. Does this not give us a solemn warning that limits are placed on the day of God's grace? There is a knock that will be the last knock. It is possible for a sinner to be lost on this side of hell. He may be pleaded with and wept over but lost! See Hebrews 10:26-27, 29, 31.

32. The reason for the sinner's ruin is placed again at his own door. He is wayward since he turns away from wisdom's beckoning voice. He despises the only cure. He dies like someone who has committed suicide. He will ignore anything that anyone says to him. Remember that every time we deliberately neglect God, we take a step closer to apostasy. God's Word gradually becomes a burden, and then we scorn it. **Fools** may seem to be spared judgment, but his **complacency . . . will destroy** them.

33. We close with the sunshine of God's promise: **"But whoever listens to me will live in safety and be at ease, without fear of harm."** Are you, reader, like God's own child, listening to him? Then you are protected by him, and no evil can reach you. You **live in safety**. You are assured that you will be kept safe. You will not even have the **fear of harm** attacking you. You will be like Noah in his ark, who was clearly being kept safe while the whole world around him was perishing. In the same way David was fearless in the moment of imminent danger because he knew that God was his refuge. The day of darkness will be to you the same as sunshine as you enter into everlasting joy (Malachi 4:1-2; Luke 21:28; 2 Peter 3:10-13).

Proverbs
Chapter 2

Wisdom, having solemnly warned rebellious scoffers, now instructs her obedient children. The deep question previously asked, "Where can wisdom be found?" is now answered. It is set before us here as **the fear of the LORD** (verse 5). It is seen as the principle of practical godliness (verses 7-9), as preserving us from besetting temptations (verses 10-19), and as a guide into the right and safe path (verse 20). So its pupils are safe (verse 21), but the ungodly who despise it will definitely be ruined (verse 22).

The way to find wisdom is easy. If this way is carefully pondered and faithfully cultivated, it will give the key to understanding the whole of the Word of God.

1. Accept my words. They should be received by a good and honest heart (Luke 8:15), a heart that is prepared by God. Read God's Book like the person who sat at Jesus' feet and listened to him speaking (Luke 10:39). Be like the Bereans who were so keen to examine the Scriptures (Acts 17:11).

Store up my commands within you. Carry them around with you as your most prized treasure (Colossians 3:16; Matthew 13:44). Let your heart be the hiding-place for the treasure. Satan can never snatch it from there.

2. *Oh, my God, let it be with me as with your beloved Son. In order that I may be under your grace, listen to me and come to me, so that my soul may live (Isaiah 55:3).*

3. If you call out for insight and cry aloud for understanding. We search for no other inspiration than divine grace to make God's Word clear. Every verse we read and meditate on gives material for prayer. David (Psalm 119:18) and his wise son (1 Kings 3:9-12) sought for this learning on their knees. The most mature Christian will continue to the end of his life to **call out for insight** and for more **understanding.**

4. But prayer must not be a substitute for diligent service. Rather, let it be a spur for it. Think of the miner's indefatigable efforts, his invincible resolution and untiring perseverance. This is the way we should **search** the sacred storehouse. To read instead of searching the Scriptures is to just skim the surface and collect a few superficial ideas. The secret of success in finding **hidden treasure** is to dig the entire field. If we do not find anything, we must dig again. We need to daily search the length and breadth and depth of our fruitful store until we are filled with God's fullness (Ephesians 3:18-19).

This habit of living in the element of Scripture is invaluable. To be filled from this divine treasury, to have large sections of the Word passing through the mind, enables us to grasp it more firmly and apply it to our lives. To benefit fully from this we must feed on our own. We may read the Scriptures with other people, but in order to **search** the Scriptures, we must be alone with God.

The church is harmed if this habit is neglected. All fundamental errors and heresies in the church may be traced to this source (Matthew 12:29). Such errors are usually based on partial or fragmentary statements about the truth. Truth separated from the Word becomes error.

5. But the mind that is prayerfully engaged in searching for divine truth will always discover the two great principles of godliness: **the fear . . . and . . . the knowledge of God.**

6. This search will never end in disappointment. **For the LORD gives wisdom, and from his mouth come knowledge and understanding.** Nobody will search in vain (Job 32:8; Isaiah 48:17; 54:13; James 1:5, 17). Apostasy from the faith has never been linked with prayerful and diligent study of God's Word.

7. Vanity (Ecclesiastes 1:8) and "foolishness" (1 Corinthians 3:19) are hallmarks of the wisdom of this world. But here is wisdom that comes from God. It looks at things as they really are, and not as they appear to be. Bishop Hall has written, "To those who are true and upright in heart the Lord will in his own good time reveal true and saving knowledge, and that sound and spiritual wisdom that will make them eternally happy." Our faithful God is **a shield to those whose walk is blameless.** His wisdom protects us from subtle sophistry that seeks to destroy our treasure.

8. The way of the saints is full of danger and beset with temptation, but it is a safe way. The Lord **guards the course of the just and protects the way of his faithful ones.** God's almighty power **guards** us even when we are at the edge of the enemy's ground.

9. Only the Lord's wisdom can guide our feet into **every good path.** In this way we will be equipped to do good deeds (2 Timothy 3:15-17). The gracious wisdom that saves the soul sanctifies the heart and life (Titus 2:11-12).

10. We have seen the good that wisdom brings us (verse 5). Now observe the evil that it preserves us from. Note where **wisdom** lives, in the

heart. Only here has it any light, life, or power. Clear knowledge floating in the head is deep ignorance. If it only glitters in the understanding, it is dry, speculative, and barren. But should it **enter your heart**, light shines out, and all the affections are engaged. How **pleasant** it is **to your soul**. Religion is then no longer a lifeless idea. It is handled, tasted, enjoyed.

11. Religion now gives **discretion and understanding** and directs all your behavior. It does not just become an external rule; it will **protect** and **guard you**, just as an army guard keeps a monarch safe. Education and high moral principles are at best only partially effective in helping people. External wickedness may be exchanged for decent formality. The foolishness of pride may be resisted, but pride in one of its many other forms may be cherished. In all these examples the principle is left unchanged. The forsaken sin only makes way for a more plausible sin, which is no less deadly a passion. The heart molded by the Gospel is the only protection from attacks that imperceptibly, yet fatally, cut us off from God.

12. The various traps that are set for the young are about to be detailed. This passage furnishes us with a frightening picture of the temptations to which our children are exposed. It should make us cry to God for their deep and complete conversion. We should pray that they may know the Gospel, not only in the conviction of their consciences and in the excitement of their feelings, but in the complete renewal of their hearts before God. This, and nothing less, will keep them safe from the traps that have been laid by their cruel enemy. Every town and village swarms with his servants, who are first of all initiated into the mysteries of his art and then become skilled teachers and instruct others in his evil work. We have been warned about one of his traps in 1:10-14. Another such warning is given here. The character of the tempter is seen from what the writer says. His **words are perverse**. They are like a polluted spring that sends out contaminated streams. How quickly the disease spreads.

13. Such people do not sin in ignorance. They have been trained to **walk in dark ways**. Once they come into contact with wicked men, they become infectious and quickly spread the disease. They are more than ready to **leave the straight paths** that they never really loved and to **walk in dark ways** that they really do love. Poisoned themselves, they now poison everyone around them.

14. They **rejoice**, like Satan himself, **in doing wrong** and so draw their fellow sinners into the net.

15. They revel in following **crooked** and **devious . . . ways**. Thus they fall deeper and deeper into sin as they follow the **crooked** path that leads to eternal ruin. Is this not an accurate picture of many children of godly parents who have been lovingly looked after but who become hardened through the deceitfulness of sin (Hebrews 3:13)? They now deserve to be abandoned by God, whom they have abandoned so callously. Young man, shun such friends. They have become hardened in their devotion to their

master's work. If only misguided sinners could see sin in all its horrid deformity and certain end! But their **devious . . . ways** hide this end from their sight. Satan presents the bait, palliates the sin, closes the eyes, and conceals the definite end of everything—hell. Wicked men cannot, will not, turn back from their **crooked** paths.

16-19. Another trap is here graphically portrayed. As before, wisdom is the most effective deliverer. **The adulteress** (verse 16) is described as one who has **ignored the covenant she made before God** (verse 17). It is little wonder that she therefore uses **seductive words** (verse 16). Her house is in the land of **death** (5:5). Eternal doom waits for her (Galatians 5:19-21; Ephesians 5:5; Revelation 21:8; 22:15). Few people who visit her return, **for her house leads down to death** (verse 18) and **none who go to her return or attain the paths of life**.

20. Wisdom guides us **to the paths of the righteous**. Clothed with this divine armor, you will have the courage Joseph had and will be able to turn your face away from the lure of sin (Genesis 39:9-10).

21. In this way you will be able to **live in the land** as its original inheritor (Psalm 37:9, 11, 22, 29, 34; Matthew 5:5). You will have the best inheritance on earth and an infinitely better inheritance in heaven.

22. The wicked, however, **will be cut off from the land**. They may enjoy the pleasures of sin for a time, but they will ultimately **be torn** from the land and will end up in everlasting ruin (Matthew 3:10).

Can anyone who has read this chapter seriously fail to value the privilege of being enlisted under the banner of the cross from an early age? Parents and teachers, ponder your great responsibility. Never stop praying for special grace and wisdom. Do not gloss over sins. What wisdom is needed to guide, to curb, to develop and improve the minds, energies, and feelings of young people!

Take care, young people. Do not imagine, even for one minute, that God will turn a blind eye on your sinful desires or that he will excuse them as the foibles of youth. Such ropes of sin will bind you for eternity if they are not broken by the power of God's grace. Shun the company of evil people as you would avoid the plague. Keep your distance from them as you would from the pit of destruction. Fill your mind with heavenly wisdom. Cultivate the taste for purer pleasures.

Proverbs
Chapter 3

1. My son, do not forget my teaching, but keep my commands in your heart. This is not given like a stern command. **My son.** It is our Father's voice speaking. This is the endearing persuasiveness of a promise. Having told us to search for wisdom, he now calls us to put this into practice when he says, **do not forget my teaching.** The deliberate forgetfulness of the heart (2:17; Psalm 9:17; 10:4), rather than a lapse of memory, is implied here.

In your heart. As the ark of the covenant was kept in the tabernacle, we must **keep [God's] commands** in our hearts (4:4; Deuteronomy 11:18; Isaiah 51:7).

Indeed, no laws except God's laws bind the heart. All obedience that is acceptable to God starts here. The heart is the first thing that wanders away from God, and it is also the first thing that returns to God. This is a crucial principle (4:23; Romans 6:17 [KJV]). All religion without this is only religion in name. Even if it is practiced in a thousand different ways, it is bound to fail (Isaiah 5:24). Even if you carried out kind deeds every second of the day, if **your heart** is not alive so that it can **keep God's commands,** the following rebuke will ring in your ears: "The multitude of your sacrifices—what are they to me?" (Isaiah 1:11). Delight and perseverance in carrying out God's will flows from God's grace working in our hearts.

2. For they will prolong your life many years and bring you prosperity. We have an obligation laid on us, and we benefit from obeying God. The reward of obeying God from the heart is a long and happy life— the best thing that can happen on earth (Psalm 34:12-13). A **life** prolonged for **many years** is promised to the righteous, and this can apply to earth as well as to heaven, as the Father sees fit.

3. Let love and faithfulness never leave you; bind them around your neck, write them on the tablet of your heart. Here **love and faithfulness**

25

are the basis of our salvation. Also, these two graces should always be held together. As F. Taylor has commented, "The lack of one of these graces buries the commendation of the other. Such a person may be loving to the poor without being faithful to God. Such a person may be faithful but have no love in his heart." As Bishop Sanderson said in one of his sermons, "As a rich sparkling diamond adds both value and luster to a gold ring, so do these virtues love and faithfulness bring extra glory to the crowns of the greatest monarchs."

But these virtues must not just be used occasionally—they must **never leave you.** You must **bind them** like jewels **around your neck** (4:21; 7:3; Deuteronomy 6:8). You must **write them** not on stone tablets but in **your heart** (7:3; 2 Corinthians 3:3).

4. Then you will win favor and a good name in the sight of God and man. God is not in your debt. But nobody serves God to no avail. We see the truth of this verse in the examples of Joseph in Egypt (Genesis 39:2-4, 21-23; 41:37-43), David in the family of Saul (1 Samuel 18:5, 14-16), and the early Christians with the people around them (Acts 2:44-47). What is better than to defeat reproach by consistent godliness? What is more acceptable to God or more edifying to the church (Romans 14:16-19)? Scripture links God's favor with man's favor. This was true of the Holy Child (Luke 2:52).

5. This is the polestar for a child of God—faith in his Father's providence, promises, and grace. This **trust** is not the mere cold assent of enlightened judgment. It is **trust . . . with all your heart.** It is a childlike, unwavering confidence in our Father's well-proved wisdom, faithfulness, and love. He is truth itself. Therefore, he wants us to take him at his word and to prove his word to the very limit of his power.

But our **trust** must not only be complete—it must be exclusive. No other confidence, no confidence in the flesh, can exist alongside it (Philippians 3:3). Man with all his pride feels that he wants something to **lean on.** As a fallen being, he naturally leans on his **own understanding** and on himself. Human power is his idol. His **understanding** is his God. Many people would prefer to have a lack of principle rather than a lack of talent. This is the history of man from the Fall on; this is the lamentable sin of every person created by God. Do we need to call this the sin of youth? How rare it is to see the younger submitting to the elder (1 Peter 5:5)! If advice is sought, is it not just to confirm what has already been decided?

Those who refuse to **lean on** their **own understanding** are those who **trust in the LORD.** For they are trusting in his divine power and are using it as a lamp, so they can find their way. The Christian on his knees, as if he throws away his **own understanding,** confesses that he is completely unable to find the way by himself. But observe how he behaves. He takes trouble to improve his mind. He conscientiously follows its dictates. In this way practical faith strengthens, not destroys, its power.

So it is our clear duty not to neglect our **understanding** but to cultivate it diligently. In a world where knowledge abounds, ignorance is the fruit of laziness. So **lean not on your own understanding. Trust in the LORD with all your heart.** Self-dependence is foolishness (28:26), rebellion (Jeremiah 2:13; 9:23), and ruin (Genesis 3:5-6; Isaiah 47:10-11). "The great folly of man in trials," as Dr. Owen has rightly remarked, "is leaning to or on his own understanding and counsels. What is the result of this? Whenever in our trials we consult our own understanding, listen to our own reason, even though they appear to be good, the principle of living by faith is stifled, and we will in this way be let down by our own counsels."

6. The next thing to note is that our trust should be constant: **in all your ways acknowledge him.** Take one step at a time, and make sure that each step is under God's direction. Always make your plans in total dependence on God. It is nothing short of self-idolatry to imagine that we can carry out even the ordinary matters of daily life without God's counsel. God loves to be consulted. Therefore, take all your difficulties to him. Before you consult your friends, consult God.

In all your ways. This includes the small things as well as the big things. In all your concerns, temporal or eternal, let God be supreme. Have we not all found the unimaginable peace of taking to God things that seem too small or personal to be entrusted to the most confidential ear? In this way Abraham acknowledged God. Wherever he pitched his tent for himself, he always built an altar for God (Genesis 12:7; 13:18).

He will make your paths straight. If we go to the Lord every morning in true humility, knowing that we do not know how to order our day, light will come down to us. We are not looking for new revelations or visible signs. Study the Word with prayer, and note how God's Spirit sheds light on it. Make sure that your will is ready to move in the direction God indicates. No step well prayed over will bring ultimate regret.

7. This warning against self-confidence is closely linked to the preceding verses. The person who is **wise in [his] own eyes** is the person who leans on his own understanding. That kind of wisdom is foolishness and self-delusion. Even a non-Christian could remark, "I suppose that many might have attained to wisdom, had they not thought they had already attained it" (Seneca). Throw that kind of wisdom away, and let your wisdom be to **fear the LORD and shun evil.** There is a striking link between the **fear of the LORD** and the fear of sin (14:27; 16:6; Genesis 39:9-10; Nehemiah 5:15; Job 28:28). Where God is honored, sin is hated, loathed, and resisted (Romans 7:18-24). It lives, but it is condemned to die (Romans 6:6). It clings to the child of God, but his heart will shun it. It often makes the body ill, and always makes the soul ill.

8. Exercising self-denial and godly discipline **will bring health to your body** and revive your soul.

9. A worldly person finds this a hard precept. But for God's servant it is a privilege to put to one side part of his **wealth** and label it, "This is for God."

Giving **the firstfruits of all your crops** was the way that God's redemption out of Egypt was acknowledged (Exodus 13:12-13; Deuteronomy 26:1-10). Should we who have been redeemed from sin, Satan, death, and hell deny this claim? As Bishop Hall has said, "Well may we think our wealth is our due, when we really owe our very selves to God."

We must **honor the LORD,** not ourselves. We should do this in a spirit of renouncing self (1 Chronicles 29:14-16; Matthew 6:1-4). Have no doubt that the Lord will add his own seal of approval to this: "Those who honor me I will honor" (1 Samuel 2:30).

11. Prosperity and adversity are part of our present situation. Each can honor the Lord. In prosperity this can be done by consecrating our wealth to the Lord (verses 9-10). In adversity this can be done by being humble and cheerful in whatever the Lord sends us. As Bishop Patrick has written, "In prosperity it is well to expect discipline; and if it is the Lord's pleasure, do not let this make you doubt God's gracious providence." In no other way does the Lord act more like a father toward us than in this. It is wonderful to be addressed as **my son** at any time, but most of all when we experience the Lord's **discipline.**

Our corruption is never so evident and our graces are never so apparent as when we are being disciplined by the Lord. We need this as much as we need our daily bread. Children of God are still children of Adam who have Adam's will, pride, independence, and waywardness.

We especially need God's grace in this so that we do not become hardened or despondent. Some people **resent** God's rebuking them, while others faint under its weight. So do not give way to heartless despondency or anxious impatience.

12. But these rules imply much more than something that is just negative. Instead of resenting God's rebuke, we are to be like the son who delights in it. Always remember that you are under the Father's discipline. So do not resent it, but hang onto his rebuking hand and pour out your soul into his heart. Kiss the rod. Acknowledge that it is humbling but also enriching. Expect a richer grace from sustaining strength than from the affliction being removed.

The Lord's discipline is like that in a family, not in a school, let alone in a prison. The Lord corrects his children and does not treat them as criminals. "I love the rod of my heavenly Father," exclaimed the saintly Fletcher. "How gentle are the stripes I feel. How heavy those I deserve." As Bishop Hall once prayed, "O God, I have made an ill use of your mercies if I have not learned to be content with your discipline." Never is Christ more precious to us than in the middle of discipline.

13. Who does not admire this glowing picture of happiness? The wisdom of this world can give no such happiness (Ecclesiastes 1:18). **Blessed is the man who finds wisdom** where he possibly least expected it, being disciplined by the Lord. David found "God's house of correction to be a school of instruction" (Trapp). Under all circumstances, however, prayerful diligence in searching for **wisdom** ensures success (2:1-6). The naturally wise man is a fool when it comes to heavenly **wisdom**. But the man of prayer **gains understanding**.

14. Here the wise man, himself enriched with **silver** and **gold**, points out to us a **more profitable** merchandise.

15. This is the search for the pearl of great price that **is more precious than rubies** (Matthew 13:45-46; 23:23; see also Philippians 3:4-8). Complete happiness will never be experienced unless this is in your mind. The man who doubts falls short of this. Determined perseverance wins the prize.

16. **Long life is in her right hand; in her left hand are riches and honor.** Note how this heavenly queen dispenses her blessings! **Her right hand** presents the promise of both worlds (verse 2; Psalm 91:16; 1 Timothy 6:8)—the rich enjoyment of the world's lawful comforts (1 Timothy 6:17) and the yet higher joy of serving the Lord and his church—a privilege for which the apostle Paul was content to be detained from heaven for a while.

Her left hand offers earthly **riches and honor**, insofar as they are good for her children. But even when they shine most brightly, they are only a faint shadow of wisdom's more durable **riches** and the **honor** of a heavenly crown.

17. What are we to say of **her ways**? Is wisdom a sullen matron who entertains her followers only with sighs and tears? Does this mean that to gain the joys of the next life we must bid eternal farewell to the benefits of this life? Is it true that "we must never more expect a cheerful hour, a clear day, a bright thought to shine upon us" (Bishop Hopkins)? This is the world's creed, and it is a slander from the great liar. In this way we are opposed as we try to follow wisdom's **ways**. They are **pleasant ways** because they have been decreed by the Lord. And if we do not find them **pleasant**, we do not know them.

The man of pleasure utterly mistakes both his object and his pursuit. The only happiness worth seeking is found here in this proverb. This happiness lives through all circumstances and copes with all the endless changes of this mortal life. The ways may be dark and lonely, but how the sunshine of reconciliation shines on them! Every step is given light from above and showered with heavenly promises. They are steps in happiness and steps in heaven. Wisdom's work is her own reward (Psalm 19:11; Isaiah 32:17). This life is strict, but it is not imprisonment. So the sacrifices of love should be **pleasant**. When the heart is free, the journey is not burdensome.

We should go beyond saying that these **ways** are consistent with being

pleasant. They are the basic principles of the most elevated pleasure. "The verdict of Christ," says Dr. South, "makes the discipline of self-denial and the cross—those terrible blows to flesh and blood—the indispensable requisite to being his disciples." And yet, paradoxical as it may appear, in this deep gloom is the sunshine of glory. For if we are naturally God's enemies (Romans 8:7), we must also be our own worst enemy and so will never be happy. Our pleasure, therefore, must be to deny, not to indulge, ourselves. We must put to death our sinful appetites, which only end in death (Romans 7:5). Even what may be called the austerities of godliness are more enjoyable than the pleasures of sin. It is far better to annoy the will than to wound the conscience. Christ's chains are glorious (Acts 5:41-42; 26:24-25). Moses did not endure his reproach as if it were a trial (Hebrews 11:26). Our principles are never more consoling than when we are making a sacrifice for them. Hannah gave up her dearest earthly joy. But did she shrink under the trial? Did she begrudge the sacrifice? No. When Hannah prayed, she rejoiced in the Lord (1 Samuel 1:26; 2:1). And as if to demonstrate that no one serves God for nothing, for the one child Hannah gave to God, five more were given to her (1 Samuel 2:20-21).

In fact, those in the world have no conception about the real nature of wisdom's **pleasant ways**. To them, religion is associated with cold, heartless forms and irritating restraints, where there is much to do but little to enjoy. But they only see half the picture. They see what religion takes away, but they do not see what it gives. They cannot comprehend that while it denies sinful pleasures, it overflows with spiritual pleasures.

18. She is a tree of life to those who embrace her; those who lay hold of her will be blessed. The glory, beauty, and fruitfulness of wisdom, the paradise of God alone, furnish the full counterpart to life apart from God (Revelation 2:7). "The tree of life was the means ordained of God for the preservation of lasting life and continual vigor and health before man sinned. So true wisdom maintains man in the spiritual life of God's grace and the communion of his Spirit" (Bishop Sanderson). Once our way was barred, and nobody could touch wisdom (Genesis 3:22-24). Now our way is opened to her in a better paradise (Hebrews 10:19-22). We sit under her shadow in great delight. For what is so refreshing as fellowship with God, access to him, boldness in his presence, and admission to his most holy delights?

Those who lay hold of her will be blessed. The promises are to those who overcome (Revelation 2—3). God honors perseverance in the weakest saint.

This lovely description of wisdom's blessing is no fanciful picture but a divine reality. Do not rest until your heart is filled with it. Pray to the Lord about this, and before long you will rejoice in experiencing it.

19. We have noted **wisdom** in human lives, with all its enriching blessings. Now we see its majesty as it is displayed in all of God's works.

"Hereby he shows that this wisdom that he speaks about was everlasting, because it was before all creatures; and all things, even the whole world, were made by it" (*Reformers' Notes*). **The earth's foundations** are so sure that they cannot be moved (Psalm 93:1). Note how this great Architect **set the heavens in place**, arranging their bright lights in their various orbits (Genesis 1:14-18; Psalm 136:5; Jeremiah 10:12)—"such a glorious canopy set with such sparkling diamonds" (Leighton).

20. The universe is a parable, a mirror of the Gospel. The manifestation of these divine acts in the field of creation opens a rich provision for our happiness. So in an even greater way the glorious demonstration of the great work of God's redemption fills us with adoring praise (Romans 11:28). "That which moves God to work is goodness; that which orders his work is wisdom; that which completes his work is power. All things, which God in these times and seasons has brought forth, were eternally and before all time in God, as a work unbegun is in the artificer, which later is brought into being. Therefore whatever we do behold now in the book of Eternal Wisdom are held in the hands of Omnipotent Power, the first foundations of the earth being as yet unlaid. So all things that God has made are in that respect the Offspring of God. They are in him as effects in their highest cause. He likewise is actually in them; the assistance and influence of his Deity is their life" (Hooker).

21. Again we listen to wisdom's voice. Her repetitions are not vain repetitions but need to be impressed on young people (Isaiah 28:9-10). They should be your much-loved treasure and your daily guide; so **do not let them out of your sight**. God's teaching is **sound judgment**, full of light and substance. Keep it so that you may have **discernment** in everything you do.

23. Keeping one's eye constantly on the Word of God prevents one's feet from slipping. When the psalmist did not pay attention to wisdom's words, he nearly fell (73:2-17).

24. The hours during which we are asleep, no less than our waking hours, are divinely guarded (Psalm 127:1-2). God's servants enjoy a childlike repose, sleeping in the Father's care without any fear. When Peter was in prison, in chains, between two soldiers, on the eve of his expected execution, when there seemed but a step between him and death, he was able to **lie down** and **not be afraid**.

25. **Sudden disaster** may come, but we are to have **no fear**. It is **the wicked** who will be ruined.

26. Child of God, run with **confidence**, for God will keep you safe, and **your foot** will not be **snared**. Noah found this security when all the ungodly were drowned. Lot found this safety when Sodom was destroyed (2 Peter 2:5-9). Luther sang his song of **confidence**: "God is our strength and refuge."

27. The wise man comes now to some practical points. He shows that

the result of selfishness is to **withhold good**. This dishonesty takes many forms: in borrowing without making any repayment (Psalm 37:21), in evading paying taxes, in keeping back wages due to employees (James 5:4; Jeremiah 22:13-17). But this instruction is deeper than this. Even if we are not legally indebted to anyone, we have an outstanding debt to "love one another" (Romans 13:8). Even the poor person is bound by this universal law to his poorer neighbor. Everyone has a claim on our love. Every opportunity to do good is our calling to do so. Kindness is not an option but an obligation. It is an act of justice, no less than an act of mercy. If we **withhold** it, that will be to our eternal condemnation (Matthew 25:41-45).

28. Christian kindness will also be carried out in the most loving way. Delay is an offense against the law of love. Too often the cold rebuttal, **"Come back later; I'll give it tomorrow"** is just a cover for selfishness. There is a hidden hope that the matter will be forgotten or dropped or taken up by somebody else.

When you now have it with you. A little given in time of need is more than a larger amount when the needy moment has passed. We should cultivate the habit of being sensitive to the needs of others, putting ourselves in their place. We should not only do good but be *prepared* to do good (Titus 3:1; 1 Timothy 6:18). The Gospel presents every neighbor to us as a brother or sister who needs our help, who is to be loved and cared for in the same way that we look after ourselves (Leviticus 19:18). Why are we so slow to acknowledge this? May the Lord deliver us from our selfishness and mold us to his own image of love and mercy.

"Was ever the hungry fed or the naked clothed with good looks or fair speeches? These are but thin garments to keep out the cold, and but a slender repast to conjure down the rage of craving appetite. My enemy, perhaps, is ready to starve, and I tell him that I am heartily glad to see him and am very ready to serve him. But still my hand is closed, and my purse shut. I neither bring him to my table, nor lodge him under my roof. He asks for bread, and I give him a compliment—a thing indeed not so hard as a stone, but altogether as dry. I treat him as an outsider, and lastly, at parting, with all the ceremonial dearness, I shake him by the hand but put nothing into it. I play with his distress and dally with that which was not to be dallied with—want, and misery, and a clamorous necessity" (Dr. South).

29. The command not to withhold good is naturally followed by the instruction not to **plot harm against your neighbor.** This treachery was a scandal even among the godless. It is generally abhorred by the world and should be doubly hated by a godly man. With the latter everything should be as clear and open as the day. A harmful **plot against your neighbor** is a serious sin (6:14-19; Deuteronomy 27:24). This is the kind of wisdom that comes from the devil (James 3:15). Such was the cunning of Jacob's sons against the unsuspecting Shechemites (Genesis 34:13-29; 49:5-7), Saul's malice against David when he was under the king's protection

(1 Samuel 18:22-25), Joab's murder of Abner and Amasa (2 Samuel 3:27; 20:9-10), and Ishmael's murder of Gedaliah (Jeremiah 41:1-2). This was part of the bitter cup of suffering our Savior drank (John 13:21). Many a wounded spirit has been cheered with our Lord's poignant sorrow (Hebrews 4:15).

30. We must not only guard against secret malice but against accusing **a man for no reason.** We must beware of becoming involved in quarrels (17:14; 18:6; 25:8-9) instead of pursuing peace (Romans 12:18). A spirit of strife is a great hindrance to holiness (Hebrews 12:14; Colossians 3:12-15) and is inconsistent for any of God's servants (2 Timothy 2:24). Irritable people are always strongly insisting on their own rights, or what they imagine is due to them from other people. How we need to earnestly seek to have Christ's own meek and loving spirit (1 Peter 2:21-23).

"O Lord, pour into our hearts that most excellent gift of charity, the very bond of peace, and of all virtues; without which, whosoever liveth is counted dead before thee" (Collect for Quinquagesima Sunday [Sunday before Lent], from the *Book of Common Prayer*).

31. What, we may ask, is there to **envy** in **a violent man?** The love of power is a ruling passion. But we have little reason to **envy** such a man, let alone **choose any of his ways.**

32. Can anyone be happy when he deliberately contradicts God's will? "For he who hateth nothing that he hath made, abhors those who have thus marred themselves. They are not only abominable, but the Lord detests the sight of them" (*Reformers' Notes*). Sinners are detested by the Lord. Saints are his delight. "They are God's friends, to whom he gives, as men used to do to their friends, his mind and counsels or his secret favor and comforts, to which other men are strangers" (Poole). "He loves them dearly as his intimate friends, to whom he communicates the very secrets of his heart" (Diodati). Is it not infinitely more worthwhile to live with God in heaven than in all the vain pomp of this ungodly world?

33. The LORD's curse is on the house of the wicked, but he blesses the home of the righteous. The contrast between **the wicked** and **the righteous** does not just affect us as individuals, but as families. The **curse** or the blessing of the Lord follows us to our homes. Many modest cottages that are lived in by a child of Abraham shine more splendidly than the princely palaces of the ungodly, for heirs of glory live there. A family altar of prayer and praise consecrates it as the temple of Jehovah (Genesis 12:8). Promises, like clouds of blessings, rest over it. God has been honored, and God will honor it (2 Samuel 6:11; Jeremiah 35:18-19). Is my **house** under the Lord's **curse** or under his blessing?

34. He mocks proud mockers but gives grace to the humble. God's mind is never more fully declared than it is against pride and **proud mockers.** Such behavior displeases man, and would, if it were possible, disturb God himself. God hates the sinner who refuses to submit himself to his righteousness and who mocks the cornerstone of salvation. How dreadfully this becomes a rock of offense for the eternal ruin of the sinner (Romans 10:3). **Proud mockers** will not escape God's frown.

A **humble** spirit, a deep conviction of utter nothingness and guilt, is a most adorning grace. Nor is it an occasional or temporary feeling, the result of some unexpected disclosure, but a habit that clothes a person (1 Peter 5:5) from head to toe. It combines the highest elevation of joy with the deepest abasement of spirit. "God pours his grace plentifully upon humble hearts. His sweet dews and showers of grace slide off the mountains of pride and fall on the low valleys of humble hearts and make them pleasant and fertile" (Leighton). But the soul that swells with pride has no room for God's humbling grace.

35. The wise inherit honor, but fools he holds up to shame. This is the last contrast made to restrain our envy of the prosperity of the wicked (verse 31). Self-knowledge, the principle of lowliness, is the essence of wisdom. **Fools** will discover the vanity of this world's glory when it is too late to make a wise choice. **Shame** is their present fruit. **Honor** even now sits uneasily on **the wise.** How solemn and complete will be the great separation in eternity.

Proverbs
Chapter 4

1. Listen, my sons, to a father's instruction; pay attention and gain understanding. These frequent repetitions are meant to wake us out of our sleep. It would have been possible for Solomon to make every sentence different and to give us something new from his mind in every proverb. But it was more appropriate for our sluggish and forgetful heart to have "rule on rule, rule on rule" (Isaiah 28:13). A genuinely wise person, like the apostle Paul in later days, exhorts like a father who is dealing with his own children (1 Thessalonians 2:11).

2. Solomon clearly speaks from the mouth of God. He declares that he gives **sound learning.** To many people, exciting, speculative, compromising, self-righteous, self-exalting doctrine is more attractive. But, young people, remember what humbles the soul before God. Remember what demonstrates the free grace of the Gospel. Remember what curbs the will, consecrates the heart, and imbues the heart with the spirit of the cross. **Sound learning,** no matter how unpalatable it seems, alone is good for the soul. **So do not forsake** it. Do not be carried away with the senseless cry, "Everybody else thinks in a different way." What is the judgment of the whole of mankind worth on the great subject of belief in God? Is this world's judgment to be preferred to the Word of God?

3. We now enter the family of "the man after God's heart," David, as he taught his child Solomon in the fear and service of the Lord.

4. We are especially privileged if we can speak of an Abraham or a David or a Lois or a Eunice who has **taught** us and bound us to the ways of God. Parents, you must remember than an untaught child will be a living shame (29:15).

Let us examine carefully this beautiful example of parental instruction. Where David's instruction begins is obvious. Where it ends is not so clear, whether it is at verse 6, [9, NIV], 10, 12, or 13, or as F. Taylor asserts, at the end of the ninth chapter. But as Geier observes, "Let the reader form his own judgment; provided that we pay due obedience to the instruction, it matters little, whether we have it in the words of David or Solomon."

Note in these verses how keen the father is about his son's heart-religion: **"Lay hold of my words with all your heart."**

5. **"Get wisdom, get understanding."** Note also how earnest this exhortation is. Many parents are like Augustine's father and advise, "Get wealth, worldly honor, or wisdom." Of his father Augustine prayed to God, "This father of mine never troubled himself with any thought of how I might improve myself toward thee."

When you have obtained heavenly wisdom, **do not forget** it or walk away from it.

6. We are to **love** wisdom. Thus Jerome wrote to a friend, "Beg now for me, who am gray-haired, of the Lord, that I may have Wisdom for my companion, of which it is written, 'Love her, and she shall keep thee.'" She is the one who can **watch over** your soul.

8. You are to **esteem** and **embrace** wisdom. Even in this life **she will exalt you** and **will honor you.**

9. Wisdom is **a garland of grace** in the church. Wisdom is **a crown of splendor** in heaven.

This is not the style of someone speaking in a detached way, trying to enforce some unimportant truth. It is the father feeling that his child's soul is perishing unless it is taught and led in wisdom's ways. Parents, do we know this anxious concern as we look for the first dawn of light on our child's soul? Is it our own first choice above all the world's glitter? Is it not only important, but all-important? It can have no place if it has not the first place. If it is to be anything, it has to be everything. Earthly wisdom may be a good pearl, but this wisdom from above is the pearl of great price. It is worth selling everything we have in order to obtain it (Matthew 13:45-46).

10. It is instructive to see a king (whether David or Solomon) who in the middle of his royal cares does not forget his domestic responsibilities.

11. Let us see the need for guidance for every step, both steps to take and steps to avoid. **The way of wisdom** will definitely lead to a happy life because it is lived in God's presence. This will happen if godly discipline has been exercised, if the Bible has been laid down as the rule of life, if habits of prayer, love for serving God, and fellowship with his people have been encouraged. The path, though sometimes rough and lonely, is a **straight** path and a path of freedom.

12. The eye that is focused on wisdom will be able to **walk** at an even pace and make progress. In this way, **when you run, you will not stumble.**

13. The animated exhortation to **hold on to instruction** shows that it is a struggle to retain our principles. Feeble, indeed, is our hold when we are only interested in wisdom because it is a novelty. Truths that are only grasped by our minds and that do not become the daily nourishment of our souls never enter into our hearts. **Hold[ing] on to instruction** is done by a personal, living faith. Jacob did this when he detained the angel (Genesis 32:26-29). The two disciples of Jesus did this when they asked him to stay with them as they walked along the Emmaus road (Luke 24:28-29). So, young Christian, **do not let [wisdom] go; guard it well, for it is your life.** May heavenly treasure be more important to you than every earthly blessing.

14. How often fellowship with **evil men** loosens our hold on instruction. Their **path** and the path of instruction lead in the opposite directions. Just to **set foot on the path of the wicked** means that you are forsaking God's way **to walk in the way of evil men.**

16. Evil men are so eager to pursue their work that **they cannot sleep.** Judas with his midnight torches (John 18:3), the early-morning meeting of the Jewish rulers (Luke 22:66), the frenzied vow of the enemies of Paul (Acts 23:12), and countless other plots against the church all vividly portray this tireless wickedness.

17. Mischief is meat and drink to these evil men. "To do evil is more proper and natural than to sleep, eat, or drink" (*Reformers' Notes*).

The evil company is loved, then the evil of the company. Eusebius mentions a young man whom St. John committed to the special charge of the bishop of Ephesus, but who by evil company was drawn away to be a captain of robbers, until St. John went after him and brought him back. Augustine's recollections of his own youthful theft was, "By myself alone I would not have done it. It was the company that I loved, with whom I did it. When they said, 'Come, let us go and do it,' I was ashamed not to be as shameless as they." To pray not to be led into temptation and yet not to watch so that we do not enter into that temptation is to contradict our prayers. It is to mock God by asking him for what we do not really want. Walk closely with God in secret, and he will spread his almighty covering over you for your safety. Avoid fellowship with those who will hinder your fellowship with God.

18. The path of the righteous is like the first gleam of dawn, shining ever brighter till the full light of day. This is a good contrast of the Christian's **path** of **light** with the dark and dangerous path of the wicked. This is not the feeble light of a candle, nor the momentary blaze of the meteor, but the grand illumination of heaven. And what a beautiful sight it is to see the Christian rise out of darkness!

Is this **full light** the picture of *my* **path**? There is no command for the sun to stand still here (Joshua 10:12). So a stationary profession of faith is rebuked. It is a rising and advancing, not a declining sun. Therefore it rebukes a backsliding state. It is not necessary that everything should be perfect at once. There may be an occasional cloud, or even (as in the cases of David and Peter) a temporary eclipse. But when did the sun fail to carry its early dawn **till the full light of day**? Do not despise the day of small things (Zechariah 4:10). But do not be satisfied with it either. Aim high, and you will come closer to reaching the mark. Religion must be a shining and progressive **light**. We must not mistake the beginning for the end of the course. We must not sit down at the entrance and say to our soul, "Take it easy now." There is no point where we may rest in complacency, as if there were no loftier heights that it is our duty to climb. Christian perfection is the continual aiming at perfection. The world of eternity will be one of **the full light of day**, where joy and light increase forever.

19. But the way of the wicked is like deep darkness; they do not know what makes them stumble. The contrast between the two paths is clear. Each has his own way. The path of the righteous is glowing light and joy. **The way of the wicked is like deep darkness.** It has no direction, no comfort, no safety, no peace. Their way is not just dark but **darkness** as a result of ignorance, error, sin, and misery. The love of sin rebels against the light. This **darkness** is deliberate and therefore accountable. The people who travel on the path of the righteous do not **stumble.**

20. These repeated injunctions (3:1; 5:1; 6:20-21; 22:17) are a good example for the Christian parent or minister. The desire for wisdom, the first step along the path, is encouraged. The means of obtaining, and the privilege when obtained, are pointed out. So keep your eye on the treasure of wisdom all the time.

21. A neglected Bible is the melancholy proof of a heart that is alienated from God. For how can we have a spark of love for him if that Book that is full of his revealed glory is despised? A superficial acquaintance with it is no good. If your ears were bored to the doors of the sanctuary, if the Word were never let out of your sight, your religion would still just be an idea and not principles, unless you **keep them within your heart.**

22. The keeping of the Word will be **life to those who find** it (see verses 4, 10, 13; 3:18). Some medicines are good for one part of the body, some for another. This is good for the body and the soul. We will enjoy vigorous **health** as we feed on this heavenly manna. We will not then bear our religion as our cross, as a cumbersome appendage. We will not drag our Christian duties around with us as if they were chains. Godliness will be a joy for us. The spirit will be aglow. The mind will be enriched with divine wisdom. The heart will be established with gospel grace.

23. The rules laid out in verses 23-27 constitute an invaluable safeguard for our Christian lives. Since we are attacked at every point, every possible place where sin may gain a foothold has to be guarded against—the **heart**, the **mouth**, the **eyes**, the **feet**.

First the **heart**, man's citadel, the center of his dearest treasure. It is frightening to think about its many assailants. Let it be guarded carefully. Never let the guard sleep at his post (Deuteronomy 4:9).

The **heart** must be known, so that it may be kept safe. Nothing is more difficult, but nothing is more necessary. If we do not know our hearts, it will be as if we knew nothing at all. Whatever else we know, to neglect this knowledge is to be a prize fool. If we do not know our weak points, Satan is well aware of them, "the sin that so easily entangles" (Hebrews 12:2).

Then, when I know my heart and feel that it is in the middle of so many dangers, the question arises, can I **guard** my own **heart**? Certainly not. This is God's work, though it is carried out through the agency of man. He works through our efforts. He implants an active principle and sustains the ceaseless exercise. When this is done in his strength and guidance, all the means of our preservation are greatly increased. Watch and pray. Nurture a humble spirit and a dependent spirit. Live in the atmosphere of the Word of God. Resist the evil world, even in its most plausible forms. This will be a conflict until the end of our lives. "The greatest difficulty in conversion is to win the heart to God, and after conversion to keep it with him" (Flavel). "What is there," asks Mede, "that will not entice and allure so fickle a thing as the heart from God?" **Above all else**, exhorts the wise man, **guard your heart**.

As Satan keeps special watch here, so must we keep special watch as well. If the citadel is taken, the whole town must surrender. If the heart is captured, the whole man—affections, desires, motives, pursuits—will be handed over. The heart is the vital part of the body. If the heart is wounded, that means instant death. Spiritually as well as naturally, the **heart . . . is the wellspring of life**. It is the great vital spring of the soul, the fountain of actions, the center and the seat of both sin and holiness (Matthew 12:34-35). The natural heart is a fountain of poison (Matthew 15:19); but the purified heart is a well of living water (John 4:14). As the spring is, so will be the streams. As the **heart** is, so will be the **mouth**, the **eyes**, and the **feet**. Therefore, **above all else, guard your heart.** Guard the spring so that the waters are not polluted. If the heart is not guarded, everything else is of no avail.

24. As we guard our hearts, we must not forget to guard the outlets of sin. What a world of evil the heart pours out from the **mouth** (James 3:5-6). Commit, therefore, both **heart** and **mouth** to divine discipline. Then let prayer and faith be the way you keep watch. Do not just shun but **put away**—yes, far away from you—**perversity from your mouth**.

25. After the **heart** and the **mouth** we come to the **eyes: Let your eyes look straight ahead, fix your gaze directly before you.** The eyes are "the lamp of the body" (Matthew 6:22). Yet, all too often they are a most dangerous inlet to sin (Genesis 3:6; 6:2; 39:7; Matthew 5:28; 2 Peter 2:14). Therefore, like Job, we need to make a covenant with our eyes (Job 31:1). Place them under heavenly restraint (Psalm 119:37). **Let your eyes look straight ahead,** "like one plowing, who must not look back" (Cartwright). **Fix your gaze directly before you.** If Eve had done so, she would have looked on God's command and not on the forbidden tree (Genesis 3:2-6). Had Lot's wife looked **straight ahead** instead of behind her, she would, like her husband, have been a monument of mercy (Genesis 19:17, 26). Achan was ruined by neglecting this rule of wisdom (Joshua 7:21). David's example calls us to godly jealousy (2 Samuel 11:2-4). The pleasures of sin and the seductions of a tempting world do not lie on God's road. So they would not meet the eyes if his people were looking **straight ahead**. It is only when Christians linger, turn off the path, or turn back that they come into sight. Follow the motto of runners—"one thing I do" (Philippians 3:13). Get your goal in focus and concentrate on it. Go onwards, upwards, heavenwards.

26. Lastly, guard **your feet**. Has not experience, let alone Scripture, shown that you need to walk carefully? Traps are laid on every path—yes, for every step you take. The wicked attempt to snare your eating, your drinking, your calling, and perhaps most of all, your serving God. You should take great care as you travel along such a dangerous path. "The habit of calm and serious thinking makes the real difference between one man and another" (Dr. Abercrombie).

27. Here, then, is the voice of wisdom. Beware of mistaking presumption for faith, temptations for God's providence. Never deviate from a straightforward command for an uncertain command. Judge each step you take so that it is in line with God's will. The pleasures of sin lie **to the right or the left**. So your eyes need to keep looking straight ahead in order to **keep your foot from evil**.

May we all have grace and wisdom to ponder these sound practical rules. The man of God must only have one standard (Isaiah 8:20). He must not think about anyone "from a worldly point of view" (2 Corinthians 5:16). He must often put the church to one side, no less than the world, in order to listen more carefully to God's command. He must discern and crush the first sign of sin, guarding every avenue of sin—the senses, the memory, the imagination, the touch, the taste. He must walk by the straight rule of the Gospel, or else he will not only make himself stumble but the church as well (Galatians 2:11-14).

Cartwright's exposition about the middle path is valuable: "It is as if the royal way was hemmed in by the sea, and to wander off the path from either side would put you in danger of being drowned. Some are too greedy, others are too ascetic. Some are too bold, others are too diffident. Some neglect the Mediator, others seek other mediators. Some flee from the cross, others make their own unnecessary crosses. Some tamper with popery, others, from the dread of it, hazard the loss of valuable truth."

Proverbs
Chapter 5

1. Ponder this chapter, you who do not know the poison and corruption of the lusts of the body. Perhaps painful experience had given the wise man **wisdom** and **insight**. So **pay attention** to it with fear and trembling.

2. Man's own strength, even the restraint of education or self-discipline, is powerless in this matter. Engrafted wisdom is the only effective safeguard. This heavenly influence teaches us to both **maintain discretion** so our souls are protected and to **preserve knowledge** so our fellow sinners can be warned (2:10-11, 16; 6:20, 24; 7:1-5; Psalm 17:4; 119:9, 11).

3. The temptation seems to be so plausible that it arrests our attention. The deluded victim only tastes, or expects to taste, the **honey;** he only hears words that are **smoother than oil.**

4. But the beginning is never as sweet as **the end . . . is bitter.**

5. Her path leads **straight to the grave.** Every step is a step nearer hell.

6. One feature of the tempter's wiliness is most remarkable. She winds herself in a thousand **crooked . . . paths,** so that everyone's different moods and circumstances can be met. She works on every weakness; she seizes every unguarded moment. She has one overriding intention in mind. Not only does she give **no thought to the way of life,** she is determined that nobody else should either. She knows that the checks of conscience must be diverted. No time must be allowed for reflection. The intrusion of one serious thought might break the spell and open the way of escape.

7. Can we wonder, then, at this display of parental earnestness, this desperate desire to force back **my sons** from playing on the edge of a precipice? **Now then, my sons, listen to me.** We are not calling for austere restraint on youthful pleasures. But the tempter's touch, her word, even her look, must be avoided.

8. Keep to a path far from her. Do not just not go and visit her, but, as she is so highly contagious, **do not go near the door of her house.** To thrust ourselves into temptation is to place ourselves outside God's protection. The snare as it approaches becomes more enticing. The voice of wisdom, therefore, is: Flee youthful desires.

9-14. This is a picture of sin. It is pleasurable for a time, but its wages are eternal death (Hebrews 11:25; Romans 6:23). Every sin of unbelievers that is not repented of on this earth will bring its perpetual torment in eternity. Sinner, the path of life is open to you. Ponder it carefully, prayerfully. May the light of the Word and the teaching of the Spirit guide you to it.

15. Desire for forbidden pleasures spring out of a dissatisfaction with present possessions. Where contentment is not found at home, it will be looked for elsewhere.

Drink water from your own cistern. The beauty of this figure is illustrated from the fact that the houses of the East each had their **own cistern.**

Love within marriage is one of the greatest earthly gifts that God, in his mercy, has granted to his fallen and rebellious creatures. So enjoy with thankfulness your own, and do not desire water from your neighbor's **well.**

18. Rejoice in the wife of your youth (Deuteronomy 24:5; Ecclesiastes 9:9). Think of her as a special gift from your Father's hand.

19. Cherish her with gentleness and purity (Genesis 24:67).

A loving doe, a graceful deer. The **doe** and **deer** were objects of special delight (see Song of Songs 2:17; 3:5) and endearment—a picture of lively delight in the wife. As Bishop Davenant beautifully observes, "Abroad the man may consider himself as tossing in the waves, but at home with his wife, as in a desired haven." Whatever interrupts the harmony of this delicate relationship opens the door to imminent temptation. Tender affection is the best defense against the desires of illicit passion. Yes, it is consecrated by the Word of God itself and is a picture of the love the Lord has for the church (Ephesians 5:25, 29).

20. With such a view as we have had of the deadly enticement of sin on the one hand (verses 9-11) and the calm happiness provided on the other by God's ordinance (verses 15-19), only the infatuated would leave the wholesome spring for the polluted waters of the forbidden stream. Unless he was stupefied, would he slight the honorable state of marriage (Hebrews 13:4) to **embrace the bosom of another man's wife?**

21. Would not the thought that **a man's ways are in full view of the LORD** stop him in his tracks? No, it doesn't. Practical atheism is the root of human depravity (Psalm 14:1-3). The eye of another person, even of a child, is a check on a sinner; yet the thought of the all-seeing God, even if it enters his mind, does not alarm, convict, or restrain him. Oh, if men would but read, would but believe their Bibles, this solemn truth that God examines all their paths would flash on their consciences.

22. If no attention is paid to reason or to the all-seeing heavenly eye, the sinner may be restrained by thinking about the trouble he will land himself in. God needs no chains or prison to bring the sinner under his hand.

Wherever such a man goes, his **evil deeds** go with him, and **the cords of his sin hold him fast,** ready for judgment. Does he think he can give them up when he pleases? Repetition forms a habit; a habit becomes a ruling principle. "Every lust deals with him, as Delilah with Samson. It not only robs him of his strength, but leaves him bound" (Archbishop Tillotson). "Thus I," says Augustine about the dreadfulness of sin, "delighted with the sickness of the flesh, and with the deadly sweetness of it, drew my shackles along with me, much afraid to have them knocked off. And as if my wound had been too hard rubbed by it, I put back my friends' good persuasions, as if it were the hand of one that would unchain me."

23. Closing his eyes against the light, **he will die for lack of discipline.** The greatness of **his own great folly** will lead him **astray**—to perdition (2 Peter 2:14-15).

But is there no remedy for this deadly curse? Thanks be to God that he provides cleansing for the impure and deliverance for the captive. The blessed Savior cleanses the leper in his precious spring. He sets prisoners free.

Proverbs
Chapter 6

1. The **son** has just been warned against the deadly wound of a stranger. Now he is cautioned against the attack from an imprudent friend. Our God has graciously made his Book not only our guide to heaven, but the directory of our common life. We are here warned against **put[ting] up security for your neighbor.** The warning is clearly against entering into rash agreements, which the young and inexperienced are particularly exposed to.

If you have struck hands in pledge for another. This was the usual way to make an agreement.

2. Often you may be **trapped by what you said** and **ensnared by the words of your mouth** by entering into agreements without making careful inquiries about what is involved. Christian prudence will keep us from entering into such agreements, for they will bring disgrace on our families, dishonor on our name, and reproach on our faith.

3. If, however, you have become trapped by making an indiscreet agreement, you must attempt to free yourself from it in the following way: **Go and humble yourself; press your plea with your neighbor!**

4. Do not take time to sleep until you have succeeded in doing this.

5. You must disentangle yourself **like a bird from the snare of the fowler.**

Our God, while he warns us against putting up security, has taken it on himself. May his name be praised for this! He has given us his Word, his bond, yes, his blood as security for sinners, which no power of hell can shake.

6. "It is a shame," said the philosopher Seneca, "not to learn morals from the small animals."

Go to the ant, you sluggard. It demonstrates the degradation of the Fall that although man was created in God's image and made wiser than any of the other creatures, he should be sent to this insignificant school for instruction!

7. The ant **has no commander** to direct her work, **no overseer** to inspect her, no **ruler** to call her to account.

8. Yet the ant **stores its provisions** with diligent foresight **in summer and gathers its food at harvest** for her winter's need.

9. So the **sluggard** should consider the ant's ways and be wise. The sluggard sleeps over his work and is half-startled when he is aroused.

10. He still pleads for **a little sleep, a little slumber, a little folding of the hands to rest.** Present ease is all he thinks about. The future he carefully keeps out of sight.

11. In this way life runs to waste. **Poverty will come,** step by step, **like a bandit and scarcity like an armed man,** with irresistible force.

Perhaps such a man excuses himself by referring to his Master's words, "Do not worry about tomorrow" (Matthew 6:34). But Tully says, "The root of the word expresses the dividing of the mind into different thoughts." So our Lord was not teaching that we should take no care about anything. Care is a duty, a parental obligation, and therefore part of being godly. But being anxious and worried is a sin (Luke 10:41; 1 Corinthians 7:32), an unnecessary burden for ourselves that shows we are not trusting God. The diligent use of providential means honors God (10:5; 24:27).

We call in a much louder voice on the spiritual sluggard. You who are sleeping away the opportunities of grace and are not trying to enter through the narrow gate, you who are taking your salvation for granted and are hoping that you will reap where you have not sown and gather where you have not scattered seed (Matthew 25:26), **Go to the ant, you sluggard; consider its ways and be wise!**

12. What a contrast between the inactivity of the sluggard and the untiring diligence of **a scoundrel and villain!** This man of Belial, as it says in the Hebrew, **goes about with a corrupt mouth.**

13. Not content with the scope of his malice, he makes all parts of him—**his eye . . . his feet and . . . his fingers**—active instruments of unrighteousness.

14. These, however, are only external manifestations. Deep within lies the powerhouse of evil. He has **deceit in his heart—he always stirs up dissension** instead of piety and love.

15. Such a pest in society brings ruin on himself, and **suddenly** he will **be destroyed—without remedy.**

16. In his heart man thinks of God as being like himself and thus able to look at sin with indifference (Psalm 50:21). Here, therefore, Solomon lists **six things the LORD hates, seven that are detestable to him.**

17. Haughty eyes. Examples of **haughty** people are Pharaoh (Exodus

48

9:16-17), Haman (Esther 7:10), Nebuchadnezzar (Daniel 4:28-33), and Herod (Acts 12:21-23).

A lying tongue. Examples of people who lied are Gehazi (2 Kings 5:25-27) and Ananias and Sapphira (Acts 5:1-10).

Hands that shed innocent blood. Examples of people who murdered innocent people are Cain (Genesis 4:8-12), Manasseh (2 Kings 21:16), and especially those who murdered God's dear Son (Matthew 27:31-38).

18. And in case we should think God only looks on outward appearances, **a heart that devises wicked schemes** is mentioned.

19. God also hates **a false witness who pours out lies and a man who stirs up dissension among brothers.** A withering blast will fall on those who, mistaking prejudice for principle, cause divisions for their own selfish ends (Romans 16:17-18). The Lord will mark them out as people who do not have his Spirit and who are sensual (Jude 19; 1 Corinthians 3:3-4). Let the wisdom of experience given by an accurate observer of himself and the church be seriously pondered: "I am much more sensible of the evil of schism, and of the separating spirit, and of gathering parties, and making several sects in the church than I was heretofore. For the effects have shown us more of the mischiefs. I am much more aware how prone many young people who profess to be Christians are to spiritual pride and self-conceit and unruliness and division, and so become firebrands in the church. I am much more aware than heretofore of the breadth and length and depth of the radical, universal, odious sin of selfishness, and the excellency and necessity of self-denial, and of a public mind, and of loving our neighbor as ourselves" (Baxter). If we are unable to "be perfectly united in mind and thought" (1 Corinthians 1:10)—"a text," says Flavel, "to be commented upon rather by tears than words"—let us at least cultivate a spirit of unity.

20. The validity of parental authority is again enforced (see 1:8-9; 4:1). God never intended young people to be independent of their parents. Instruction from every quarter is valuable. But from parents, always supposing them to be godly parents, it is the ordinance of God. They will bring you *God's* Word, not their own.

21. Therefore, **bind them [your father's commands] upon your heart forever,** as your rule, and **fasten them around your neck,** so that they may adorn you.

22. Let the law be your friend at all times and in all circumstances. It is to be a **guide** by day and a solace **when you sleep.** It will be a friend **when you awake.** Take care that nothing hinders your early conversations with this faithful counselor before the world comes in. This is the best way to keep the world out. "Happy is the mind to which the Word is an undivided companion" (Bernard).

23. A lamp so full of **light** in this dark world is an inestimable gift. Its **corrections** and the **discipline** of our wayward will are to us **the way to**

life (Psalm 19:11; 2 Timothy 3:16-17). This **lamp** and **light** is especially valuable against sensual temptation (2:10-11, 16-19; 5:1-8; 7:1-5).

24. Those who choose their own light fall into the snare of a **smooth tongue.** The neglect of parental warning will in the end produce the bitter situation of unavailing repentance (5:11-14).

25. Here Solomon gives our Lord's own rule (Matthew 5:28). Resist **lust** as soon as it arises **in your heart.** Many people have been deluded by vain **beauty** and wanton **eyes.**

26. Such victims have been bought for the price of **a loaf of bread. The adulteress preys upon your very life.** Like the insatiable hunter who never loses sight of his prey until he has killed it, the seducer never ceases to solicit until she has succeeded in preying **upon your very life.**

27. Yet neither the present miseries, nor the known end of this wretched course can draw away the foot that has dared to tread the forbidden path. Self-confidence sees and fears no danger. "I can look after myself. I need not go too far, and I will come to no harm." But the temptation acts on a congenial nature like fuel, not water, on the fire. He might as well expect to **scoop fire into his lap without his clothes being burned.**

28. He might just as well expect to **walk on hot coals without his feet being scorched** as to go willfully into sin and escape the punishment.

29. Sin and punishment are linked together by a chain of unbreakable stone. "The fire of lust kindles the fire of hell" (Henry). It is no good for such a man to later on complain about the strength of the temptation. Why did he not avoid it?

30. Men do not despise a thief if he steals to satisfy his hunger when he is starving. This should not be used as an excuse for a thief to go unpunished.

31. He must pay full restitution. **Sevenfold** is not to be taken literally. Fourfold or fivefold was the limit of the divine requirement (see Luke 19:8). Let him earn his living through honest work. If the fruits of his labors fail, let him, trusting in God, seek the help of his fellow creatures. If he has faith to trust, he will not be forced to steal. Yet his extreme temptation makes him an object of pity rather than of scorn: **men do not despise a thief** (verse 30).

32. But the sin of the adulterer claims no sympathy. His plea is not a cry of hunger but of lust, not want but wantonness. He does not lack bread— he **lacks judgment.** He is willingly given over to his sin. In this way he **destroys himself.**

33. He is wounded, but not like a soldier or Christian martyr. He is not full of honor but of **disgrace.** His name is full of **shame.**

34. The tremendous passions of **jealousy** and **revenge** shut out all forgiveness.

35. No **bribe** will be accepted. No **compensation,** no matter how **great it is,** will be enough.

Such are the many sins that flow from breaking God's holy commandment. "Oh, how great iniquity," exclaimed the godly Augustine, "is this adultery! How great a perverseness! The soul, redeemed by the precious blood of Christ, is thus for the pleasures of an hour given to the devil, a thing much to be lamented and bewailed; when that which delighteth is soon gone, that which tormenteth remaineth without end."

And will not this frightening picture of sin and its consequences (which Solomon, alas, was only too well qualified to draw) teach us to avoid everything that may be temptation, to be sensitive to the first intimations of its becoming so and to close every avenue of sense to its seductive poison? Let us learn to seek divine strength to watch and pray and, as we think that we stand, to take heed in case we fall (1 Corinthians 10:12).

Proverbs
Chapter 7

1. The study of wisdom in the Word of God is now commended to us with affectionate earnestness and with a variety of beautiful images. Let us ponder these valuable rules and see how we can put them into practice in our lives.

Let the whole mind and heart be occupied with this. **Keep** it as the daily means of life. Sir Matthew Hale told his children, "If I omit reading a portion of Scripture in the morning, it never goes well with me through the day." **Store up my commands,** we are told, not on our shelves but in our hearts.

2. Keep a jealous regard for the law. What care is necessary to **guard . . . the apple of your eye,** that most tender part of the most tender part of the body! With the same care preserve the integrity of the law. Let every part of it have its full weight. To explain it away or to lower its requirements breaks down the barrier and gives temptation an easy way in. The sensual sinner is often a covert infidel.

3. Let God's commands be at hand for constant use. **Bind them on your fingers.** In this way they will always be in sight, so they may be ready whenever they are needed. So they can be used in a practical way, **write them on the tablet of your heart.** *Oh, my God, this is your almighty work! But you have promised to do it for your people (Jeremiah 31:33). I take hold of your covenant. Lord, seal your promised grace on me!*

4. Let **wisdom** be the object of tender affection, as a **sister** or **kinsman.**

5. Man must have the object of his delight. If wisdom is not loved, lust will be indulged. The Bible therefore, not merely read but cherished, proves a sacred exorcist to expel the power of evil (2:10, 16; 6:23-24; 23:26-27).

6. Solomon now paints the deadly snare of **the wayward wife** (verse 5) with a master's hand and with exquisite faithfulness to detail.

7. **A youth who lack[s] judgment** is in the company of young people as **simple** as himself.

9. Under the cover of **twilight** he makes his way to the prostitute's house.

10. There the woman comes out **to meet him**.

11. Her dress, her intent, her **loud and defiant** voice, **her feet** at this late hour, not staying **at home,** all reveal who she is.

12. **At every corner she lurks**, waiting for her prey.

13. Her **brazen face** shows that she has the forehead of a prostitute (Jeremiah 3:3).

14. She allures her victim with the garb of sanctity. She has just been engaged in special religious duties. **"I have fellowship offerings at home; today I fulfilled my vows."**

15. She **came out to meet** her lover, that they might feast together.

18. They fill themselves with every indulgence. **"Come, let's drink deep of love till morning; let's enjoy ourselves with love!"**

19. Her **husband** is not named, as that might have awakened the youth's conscience. **"My husband is not at home; he has gone on a long journey."** Meanwhile, they take their fill of love without fear of interruption. Unarmed with principle, the weakness of resolution yields to the seduction of lust, and her unsuspecting prey rushes on to ruin.

Trace this sad end to its source. Was not idleness the parent of this mischief? The loitering evening walk, the late hour, the vacant mind all bring the youth into contact with evil company. Was this not courting sin and tempting the tempter? How valuable self-discipline, self-control, constant employment, and vigorous activities are in keeping us from danger and preserving us under God's blessing.

See also the base varnish of religion. It is often used as a cover for sin (1 Samuel 2:22; 2 Samuel 15:8-11; John 18:28). "She dared not play the harlot with man until she had played the hypocrite with God and stopped the mouth of her conscience with her fellowship offerings" (Gurnall). It is a well-known fact that the favorite mistress of Louis XIV was so rigid in her religious duties that her bread was weighed during Lent, in case she should break the austerity of fasting. The adulteress in the Book of Proverbs is pictured as if she was reaping the reward for her religious observances. Beware of any voice, even if it comes from the most revered quarter, that manifestly encourages forbidden indulgence.

Observe also the infatuation of the snare. "Man cannot be ruined till he has been made confident to the contrary. A man must get into his victim's heart with fair speeches and promises before he can come at it with a dagger" (South). Thus the adulteress's flattering speech chained the young blindfolded for destruction. As the ox goes to the slaughter, unconscious of his fate, perhaps dreaming of rich pasture, or as a fool goes to the stock, careless and unfeeling, so does this poor deluded victim rush on with pitiable mirth or indifference **till an arrow pierces his liver** (verse 23). He is **like a bird darting into a snare, little knowing it will cost him his life** (verse 23). What will recollection bring but the fragrance of exciting perfume (verses 16-17), changed into the bitterness of wormwood and gall? The short night of pleasure is succeeded by the eternal night of infernal torment. A cup of pleasure is replaced by an ocean of wrath (verse 27).

Lastly, note the danger of venturing into temptation. Could we expect any other results when we saw the youth going toward her house? He intended merely his own idle gratification, and when he yielded, it was probably not without some struggle. But it is a just judgment that those who do not fear temptation fall. "Who would avoid danger must avoid temptation to sin. Who would avoid sin must avoid temptation to sin" (Geier). Self-confidence has ruined many a promising profession.

24. In the hand of a licentious poet or painter this picture might contaminate the unsanctified imagination. But as it stands on the page of inspiration, it is God's solemn warning to **sons**, whether in years, understanding, or experience. **Now then**, now that you have seen the end of sin (verses 22-23), **listen to me.**

25. Do not let your heart turn to her ways or stray into her paths. An impure thought, an idle look, foolish company, are **her ways**. Dread the first step, and do not imagine that you can stop yourself when you want to. Familiarity with sin weakens our abhorrence of it. Soon you will begin to love the object of detestation. Too late you will find that you have chosen her house as your home.

26. Many are **slain** in this way. It is the Almighty's miracle of power and grace that plucks the child of God from the brink of destruction.

The Gospel presents only one remedy. The love of Christ counters the love of lust. "If impure love solicits, remember the holy love of thy Savior to thee, proved by his most shameful death. Think of him as looking into thy heart boiling over with corruption, showing thee his wounds, and moving thee to a reciprocal love of himself" (Geier). The crucifixion of the flesh by a living union with him will keep us from iniquity (Galatians 5:24). The person who walks with God in gospel freedom and Christian discipline and watchfulness is safe.

27. But if sin is not mortified by these principles, sooner or later it will break out; if it does not result, as here, in open disgrace, it will defile the conscience and quench the Spirit and by a certain, though perhaps imperceptible, course bring the soul and body to hell (Romans 6:21; James 1:14-15), **to the grave, leading down to the chambers of death.**

Proverbs
Chapter 8

1. Does not wisdom call out? Does not understanding raise her voice? Now we listen to the call of heavenly **wisdom**, to the voice of the Son of God. We assume the speaker to be personal—essential **wisdom**. This description could not without unnatural force apply to an attribute. It sets out his personal existence (verses 24, 30). It sets out his personal characteristics: He is appointed from eternity for a distinct office (verse 23); he was the efficient cause in the work of creation (verses 27-30); he has **sound judgment** (verse 14), which being an attribute itself could not be the property of an attribute; he has strength (verse 14), an independent quality, not a property of **wisdom**; he has personal authority (verses 15-16); he leads into the ways of truth (verses 19-20); he enables people to inherit God's gifts (verse 21). This passage also sets out his personal affections: hatred (verse 13), love (verse 17), joy (verses 30-31). He also gives personal promises (verse 21). He also commands obedience as a matter of life and death (verses 32-36). Whether Solomon fully understood his own words may be an open question (compare 1 Peter 1:10-11). But receiving the words as from God, weighing their natural meaning, and comparing them with other Scriptures, we are certain that they describe not an attribute but a person—eternal, omniscient, in the most endearing relationship to man, the Creator, Mediator, and Savior.

Careless soul, will your divine call be ignored when the allurements of sin and vanity have the power to arrest your ear? "Imagination cannot form to itself a more exquisite and affecting piece of scenery than that exhibited by Solomon in the Book of Proverbs. In his seventh chapter he introduces the world by its meretricious blandishments alluring the unwary to the chambers of destruction. In the succeeding chapter, by way of perfect contrast, appears in the beauty and majesty of holiness the Son of the Father, the true and eternal Wisdom of God, with all the tender love and affectionate concern of a parent, inviting men to the substantial joys and enduring pleasures of immortality in the house of salvation" (Bishop Horne).

2. Can ignorance be pleaded? **Does not wisdom call out?** (verse 1). Her cry is not in the middle of the night or on the street corners, but **on the heights along the way, where the paths meet.**

3. She cries out **beside the gates leading into the city.** Has she not followed you to your places of business, of pleasure, and of sin?

4. Does she not **raise [her] voice to all mankind** in the Bible, in the family, in the preached Word? The loudness and the perseverance of the **voice** is that of an earnest friend who warns of danger. For would she have cried so loud or continued for so long if she had not loved your soul, if she had not known the wrath that was hanging over you, the hell that was before you?

5. The great Teacher calls the **simple** and the **foolish** to **gain understanding.**

6. And where else can they hear such **worthy things?** They are worthy of the attention of princes, as they are about our Lord's glorious person, his everlasting covenant, his rich and sovereign love to sinners (verses 12-31).

7. Often the truth of God, by the tradition of men or the subtlety of the father of lies, becomes virtually a principle of error (Galatians 1:7-9). No wonder wisdom says, **My lips detest wickedness.**

8. Scriptural difficulties belong not to the Book itself, but to man's blind and corrupt heart.

9. The carnal mind cannot understand the Bible, any more than the blind can see the midday light of the sun. But "it is easy to all who have a desire for it and who are not blinded by the prince of this world" (*Reformers' Notes*). "What wonder if the unlettered and despised Christian knows more of the mysteries of heaven than the naturalists, though both wise and learned. Christ admits the believer into his heart, and Christ is in the heart of the Father" (Leighton). Wisdom not only opens up the truth but opens men's hearts to receive it. There will be, indeed, great truths they cannot understand. But they will grasp important, saving truths. Here "the wisest Solomon may fetch jewels for ornament, and the poorest Lazarus bread for life" (Bishop Reynolds).

10. Come then, sinner, sit with one of old, at the feet of your divine Teacher. **"Choose my instruction instead of silver, knowledge rather than choice gold."**

11. Enrich yourself with his satisfying and enduring treasures. For **nothing you desire can compare with her.** Will not God's children daily draw more abundantly from these treasures? Oh, let those treasures not be, like the pomp of this world, just looked on, but actively sought after and increasingly enjoyed.

12. **"I, wisdom, dwell together with prudence; I possess knowledge and discretion."** How adorable is the Being here before us!

Prudence is usually only thought to be a moral quality. Here we see that it is an attribute of deity. The humanity of our beloved Lord was filled with this perfection (Isaiah 11:2). With what divine acuteness of **wisdom** did he **possess knowledge and discretion** and so put his enemies to shame (Matthew 9:4-8; 22:15-46)!

13. "**To fear the LORD is to hate evil; I hate pride and arrogance, evil behavior and perverse speech.**" Such is the holiness of divine wisdom. She lives with **prudence**, but she cannot live with **evil**. Therefore, **to fear the LORD**, which is her very nature, **is to hate evil.** Thus regarding **pride** in all its forms, **arrogance** of spirit, **evil behavior and perverse speech,** the wisdom of God declares without reserve, "**I hate** them." A proud disciple of a lowly Savior—how offensive is this contradiction to our Master! What a stumbling-block this is to the world.

14. "**Counsel and sound judgment are mine; I have understanding and power.**" This **counsel** is not, as with man, the fruit of deliberation but divine intuition. It is not that it flows from God, but that he is himself the essence, the fountainhead. It is not that he has **understanding** to order and govern the world. Rather, he *is* **understanding.** All is in him. Everything is derived from him.

15. He proclaims himself to be the source of power and authority, no less than of counsel and judgment. "KING OF KINGS AND LORD OF LORDS" was the mysterious name written on his robe (Revelation 19:16). Yet his crown does not displace the regal diadem from the brow of earthly rulers, nor is the scepter to fall from their hands. These symbols of power are to be held, but in subordination to his own.

"**By me kings reign.**" This happens not only by permission but by appointment. They bear his name and are stamped with his authority (Exodus 22:28; Psalm 82:6; John 10:35).

16. "**By me princes govern, and all nobles who rule on earth.**" Scripture lays down a truth that offends men: There is no power but of God; the powers that be are ordained of God. Rulers are ministers of God, not servants of the people (Romans 13:1-6). And all things, all power in heaven and on earth, were delivered to our Lord by his Father (Matthew 11:27; 28:18).

17. "**I love those who love me, and those who seek me find me.**" Now look at the grace of this divine Person toward **those who love** him. By nature nobody is interested in God's grace (Romans 8:7). But his free grace first implants **love** in their hearts and then cheers them with the assurance of his own love (1 John 4:19; John 14:21). We love because we are drawn to God (Jeremiah 31:3).

We **seek,** not by the impulse from within, but by the grace from above, and seeking we **find** (Isaiah 45:19; Jeremiah 29:13; Matthew 7:7-8).

18. What a treasure seekers find! This fading world offers a poor portion. But those who seek find the **riches and honor** of eternity. That is why these riches are described as **enduring wealth and prosperity**.

19. Is not this **fruit . . . better than fine gold? It surpasses choice silver.**

20. When our way is blocked, how valuable is Wisdom's counsel, which leads to **the way of righteousness**.

The sober-minded Christian is equally remote from formal service and enthusiastic delusion. The intelligent and spiritually-minded churchman is both separate from exclusiveness or idolatry on the one side, and from indiscriminate Christianity on the other. He values highly his scriptural ordinances, but he does not mistake them for the substance of the Gospel, and he does not substitute self-induced effervescence in their place. This is the *Via Media*, Christian duty, consistency, and fruitfulness.

21. Even now from his royal bounty does Wisdom make **their treasuries full**. But an even more joyful day is yet to come when the redeemed will unite in their testimony that one Christ has abundantly filled us all!

22. Only a perverse mind can suppose an attribute here. So glorious are the rays of the eternal supreme deity, his distinct personality, his essential unity, that the mysterious, ever-blessed Being now undoubtedly stands before us. To receive his own revelation of himself is our great privilege.

How clear is his essential unity with the Father. **"The LORD brought me forth,"** for he was present with him in the heart of the deity. Every movement of the divine mind was infinitely known, every purpose of divine counsel eternally present and fully developed. The mode of his existence in the Godhead (and this is all that is revealed of this inscrutable subject) is generation. He was **brought . . . forth,** the only begotten Son, a term that it is much safer to adore than to expound, expressing, as it does, what is unsearchable. "Take care," says an old expositor, "that in this generation we invent nothing temporal, carnal, or human. But rather let us worship this generation, beholding it by faith; and let us take heed from searching further than Scripture teaches us. Otherwise we should deserve to be blinded and punished for our great curiosity."

No less clear is his eternal existence. He was in the beginning. He was **"the first of his works."** He was "destined and advanced to be the Wisdom and Power of the Father, Light and Life, and all in all, both in the creation and the redemption of the world" (Henry).

23-29. Connected with his eternity was his agency in the work of creation. **"I was appointed from eternity, from the beginning, before the world began"** (verse 23). The whole detail of the creative work is here laid out. Thus uncreated wisdom displayed in clear and undoubted glory "the divinity and eternity of Wisdom, meaning thereby the eternal Son of God, Jesus Christ our Savior" (*Reformers' Notes*).

30. Next he describes his unspeakable blessedness in communion with his Father. **"I was filled with delight day after day, rejoicing always in his presence."** He was in the heart of his Father as he delighted in his presence. So God is "willing that by the Son we should approach him, in the Son we should honor and adore him, and honor the Son as himself" (Scott).

31. But the wonder of wonders remains that he who was his Father's infinite delight and was infinitely delighting in him should find his delight from all eternity **in mankind.** How wonderful that he should, as it were, long to be with us, **rejoicing in his whole world.** On this foundation is our confidence, rest, and security.

32. "Now then, my sons, listen to me." It is no mean and undeserving person who is calling. It is none other than the Wisdom of God, the source of all light and knowledge (verses 12-14), the King of kings (verses 15-16), the loving rewarder of his children (verse 17), the rich portion and unfailing guide of his people (verses 18-19).

Look at him once again in his divine glory as the only-begotten Son of God (verses 22, 24), the Mediator in the everlasting councils of redemption (verse 23), the almighty Creator of the world (verses 27-30), the adorable Friend of sinners (verse 31). How should his divine majesty and condescending love endear his instruction to us! Yet his promised blessing is only for those who carry out what they hear him say and for **those who keep [his] ways** with godly fear, constancy, and perseverance, keeping their eye on **his ways,** their hearts toward them, and their feet in them. Yes, such people will be **blessed.**

33. "Listen to my instruction and be wise; do not ignore it." What a happy moment it is when the cold, dead indifference is gone. For it is an unimaginable delight to take on such a yoke. *Oh, my Prince, my Savior, you have founded your dominion on your blood. You rule only so that you may save. Take to yourself the glory and your victory. I am yours, not my own, forever.*

34. This is the hearing of faith, the voice of Christ in the inmost man, the impression of his Word on the heart (John 5:25; Revelation 3:20). The effect is untiring diligence and patient expectation, like the priest **waiting** at the **doors** of the tabernacle for the assured blessing (Exodus 29:42) or those **watching** at the temple gates for his return from his holy ministrations (Luke 1:10, 21). This willing and constant attendance on sacred ordinances indicates a healthy appetite for heavenly sustenance. Wisdom's child will always be familiar with wisdom's gates. Listen to the Lord's rebuke: "Wake up! Strengthen what remains and is about to die" (Revelation 3:2). "The places where the Gospel is faithfully preached are 'the gates and posts of the doors of Wisdom,' at which Christ would have his disciples to 'wait daily.' And may not Christians, consistently with other duties, redeem time for this waiting as well as the children of this world find time for their vain amusements, who yet do not neglect their one needful thing? Is not the time spared from attending on a weekday often spent in unprofitable visits or vain discourse? Should not ministers be 'instant in season, and out of season,' in preaching the word, and should not the people be glad of an opportunity of hearing it?" (Scott).

35. "The smiles of God make heaven; and those who obtain the favor of the Lord have a heaven on earth" (G. Lawson). Set this expectation before your eyes in waiting on your God: "I am seeking life for my soul. I will wait at the doorposts, missing no opportunity to receive the means of grace. I shall not wait in vain."

36. If only the sinner, the careless sinner, not the daring and ungodly only, would ponder how his heartless neglect of wisdom **harms himself.** How cruel he is to himself while he is despising his Savior. Every allurement of sin is the temptation of suicide, soul-murder. When people grab hold of it, it is as if men were in love with damnation. "**All who hate me love death.**" They **love** what will be their **death** and push away from them what would be their life. Sinners die because they want to die. So they are left without any excuse.

Proverbs
Chapter 9

1. Wisdom has built her house; she has hewn out its seven pillars. We have delighted to contemplate the divine Savior in his glorious majesty, and especially in his wonderful love to the sons of men (8:22-31). Here his love is poured out before us. The parable of the marriage feast clearly identifies the speaker. Then the King made the feast and sent his servants to invite the guests (Matthew 22:1-4). Here **wisdom** is a queen, which was the Eastern custom.

Built her house. This is the church of the living God, which is firmly set on the **pillars** of eternal truth (1 Timothy 3:15; Ephesians 2:20-22; Hebrews 3:3-4). The great sacrifice supplies her feast (1 Corinthians 5:7; Psalm 36:8; Isaiah 25:6).

2. She has prepared her meat and mixed her wine and so has amply provided for **her table.**

3. Wisdom is attended by **her maids.**

4. She cries to **all who are simple,** who are ignorant of their danger (22:3) and easily deceived (14:15), and **to those who lack judgment,** who have no understanding about their need or desire for the blessing.

"**Let all . . . come in here.**" Here is a feast not to see, but to enjoy.

5. "**Come, eat my food**" (the bread of life) "**and drink the wine**" of the Gospel of grace and joy.

Are not all comers welcome to the gospel feast? The Master's heart flows along with every offer of his grace. His servants are ministers of reconciliation (2 Corinthians 5:18-20). Their message is to tell of the bounty of Messiah's house and to invite sinners to him. All the blessings of the Gospel are set before you—love without beginning, end, or change. Honor the liberty of his mercy. Let him have the full glory of his own grace, who invites you to a feast when he might have frowned on you and sent you to hell. Calvin speaks of the pleading invitations of Christ as "his sweet and more than motherly allurements" and beautifully adds, "The word of God is never opened to us, but that he with a motherly sweetness opens his own heart to us." Let this heavenly hope be enthroned in your soul, displacing every subordinate object from its hold on your affections, eclipsing the glories of this present world, absorbing your whole mind, consecrating your whole heart.

6. The very severities of the Gospel prepare the way for its consolations. But these blessings can never be appreciated until the **simple leave** their **ways.** You must either **leave** them or Christ (James 4:4). To live in them is to remain in the company of the dead (21:16). To **leave** them is to **walk in the way of understanding** (13:20). Are they more to you than salvation? To be the friend of the world is to be the enemy of God. You must separate yourself from anything that is unholy, so you can be welcomed by the Almighty (2 Corinthians 6:17-18).

7. Wisdom's messengers must discriminate in the proclamation of their message. Though the simple welcome it, **a mocker** and **a wicked man** will rebel. You must distinguish between the ignorant and the deliberate **mocker.** Paul once "acted in ignorance and unbelief" (1 Timothy 1:13). But his fellow countrymen deliberately refused the blessing and shut themselves out from the free offer of salvation (Acts 13:45-46, 50).

One cannot think of the **mocker** without compassion. Under an assumed happy life, he would envy, as Colonel Gardiner did, his own dog. "I hate life," said Voltaire, "yet I am afraid to die." Such is the bitterness of the soul linked with rebellion against God.

Yet, in dealing with him, Solomon gives us here the rule of Christian prudence. The Gospel is too holy to be exposed to scoffing fools (Matthew 7:6). Why should we correct and rebuke when more harm than good will be the result? Avoid irritations. Wait for the favorable opportunity. Sometimes a sad, serious, intelligible silence is the most effective reproof.

8. A wise man is happy to encourage timely reproof (28:23). Conscious of his own feelings, **he will love you,** his reprover, as a friend of his best interests.

9. The **wise** will be instructed and taught from the lowest person, so that he can become **wiser still** and **add to his learning.**

Wisely to give and humbly to receive reproof requires much prayer, self-denial, love, and sincerity. Faithful are the wounds of a friend (27:6). Happy is the church that receives the loving admonitions of the Christian pastor with humility and thankfulness. As was observed of Mr. Martyn, "He felt reproof to be 'a duty of unlimited extent and almost insuperable difficulty.' But, he said, 'the way to know when to address men and when to abstain is to love.' And as love is most genuine where the heart is most abased, he resolved not to reprove others when he could conscientiously be silent, except he experienced at the same time a peculiar contrition of spirit."

10. "The fear of the LORD is the beginning of wisdom, and knowledge of the Holy One is understanding." The repetition of this weighty sentence (see 1:7) deepens our estimate of its importance.

The fear of the LORD was a lovely grace in the perfect humanity of Jesus (Isaiah 11:2-3). The child of God has only one dread—to offend his Father. The child of God has only one desire—to please and delight in him.

Here **the fear of the LORD** is combined with knowledge of the Holy One. The parallelism with the former clause seems to demand this meaning. The application of the plural number to the sacred name is used elsewhere by Solomon (1:1-20; Ecclesiastes 12:1) as well as by other inspired writers (Genesis 1:26; Job 35:10; Isaiah 44:5). [Editor's note: Though a plural form in the Hebrew, the word *Elohim* can be treated as a singular, when it means the one supreme Deity.] Bishop Horsley remarks, "God is the only Being to whom the same name in the singular and in the plural may be indiscriminately applied. And this change from one number to the other, without anything in the principles of language to account for it, is frequent in speaking of God in the Hebrew language." The reason for this strange use of language is obvious to anyone who receives with implicit and reverential faith the scriptural revelation of the divine essence.

If all men knew **the Holy One**, who would not fear the Lord (Revelation 15:4)?

11. Many . . . days and **years . . . added to your life** were God's reward in the Old Testament (3:2, 16; 4:10; 10:27). The prospect of **years** being **added to your life** is unimaginably joyful, as it speaks of endless eternity and being fully satisfied with the enjoyment of heaven.

12. "If you are wise, your wisdom will reward you; if you are a mocker, you alone will suffer." The consequences of our conduct, good or bad, rebound on ourselves. God does not benefit from what we do, and he is beyond the reach of any harm being done to him. The **wise** man's light is a blessing to the church and to the world (Matthew 5:14, 16). And he will receive a **reward** for his **wisdom**.

The **mocker** is a burden to his minister and a stumbling-block to his church. But he hurts nobody more than himself. Everybody must bear his own burden, and whatever a person sows, that will he reap (Galatians 6:5, 7-8).

13. Wisdom's free and gracious invitation has been set before us. And we might almost ask, who could resist it? Now we have an allurement from the opposite direction. For sin is no less keen to destroy than wisdom is to save. The distinct character of **Folly** as alluded to here can be seen from the previous descriptions of it (chapters 2, 5, 7). The lusts of the body are in open opposition to divine wisdom. "The delight of the soul fixed on anything but God and his grace is spiritual adultery" (Diodati).

14. With utter shamelessness Folly dares to present herself **at the highest point of the city.**

15. She allures anyone who might **pass by, who go straight on their way.**

17. May not some **stolen water,** some **secret** indulgences, be allowed? Ah, sinner, there is no such thing as **secret** sin. All is exposed before God's eye.

But the strength of this temptation is that they are forbidden pleasures. Restraint provokes the dormant power of sin, just as children do what is forbidden just because it is forbidden. When Augustine describes how he stole fruit from the pear tree, he says that he did not do it because he was hungry, as he threw away most of the fruit, but for the mere pleasure of sin as sin. He did it to break God's law. It is instructive to see how he traces the sin to its root, as the psalmist also did (51:5). *Behold my heart, O Lord, which you have had pity on in the very depth of the bottomless pit.*

18. How will all this end? Satan shows only the sparkling cup and the glaring light. Ask to look into the inner room. The blinded fool has deliberately closed his eyes, or else he would **know that the dead are there, that her guests are in the depths of the grave.**

Proverbs
Chapter 10

1. The proverbs of Solomon: A wise son brings joy to his father, but a foolish son grief to his mother. The previous chapters have beautifully set out the nature and value of heavenly wisdom and contrasted it with the fascinations of sinful folly. We now come to what are more correctly (not excluding the foregoing) **the proverbs of Solomon.** They are for the most part unconnected sentences, remarkable for profound thought and acute observation, expressed in an antithetical or illustrative form. They comprise a divine system of morals that should be universally applied. They are a treasure of wisdom in all its varied details. They apply to the individual, the family, and governments. The previous chapters form a striking introduction to the book. The glorious description of the great Counselor (chapters 1 and 8) commends to us his gracious instruction concerning the principles of true happiness and practical godliness.

This first verse may have been placed at the beginning to point to the value of a godly education in its personal, social, and national influence, which are linked to both time and eternity. The child who has been prayed over, instructed, and disciplined will in the Lord's time choose the path of wisdom and so bring **joy to his father.**

Many a **mother,** alas, has **grief** brought to her by her **foolish son.** In such cases, has not indulgence instead of restraint, pleasure instead of godliness, the world instead of the Bible educated the child?

2. Ill-gotten treasures are of no value, but righteousness delivers from death. The most substantial earthly **treasures are of no value** (23:5; Matthew 6:19). **Ill-gotten treasures** are even less valuable. "A man may seem to benefit from them and to live a wonderful life for a time" (Bishop Sanderson). But what was the benefit of Naboth's vineyard to Ahab when in his ivory palace he was withering under God's curse? How did Judas benefit from his thirty pieces of silver? They did not deliver him **from death;** instead, their intolerable sting plunged him into eternal death. A

67

godly person is told to seek **righteousness**. Take up the prayer and confidence of the man of God: "May integrity and uprightness protect me, because my hope is in you" (Psalm 25:21).

3. The LORD does not let the righteous go hungry but he thwarts the craving of the wicked. To spiritualize the temporal promises diminishes their effect in our lives. They are not restricted to the old dispensation. "Yet the promises require faith, whereby we believe that God helps us" (Cope).

4. Lazy hands make a man poor, but diligent hands bring wealth. Daily observation confirms the fact that **lazy hands** bring poverty, while **diligent hands bring wealth**, the reward of the harvest. Industry was the law of paradise (Genesis 2:15), and although it now bears the stamp of the Fall (Genesis 3:19), it is still a blessing and under God's providence brings **wealth**. The Lord's favors were never given to loiterers. Moses and the shepherds of Bethlehem were keeping watch over their flocks (Exodus 3:1-2; Luke 2:8-9). Gideon was busy in his threshing floor (Judges 6:11). "Our idle days," as Bishop Hall has observed, "are Satan's busy days."

5. He who gathers crops in summer is a wise son, but he who sleeps during harvest is a disgraceful son. Indolence has just been contrasted with diligence. Forethought is here contrasted with improvidence. The **wise son . . . gathers** his blessing at the appropriate time. It is as much the will of God that the young should gather knowledge as that the farmer should gather his harvest. How often we can trace poverty of mind, enervation of character, and unprofitable habits to sleeping **during the harvest**. "He who idles away the time of his youth will bear the shame of it when he is old" (Henry). "If it should ever fall to the lot of youth to peruse these pages, let such a reader remember that it is with the deepest regret that I recollect in my manhood the opportunities of learning that I neglected in my youth; that through every part of my literary career I have felt pinched and hampered by my own ignorance; and that I would at this moment give half the reputation I have had the good fortune to acquire if by doing so I could rest the remaining part on a sound foundation of learning and science" (Sir Walter Scott).

Look again at the large harvest of opportunity in working for God. So while we have time, let us do good (Galatians 6:10). What a wonderful privilege it is to gather with Christ in such a harvest (Matthew 12:30). And how **disgraceful** it is to do nothing when there is so much to be done.

May the Lord keep me from being like **he who sleeps**, perhaps in the very house of God, instead of listening to the voice from heaven. This brings shame on my minister, my church, and my Lord.

6. Blessings crown the head of the righteous, but violence overwhelms the mouth of the wicked. Is not affliction the lot **of the righteous** (John 16:33; Acts 14:22; 2 Timothy 3:12)? Yet how abundantly it is compensated for by the **blessings** that **crown the head of the righteous.**

These **blessings** are temporal (Deuteronomy 28:1-6; 1 Timothy 4:8) and spiritual (Isaiah 32:17). These **blessings** are from man (16:7; Job 29:11-13) and from God (Psalm 3:8; 5:12; Isaiah 64:4-5; Matthew 5:3-12).

7. Truly **the memory of the righteous will be a blessing** to his family and to the church. This applies to a godly parent (31:28), a faithful minister (Hebrews 13:7), a righteous king (2 Chronicles 35:24-25), a public benefactor (2 Chronicles 24:6), and a self-denying Christian (Mark 14:9). "No spices can so embalm a man, no monument can so preserve his name and memory, as a pious conversation [conduct], whereby God has been honored, and man benefited. The fame of such a person is in the best judgments far more precious and truly glorious than is the fame of those who have excelled in any other deeds or qualities" (Barrow).

No such honor belongs to **the wicked.** Even now their memory **will rot** in corruption. "You may choose," said godly Bishop Pilkington, "whether you will be remembered to your praise or to your shame."

8. The wise in heart accept commands, but a chattering fool comes to ruin. The **heart** is the seat of true wisdom, and a teachable spirit is the best proof of its influence. For whoever knows himself is grateful for further light. As soon as the **commands** come down from heaven, the well-instructed Christian will **accept** them, like his father Abraham (Hebrews 11:8; Genesis 22:1-3).

But look at the person who professes to be religious but is devoid of this wisdom in his heart. We find him a man of creeds and doctrines but not of prayer. He prefers to ask curious questions rather than listen to simple truths. He is occupied with other people's business and neglects his own. He wanders from church to church and from house to house like **a chattering fool.** He will come **to ruin** and fall into disgrace, beaten with the rod of his own foolishness. Let us look at this picture as a beacon against the foolishness of our own hearts. Young Christian, beware of a specious religion that has no humility, consistency, and love because it is separated from a close walk with God.

9. The man of integrity walks securely, but he who takes crooked paths will be found out. A Christian should be a **man of integrity,** though he is not a man of sinless perfection. He **walks** willingly before God, not before men. Impurity does indeed defile the holiest activity. Nature's cry is, "Show me an easier path." **The man of integrity walks** under the shield of the Lord's protection, his providence, and the shadow of his promises. There will be difficulties, but a deliverance will be provided, just as the Babylonian exiles were delivered through the fire from the infinitely greater danger of apostasy (Daniel 3:21-29).

Because Peter did not walk in the right way, he denied the foundation of the Gospel (Galatians 2:14). So we must learn the value of this principle for an enlightened and full reception of the truth, that we may welcome a Ruler as well as a Savior (Acts 5:31). We must combine his scepter with his sacrifice, his holy precepts with his precious promises. In this way we will put into practice the rule of the Gospel in everything we do. "The man conscious to himself of an honest meaning, and a due course of prosecuting it, feels no check or struggling of mind, no regret or sting of heart. He therefore moves quickly forward with courage, as there is nothing in him to stop him, distract him or disturb him" (Barrow).

But to bend God's rules and to follow **crooked paths** will shake our confidence far more than the heaviest cross. God's eyes see everything that you do, and you **will be found out** and brought to shame. In this way Jacob was punished to the end of his days. Peter was openly rebuked (Galatians 2:11-14). Judas and Ananias are examples that are recorded in the annals of the church to the end of time.

10. He who winks maliciously causes grief, and a chattering fool comes to ruin. The intended contrast here is between the man who brings trouble on his fellowmen and the man who brings trouble on himself. The first is a plague to his neighbor because he is God's enemy. And because the **fool** despises wisdom (1:7), he **comes to ruin**.

11. The mouth of the righteous is a fountain of life, but violence overwhelms the mouth of the wicked. The indwelling Spirit, a well of living water, is the glorious privilege of **the righteous** (John 4:14; 7:38). So his **mouth,** replenished from the heavenly source, **is a fountain of life,** sending out refreshing waters (16:22). The precious gift of speech is thus consecrated to God's service.

Servant of God, honor your great privilege of ministering a blessing to the church in this way (verse 21; 15:7; Ephesians 4:29). How much you owe to God's grace who has made your **mouth . . . a fountain of life,** while **violence overwhelms the mouth of the wicked**. The latter find that they turn against themselves and are covered with confusion.

12. Hatred stirs up dissension, but love covers over all wrongs. Here is a simple but forceful contrast. **Hatred,** however disguised by a smooth exterior, is the selfish principle of man (Titus 3:3). Like an underground fire, it constantly **stirs up** mischief and creates or keeps alive envy and criticisms. When this **dissension** is set on fire, God's name is greatly dishonored. Is this not a matter for much prayer, watchfulness, and resistance?

Let us study 1 Corinthians 13 in all its detail. Let it be the mirror for our hearts. **Love covers,** overlooks, speedily forgives, and forgets. Full of candor and inventiveness, it puts the best construction on doubtful matters and does not expose the faults of a brother. Oh, let us put on the Lord Jesus in his spirit of forbearing, sacrificial love, and let us forgive as we have been forgiven by Christ (Colossians 3:13). Geier has commented, "It is one thing to cover sin before men, another thing to cover it before God. The first is an act of love (1 Corinthians 13:4; Galatians 6:2). The last requires an infinite price, equal to the turning away of the eternal wrath of God (Romans 3:25; 1 John 1:7; Psalm 32:1)."

13. Wisdom is found on the lips of the discerning, but a rod is for the back of him who lacks judgment. Solomon and his son admirably illustrate this contrast. The **wisdom that is found on the lips** is the fruit of a **discerning** heart. The whole world came to hear Solomon's **wisdom** (1 Kings 4:31; 10:1). Rehoboam lacked **judgment,** but his father was full of discernment. Rehoboam's foolishness was like **a rod for** his **back.** The **rod** was the usual form of corporal punishment under the Mosaic law. Learn to seek **wisdom** from the **lips** of the wise. The lack of this **wisdom,** or rather the lack of a heart to seek it, will bring us under the **rod.**

14. Wise men store up knowledge, but the mouth of a fool invites ruin. Solomon showed that he deserved the title of "wise man" by the way he used to **store up knowledge.** No wonder that wisdom is found on the lips, for "out of the overflow of the heart the mouth speaks" (Matthew 12:34). Jerome mentions about his friend Nepotian, "By daily reading and meditating in the sacred volume, he had make his soul a library of Christ." If you **store up knowledge** when you are young, what a valuable treasure will be accumulated, although it will only be enough to meet the coming trials. Add something every day to your storehouse. For lack of sound wisdom the **fool** only opens himself to his own **ruin,** for he is in constant rebellion against God.

15. The wealth of the rich is their fortified city, but poverty is the ruin of the poor. This means exactly what it appears to say. **The wealth of the rich** man fences him in and protects him from many invading evils. But this leads him to rest on human protection as his comfort and security in life. All thoughts about God are blotted out, and man becomes a god to himself.

The poor have no such defense. They live in a city that has no walls and are exposed to every attack (14:20; 19:7; 22:7; John 7:48-49).

So we are ready to agree how happy the rich are and how wretched the poor are. But God's Word teaches us something other than this. God has chosen the poor of this world who are rich in faith (James 2:5). Think of Jesus sanctifying the state of poverty by his own blessed example (Luke 2:7-12; 8:3; Matthew 8:20). Think of the riches of his grace, raising the poor from the mire.

Both states have their besetting temptations, and both need God's special grace. Both are safe—when the **rich** are poor in spirit and large in heart (1 Chronicles 29:14), and when the **poor** are rich in faith and are content with acquiring godliness (1 Timothy 6:6-8). See also James 1:9-10.

16. The wages of the righteous bring them life, but the income of the wicked brings them punishment. Work, not idleness, is the stamp of a servant of God. So even the duties of our daily life should lead us in the way of **life** (Jeremiah 22:15-16). God works in us, by us, with us, and through us (Isaiah 26:12). We work in and through him. Remember, "A man reaps what he sows" (Galatians 6:7).

17. He who heeds discipline shows the way to life, but whoever ignores correction leads others astray. It is unimaginable mercy that **the way to life** has been opened up for us. **Discipline** sets the way before us. **He who heeds discipline** cannot fail to find **life** and to enjoy it. The more we value **discipline**, the more we will take note of every practical lesson we learn in the heavenly school. But the person who **ignores correction** is deaf to the voice that would save him from ruin.

18. He who conceals his hatred has lying lips, and whoever spreads slander is a fool. Scriptural history from the first chapter of fallen man abundantly illustrates this proverb. Consider the hidden **hatred** of Cain talking with his brother (Genesis 4:8), Saul plotting against David (1 Samuel 18:20-22, 29), and the enemies of the church on the return of God's people to Jerusalem from Babylon (Ezra 4:1-16; Nehemiah 6:2).

Is this root of bitterness mortified in the Christian's heart? Is there any insincerity in our meetings with those to whom we feel, if not **hatred,** at least strong repugnance? In the language of polite courtesy there is much that is hollow, if not false. Do we really mean what we say? Are not our outward actions often at variance with our inner feelings? Do we not often boost our own reputation at the expense of somebody else's? "Occasions of evil report can never be lacking to them who seek or are ready to embrace them. No innocence, no wisdom can in any way prevent them, and if they are admitted as grounds of defamation, no man's good name can be secure. It is not every possibility, every seeming, every faint show or glimmering appearance that is sufficient to ground bad opinion or reproachful discourse concerning our fellow creature. The matter should be clear, notorious, and palpable before we admit a disadvantageous conceit into our head, a distasteful resentment into our heart, a harsh word into our mouth about him. Justice requires full proof. 'Charity thinketh no evil, and believeth all things' for the best. Wisdom is not forward to pronounce before full evidence" (Barrow).

This spirit is in God's eyes **slander,** an offense against the new commandment of love that is the hallmark of all the disciples of Jesus (John 13:34-35). *Lord, purge our hearts from these hateful, hidden corruptions.*

19. When words are many, sin is not absent, but he who holds his tongue is wise. Hypocrisy and slander are not the only sins of the tongue. Indeed, considering the corrupt spring from which they flow we cannot think of **words,** much less **when words are many,** without **sin.**

There is the sin of *egotism.* Our own mouth praises us, but no one else (27:2). We love to hear ourselves talk and to present our own judgments intrusively.

There is also the sin of *vain babbling.* The fool talks forever about nothing, not because he is full, but because he is empty; not in order to give instruction, but for the pure love of talking. This wantonness is a sin of the flesh, trifling with the most responsible talent, when "conversation

72

is," as Bishop Butler rightly says, "merely the exercise of the tongue; no other human faculty has any place in it. One meets with people in the world who never seem to have made the wise man's observation that 'there is a time to keep silence.' These times, one would think, should be easily discerned by everybody; namely, when a man has nothing to say, or nothing but what is better unsaid." The government of the tongue is, therefore, a searching test of the soundness of our religion. Since the **sin** is linked to **many . . . words**, it is surely **wise** to hold our **tongue**—not in silence, but in caution; to weigh our words before uttering them; never speaking except when we have something to say; speaking only just enough; considering the time, the person, and the circumstances. "Light words weigh heavy in God's balance" (Nicholls). Never let us think of these sins as anything less than the nails that pierced our Lord's hands and feet. Thus we will become like the one who **holds his tongue**. See also Psalm 141:3.

20. The tongue of the righteous is choice silver, but the heart of the wicked is of little value. If our **tongue** is our shame in giving voice to sin (verses 18-19), is it not also our glory? Our words should be **choice silver**, refined of this world's dross, shining with heavenly brightness.

21. Note how useful this part of the body can be. If we are living with God, it will diffuse heavenly leaven. **The lips of the righteous nourish many.** We are to feed the church with our words. Of Bishop Ridley, the martyrologist Foxe records in his own beautiful style: "To his sermon the people resorted, swarming about him like bees, and coveting the sweet flowers and wholesome juice of his fruitful doctrine." And as our great Master broke the bread and give it to his disciples for them to distribute (Matthew 14:19; Mark 6:41; Luke 9:16; John 6:11 [KJV]), so does he now give to his servants heavenly provision that is suitable for the needs of those in their charge. And every Sunday the wonderful miracle is set before us. The imperishable bread multiplies as it is broken. The hungry, the mourners, the weary, and the faint—yes, all who feel their need are refreshed and invigorated.

As for the **fools,** they may have boxes full of treasure, but their hearts are empty of **choice silver** (verse 20). So far from feeding other people, **fools die for lack of judgment.** They die from a heart that does not seek discernment. "They die of famine in the middle of the rich pastures of the Gospel" (Schultens).

22. The blessing of the LORD brings wealth, and he adds no trouble to it. We were told in verse 4 that **diligent hands bring wealth.** Here we see that **the blessing of the LORD brings wealth.** There is no inconsistency here. The one notes the primary source of wealth; the other points to the instrumental source of wealth. Neither can be effective without the other. The sluggard looks for prosperity without diligence; the atheist looks for prosperity only from being **diligent.** The Christian, armed with

God's blessing, is **diligent**. This wise combination keeps him active and at the same time humble and dependent on God (John 6:27).

To **the blessing of the LORD** the divine hand **adds no trouble**. This is true in the sense that the Lord **adds no trouble** that he does not turn into a blessing. Accumulation of riches may be the accumulation of sorrows. Lot's covetous choice was fraught with bitterness (Genesis 13:10-11; 14:12; 19:15; 2 Peter 2:8). Ahab wore a crown but lay on his sickbed discontent (1 Kings 21:4). The rich man's rejection of Christ was the source of present and everlasting sorrow (Luke 18:23-25). Happy are those who know what it is to be in need and also know what it is to have plenty and are content in both situations (Philippians 4:12).

23. A fool finds pleasure in evil conduct, but a man of understanding delights in wisdom. Are we sufficiently careful not to indulge our wit or humor at another person's expense? For to behave in such a way is utterly selfish. Young people cannot be taught enough to consider the feelings of others and to be considerate.

A man of understanding is too wise to take reckless delight in harming his neighbor. Let us who bear the name of our Lord cultivate his self-denying, loving mind (Philippians 2:4-8).

24. What the wicked dreads will overtake him; what the righteous desire will be granted. We know that **the wicked** will be found in their sins, being fearful of their doom and without hope.

But if what **the righteous desire** is **granted**, faith and patience will be tested. Growth in grace is given by deep and humbling views of our corruption. Longings for holiness are fulfilled by painful affliction. Prayers are answered by crosses. But all things that are necessary will be **granted**.

25. When the storm has swept by, the wicked are gone, but the righteous stand firm forever. Suddenly, like a **storm . . . the wicked** are swept away. All his hopes, pleasures, and dependencies, all his opportunities of grace and God's offers of mercy, are swept away in a moment forever. But he who does God's will lives forever (1 John 2:17); he will **stand firm**. Faith has attached him to the Rock of Ages and has built his house on that Rock, and no storm can uproot him (Matthew 7:25).

But remember that this is the confidence of **the righteous**. Sin, when it is indulged in, will shake this foundation far more than all the outward attacks of earth and hell. So hold fast in godly fear. Then you can look at trouble; you can look into the face of death itself and without dismay say, "I am safe." See also Romans 11:20.

26. As vinegar to the teeth and smoke to the eyes, so is a sluggard to those who send him. This is a striking picture of how annoying the **sluggard** is to those who employ him. If a fire needs putting out, if medical assistance is necessary, an urgent message has to be sent. In such a situation **a sluggard** is a worthless person to have around. Common prudence dictates the selection of active and industrious servants.

The **sluggard** can disappoint and provoke his earthly master. So we must ensure that we are not sluggards to our heavenly Master. Those who professed faith at Laodicea were especially hated in God's sight (Revelation 3:16). The slothful minister is accountable to the one who sends him. When he hears the Master's call to go into his vineyard, he disobeys at his peril (Matthew 20:7; 25:30).

27. The fear of the LORD adds length to life, but the years of the wicked are cut short. Here **the fear of the LORD** is not a single grace. It includes the substance of all godly inclinations, for all come from one source. Those who **fear** the Lord are essentially different from **the wicked**, who fear those whom they hate. The child of God fears him whom he loves. **The fear of the LORD** is rightly contrasted with **the wicked** because the latter have rejected the grace of God. Excessive worldliness depletes the spring of life and often brings it to an untimely end.

28. The prospect of the righteous is joy, but the hopes of the wicked come to nothing. The fear of the Lord, so far from being opposed *to*, is often connected *with* **the prospect of the righteous**. This may well be called **joy**, as it is "accompanied with sweet patience, joyful hope, and crowned with a happy issue" (Diodati). It has its origin in eternity (Titus 1:2). Its substance is Christ and heaven. The foundation is the work of Christ (1 Peter 1:3, 21). Do I grasp this hope? Then, as a godly man exclaimed, "Let who will be miserable; I will not, I cannot!" Christian, make the ground of your hope sure (2 Peter 1:10). Manifest its **joy** as becomes an heir of glory. Do not let a drooping spirit make the world think that you have a scanty hope. Being full of doubt leaves believers and unbelievers nearly on the same level. A clear understanding of this infinite **joy** stimulates our being "all the more eager to make [our] calling and election sure" (2 Peter 1:10).

29. The way of the LORD is a refuge for the righteous, but it is the ruin of those who do evil. Coming into **the way of the LORD** was strength to the upright Nicodemus. The weakest believer will, in the Lord's strength, march on and not faint. When we look at our own resources, we might "as well despair of moving sin from our hearts as of casting down the mountains with our fingers" (Bishop Reynolds). Yet none of us needs to shrink from the confession that we can do all things through Christ who strengthens us (Philippians 4:13).

No such resources support **those who do evil**. They are prisoners instead of soldiers. They do not realize that they need strength. The Judge will tell them to go away from him, and this will be their **ruin** (Luke 13:27).

30. The righteous will never be uprooted, but the wicked will not remain in the land. We know that **the righteous** "enjoy in this life by faith and hope their everlasting life" (*Reformers' Notes*). This is a confidence that neither earth nor hell can shake (Romans 8:38-39).

As far as **the wicked** are concerned, it is not a question of their having their confidence **uprooted** because they have never had this confidence. They have no title as **the righteous** do. They are not God's sons or heirs of the earth.

31. The mouth of the righteous brings forth wisdom, but a perverse tongue will be cut out. Here is another picture of the fruitfulness of a gracious tongue. It **brings forth wisdom.** This gift needs to be deeply pondered and carefully cultivated. This will be applied in different ways by different people. How, what, when, and to whom to speak is a matter of great **wisdom. A perverse tongue** provokes its own ruin. It **will be cut out** (8:13; 18:7; Psalm 12:3; 52:1-5; 120:3-4; Numbers 16:1-33). *Oh, my God, how much I owe you for the bridle of discipline that restrains me from self-destruction!*

32. The lips of the righteous know what is fitting, but the mouth of the wicked only what is perverse. Let the minister of God study to clothe his most unpalatable message in the most **fitting** way. Let him mold it in all the sweetness of persuasion (2 Corinthians 5:11, 20), compassion (Romans 9:1-3; 2 Corinthians 2:4), and sympathy (Titus 3:2-3; 2 Corinthians 11:29). He must always gain his people's ears, that he may win their hearts.

Proverbs
Chapter 11

1. The LORD abhors dishonest scales, but accurate weights are his delight. How valuable is the Book of God for the minute details it gives on how we should behave. **Scales** and money are necessary for daily life. Underhanded dealings and hard bargains struck with self-complacent shrewdness are **dishonest scales**. They are forbidden by the law (Leviticus 19:35) and by the Gospel (Matthew 7:12; Philippians 4:8). They are hated by God, and they are an abomination to God (20:10; Deuteronomy 25:13-16; Amos 8:5-7).

But we must not just treat this proverb as a moral maxim. It was given as a warning to a flourishing Christian church (1 Thessalonians 4:6). Is it not a solemn thought that God's eye notes all our everyday dealings in life? He either **abhors** them, or else they are a **delight** to him.

2. When pride comes, then comes disgrace, but with humility comes wisdom. We know that **pride** was the main reason for the Fall (Genesis 3:5); and it still lives in fallen man (Mark 7:22). God shames men because they do not know their limits and because they refuse to stand on the low ground on which he has placed them (Luke 18:14; Isaiah 2:17).

Such is the folly of **pride, but with humility comes wisdom.** There is no greater proof of proud folly than only to believe what we understand. Happy is the humble spirit that comes to God's revelation, as it were, without any will or mind of its own. It must then humbly receive what God is pleased to give and be willing—yes, thankful—to be ignorant when God forbids us to intrude (Colossians 2:18).

3. Integrity is a most valuable guide in every perplexing situation. The single desire to know God's will so that we may do it will always bring light on our path (Psalm 143:10). **The unfaithful** who indulge in **duplicity** neglect this godly principle and so are **destroyed.**

4. In vain will the rich men of the earth seek a shelter from the wrath of the Lamb (Revelation 6:15-17). They and their hopes will perish together.

One of Bunyan's graphic and accurate sketches represents Ignorance ferried over the river by Vain Hope. Ignorance then ascends the hill alone, without encouragement, and is ultimately bound and carried away. "Then I saw," he adds with fearful solemnity, "that there was a way to Hell, even from the gates of Heaven." "They were not living, but lying hopes, and dying hopes" (Leighton). What a contrast this is to the anchor that is the hope of the soul (Hebrews 6:19).

8. The righteous man is rescued from trouble, and it comes on the wicked instead. These two classes of people change places in the dispensations of God. The same providence often marks divine faithfulness and retributive justice. The Israelites were delivered out of the trouble of the Red Sea, but the Egyptians were drowned by it (Exodus 14:21-28). Mordecai was **rescued** from the gallows, on which Haman was then hanged (Esther 5:14; 7:10). Peter was snatched from death, while his persecutors and jailers were condemned. We do not always see the same outward manifestation of God. But the love is always the same. That should make us fall in the dust and build our confidence on an unshakable foundation.

9. With his mouth the godless destroys his neighbor, but through knowledge the righteous escape. Haman, under the pretense of loyalty, sought to destroy a whole nation (Esther 3:8-13). Ziba, under the same false cover, wanted to destroy **his neighbor** (2 Samuel 16:1-4; compare 19:26-27). The lying steward from mere willfulness ruined his brother. Such is the hypocrite's **mouth.** It may be a small part of the body, but it is filled with sin and is itself set on fire by hell (James 3:5-6). When such a person is in the church, he is a wolf in sheep's clothing devouring the flock (Matthew 7:15).

But **the righteous escape . . . through knowledge.** They **escape** "by the light and direction of the Holy Spirit, and by the living knowledge of God's word, which gives to the faithful man enough wisdom to keep him safe" (Diodati). Learn the value of solid **knowledge.** Feeling, excitement, and imagination can expose us to an unsteady profession. **Knowledge** supplies principle and steadfastness. So to your faith add **knowledge** (2 Peter 1:5). Guard against plausible error, which is usually built on some single truth and pressed beyond its limit.

10. When the righteous prosper, the city rejoices; when the wicked perish, there are shouts of joy. The world, despite the natural hostility of the heart, gives testimony to consistent godliness and **rejoices . . . when the righteous prosper.** Their elevation to authority is a matter of general joy.

11. But the wicked are only a curse on the community. So it is a matter of great exultation when they **perish** (verse 10). Such was the joy of Rome on the death of Nero, and the public rejoicing during the French Revolution at the death of Robespierre. The people of God unite in shouts of joy, but not from any selfish feeling of revenge, much less from unfeeling hardness toward their fellow sinners. But when an obstacle to the good cause is removed, when God's justice against sin and his faithful preservation of his church are displayed, should not every feeling be absorbed in a supreme interest in his glory? Should **the upright** not shout? The alleluia of heaven is an exulting testimony to the righteous judgments of the Lord our God, bringing on his glorious kingdom (Revelation 19:1-2).

12. A man who lacks judgment derides his neighbor, but a man of understanding holds his tongue. Pride and uncharitableness show a man to be devoid of **judgment.** He is ignorant of himself, his neighbor, and his God. For could he delight in magnifying the speck in his brother's eye had he the **judgment** to view the plank in his own eye (Matthew 7:3-5)? Could he **deride his neighbor** if he really knew him to be as he himself is? This kind of blindness shows that he **lacks judgment.** "It denotes the lack of a right state of mind, judgment, and affections. Such a man is without heart to what is wise and good" (Scott).

A man of understanding may see much in **his neighbor** to stir his pity and excite his prayers, but nothing to deride him about. Self-knowledge shows the **man of understanding** to be the man of love. "He will keep himself from speaking or doing anything in scorn of another" (Diodati).

13. A gossip betrays a confidence, but a trustworthy man keeps a secret. Another breach of love is reproved here. The Gospel does not shut us up in our own private interests, as if we had no sympathy for our neighbor. It is a universal brotherhood of love. Yet it rebukes a **gossip** who, having no business of his own, traffics with his neighbor's name and honor and sells his scandals for gain or wantonness. It is not safe to be close to this cruel man who trifles with the happiness of his fellow creatures. For as readily as he **betrays a confidence** about a neighbor to us, so he will betray **a confidence** about us to someone else. All the bonds of friendship are broken into pieces. Let ears and lips be closed against him. Christian consistency includes the faithful spirit. It gives us great peace of mind to have a friend who is **a trustworthy man** who is able to **keep a secret.**

14. For lack of guidance a nation falls, but many advisers make victory sure. Even in personal matters the value of a wise counselor is generally admitted. **A nation,** therefore, without **advisers** is like a ship in the middle of rocks without a pilot and is in imminent danger. May the good Lord deliver us from the deserved national judgment of weak and blinded advisers.

David and Solomon, though themselves especially endowed with wisdom, governed their kingdoms with the help of wise advisers (compare Psalm 119:98-100 with 2 Samuel 15:12; 17:14; 1 Kings 12:6). The more there were of such advisers, the safer the people were. To one such wise adviser a heathen ruler owed the safety of his nation during a famine (Genesis 41:38-57).

The church too has often been preserved by this blessing (Acts 15:6-31).

15. He who puts up security for another will surely suffer, but whoever refuses to strike hands in pledge is safe. This is a repeated warning against putting up **security for another** (see 6:1-5) and is meant to inculcate circumspection, not to excuse selfishness or to dry up the sources of helpful sympathy. This must not be done for a stranger (27:13) whose character is unknown to us. For such incautious kindness, too often done at the expense of the family, will make us **suffer.**

We cannot forget one exception. The blessed Jesus, from his free grace, unsought and unasked (John 19:15, 17-18; Philippians 2:6-8), became surety, not for a friend, but for a stranger. He became one with us in nature, that he might be one with us in law. He took our place under the curse of the broken law (Galatians 3:13). He put his soul in our soul's place to the fullest extent and then in our nature paid the debt, which all the angels of heaven could never have discharged. Oh, this was suffering indeed! Sin was as thoroughly punished as it was thoroughly pardoned. So all that is left for us to do is to fall down before this grace and to spend our days, as we will spend eternity, adoring this wonderful manifestation of divine glory (Revelation 1:5-6; 5:12).

16. A kindhearted woman gains respect, but ruthless men gain only wealth. Everywhere the great value of godliness greets us. What admirable characteristics it gives to women (31:10). **A kindhearted woman** is known, not by her outward beauty, but by her "inner self" (1 Timothy 2:9-10; 1 Peter 3:3-4). Deborah was "a mother in Israel" and the adviser of a wayward people (Judges 4:4; 5:7). Esther used her influence over her heathen husband for the good of her nation (Esther 7:3-4; 9:12-13, 25). Dorcas was commended for her active usefulness (Acts 9:36). Such people should always receive honor and **respect.**

17. A kind man benefits himself, but a cruel man brings trouble on himself. Kindness is not natural benevolence, without God or godliness. It is the fruit of the Spirit, the image of our Father, and being gripped by the love of Christ (Galatians 5:22; 2 Corinthians 8:9; Colossians 3:13). It is not pity in words and looks. It is when our neighbor's trouble descends into the depths of our hearts and draws out from there our inner compassion. On the great day God will honor this before the assembled universe (Matthew 25:34-36).

It is no less certain that **a cruel man** will bring down disaster **on himself.** Unsubdued passion is like carrying around the very elements of hell. Joseph's brothers suffered for the way they had dealt with their brother in such a cruel way (Genesis 42:21). The treasures of selfishness will wound us (James 5:1-3). *Oh, my God, save me from the tyranny of my own lust. May your perfect image of mercy be my standard and my pattern!*

18. Both masters that claim the allegiance of the heart offer rewards. Did Satan fulfill all his promises (Genesis 3:4-5; Matthew 4:8-9)? No. **The**

wicked man earns deceptive wages, and his life ends in disappointment (Hebrews 3:13; Romans 6:21). Pharaoh's plan to exterminate the Israelites ended up increasing their number and being the downfall of himself and his people.

But the **sure reward** of the righteous makes a great contrast. No sinner since the fall of man has ever known the full reward of righteousness in this life. It may now be given as afflictions, with God's grace to support you so you can triumph over them. It will probably be given to us as it is given to the farmer who has to patiently wait for the harvest. But whenever it is given, no matter how long it is delayed, it is a **sure reward**. Remember, **righteousness** is the seed, and happiness is the harvest.

19. Righteousness not only delivers from death—it is the way that **life** may be attained. If righteousness is our main goal, God will make it our best friend. The man who **pursues evil** will be convicted of his sin in the end. He will say, "Had I but sown righteousness in God's service, I would have been infinitely happy." The joy of **the truly righteous man** will be wonderful (Revelation 22:12).

20. The **perverse** and the **blameless** are often contrasted. In all the contests between God and man, the question is, whose will is going to prevail? We should be grateful to the school of discipline that makes us feel the privilege of being subject to Christ (Psalm 119:67, 71). A **perverse heart** is especially hated by God, most of all when it is cloaked by external religion (Luke 16:15).

21. Those who are righteous will go free. "The best way for any man to do his children good is to be godly himself" (Dodd and Cleaver). Is this not an encouragement to parental faith as we leave our children to face this evil world?

22. Like a gold ring in a pig's snout is a beautiful woman who shows no discretion. Here is a most distasteful, yet apt comparison! Let us see things as the Bible shows them to us. Beauty is indeed to be honored as a gift from God. Yet in itself it is a fading vanity. If the **woman** lacks **discretion**, her beauty is as misplaced and as unbecoming as **a gold ring in a pig's snout**. Is the ornament going to make the filthy animal beautiful? No. This unnatural combination makes it forever an object of disgust. All the charms of beauty are lost on a foolish **woman**. Instead of retaining her honor, she only brings disgrace on herself.

"Lightness and fantastic clothing is the very sign hanging out that tells a vain mind lives within. The soul fallen from God has lost its true worth and beauty. Therefore it basely descends to these mean things, to serve and dress the body and take with it unworthy borrowed ornaments, while it has lost and forgotten God and does not seek him and does not know that he alone is the beauty and ornament of the soul, and his Spirit and grace his rich attire" (Leighton). Many a lovely form enshrines a rebellious mind. All external, even intellectual, accomplishments that have **no dis-**

cretion end in barrenness. We entirely depend on God's grace for him to fruitfully use his own gifts in us.

→ **23. The desire of the righteous ends only in good, but the hope of the wicked only in wrath.** "Desire is the wing of the soul, whereby it moves and is carried to the thing that it loves, as the eagle to the carcass, in the Scripture proverbs (Job 39:30; Matthew 24:28), to feed itself and to be satisfied with it" (Bishop Reynolds). **The desire of the righteous** must be **good** because it is God's own work. It must end **only in good** because it centers on God himself. God in Christ is the status of the righteous person, and what earthly status can compare with that? If I only subordinate my desires to his, I shall be happy. "Thou didst put into my mind good desires; and thou wilt bring me the same to good effect" (Collect for Easter Day).

But the hope of the wicked is directly opposed to God's will. Oh, let me daily test my desires by the true standard, and discipline them, that they may be fixed on the true object, so that I may delight myself in the Lord.

24. God scatters his blessings richly around, and those who have the same spirit do the same. But the man who **withholds unduly** will become poor. Generosity is the way to plenty. Have faith in God. Giving generously in his name will make us rich.

25. "How often, when my heart has been cold and dead, have I been quickened by the loving-kindness of the Lord upon doing something kind and loving for a fellow-creature, and more especially for a fellow Christian" (Venn). The minister is refreshed by his own message of salvation to his people. The Sunday school teacher learns many valuable lessons in the work of instruction. Every spiritual gift, every active grace, is increased by exercise, while its efficiency withers by neglect (Matthew 25:29).

26. People curse the man who hoards grain, but blessing crowns him who is willing to sell. This is a piece of sacred "political economy." It reminds us that we are the stewards of God's gifts (2 Corinthians 9:11). To use them for our own interest, without due regard for our neighbor, is being unfaithful to God (Matthew 25:26-27). A flagrant sin, therefore, is to withhold the very staff of life. This may be a prudent restraint in time of scarcity; but a selfish spirit that makes the poor suffer will bring a piercing curse. Would that the cry for the bread of life were as earnest and universal as for the bread that perishes!

27. He who seeks good finds goodwill, but evil comes to him who searches for it. Man is born for action, as the sparks fly upward or the stone tends downward. All of us are living with a stupendous measure of vital activity for **good** or for **evil**. Man was never intended, least of all the Christian, to be idle. Our divine Master went about doing **good**, always actively helping people. Anyone who does not live like this is a counterfeit. Usefulness is everything. We should feel ashamed of our depravity— that we could ever spend a day without seeking **good**. Nor must we wait to have opportunity brought to us. We must seek it diligently, getting up early and springing with joy to the work. Let us wake to the conscious responsibility of having the means of blessing our fellow sinners in our hands. Let us each do what we can. Whether this is a little or a lot, do it prayerfully, and faithfully. Do not be put off by trifling obstacles. Do not let your inability to do a great deal prevent you from doing what you are capable of. God honors a little strength (Revelation 3:8), the single talent (2 Corinthians 8:12), provided that it is dedicated to his service. And "filling up every hour with some profitable work, either of heart, head, or hands," as Brainerd has rightly observed, "is an excellent means of spiritual peace and boldness before God." "Religious people are heavy and moping and cast down principally because they are idle and selfish. Living and working for God and to save souls is the only way to know more and more of his truth and his salvation" (Venn).

The ceaseless energy of Satan's servants in seeking **evil** puts to shame our indifference! What is going to be the fruit of my diligence? Will it be a blessing or a curse to my fellow sinner? *Oh, my God, may it be from you, and for you!*

28. Whoever trusts in his riches will fall, but the righteous will thrive like a green leaf. Here is the cause and misery of the Fall. Man is to seek his rest in God's blessing rather than in himself (Jeremiah 9:23-24). **Riches** are one of his false grounds for trusting (10:15; Luke 12:19). He depends on them, as the saint depends on his God. And is not this the denial of the God who is above? This is a most unpopular truth, and it is one that only the heart crucified to the world by the cross of Christ can receive. The possession of riches in itself need not be a sin. See the gifts of God to Abraham, to David, and to Solomon. But it is a sin to trust in riches (Mark 10:23). The person who trusts in **riches** is bound to be disappointed by them in the end.

But **the righteous** are not like the blossom or leaf that is shaken off the tree and falls to the ground. They are **like a green leaf.** They abide in the true vine and are full of life and fruit (John 15:5). There may be, as in nature's winter, times of apparent barrenness. But the spring returns, and then the leaf will **thrive.** Does not this prospect fill us with joy and praise?

29. He who brings trouble on his family will inherit only wind, and the fool will be servant to the wise. A home that is united within itself flourishes under the special favor of God. But a home that is divided will be destroyed. Often an irreligious head of the home blights the comfort of the **family.** Indeed, he cannot neglect his own soul without harming **his family.** He deprives them of the blessing of holy prayers and godly example, while he **brings trouble** on them with the mischief of his ungodliness. And he himself **will inherit only wind,** in utter disappointment. Prayerless, careless parents, ponder the tragedy of bringing a curse instead of a blessing on your families!

30. The fruit of the righteous is a tree of life, and he who wins souls is wise. Here is **the fruit** of the **green leaf** (verse 28). The whole life of **the righteous**—his influence, his prayers, his instruction, his example—**is a tree of life.** What the **tree of life** was in paradise, it will be in heaven, as well as in the wilderness. It will be fruitful, nourishing, and healing (Revelation 22:2; 2:7; Proverbs 3:18; 15:4). "And surely he who by these means wins souls to righteousness and salvation is wise indeed" (Bishop Horne). Only he who bought them by his blood can win sinners to himself; yet he has set apart men for the work of "drawing souls to God, and to the love of him, sweetly gaining and making a holy conquest of them to God" (Diodati). This is the wisdom of our divine Master. He taught the people as much as they were able to understand (Mark 4:33). The great apostle became all things to all men, so that he might save some of them (1 Corinthians 9:20-22; 10:33). God grant that no minister of Christ may spend a day without working to win at least one soul for heaven.

But, blessed be God, this **fruit**, this wisdom, is not confined to the sacred calling. Do we love our Lord? Arise, let us follow in this happy work, and he will honor us. The righteous wife wins the soul of her husband by the wisdom of meekness and sobriety (1 Peter 3:1-2). The godly neighbor wins his fellow sinner by the patient energy of faith and love (James 5:19-20). "A soul is a kingdom. As many as we can bring back to God are so many kingdoms reconquered" (Quesnel). Every soul won by this wisdom will be a fresh jewel in the Savior's crown, a polished stone in the temple, in which our Lord will be honored throughout eternity.

31. If the righteous receive their due on earth, how much more the ungodly and the sinner! Every perfection of God is glorified in this dispensation on earth. As a wise Father, he will not give his children free rein to sin. As a holy God, he must show in them his abhorrence of it. As a faithful God, he will make the chastisements of his rod the means of their restoration. But blessed be God, all the penal curse has been taken away. We receive our **due on earth**, not, as we deserve, in hell. We are punished here, that we might be spared forever and prepared for heaven (Hebrews 12:10).

If the children are scourged, much more are **the ungodly and the sinner**. See 1 Peter 4:18.

Proverbs
Chapter 12

1. Whoever loves discipline loves knowledge, but he who hates correction is stupid. Here **knowledge,** as the contrast teaches, chiefly implies **discipline,** which is most necessary to acquire spiritual **knowledge.** This is so contrary to our proud hearts that the submission of the will is our only road to Christian attainment.

Irritable pride **hates correction.** If we find that we are upset when our faults are pointed out to us, that shows we lack not only grace but understanding. We are behaving as if we were stupid, "like the horse, which bites and kicks out at the man who performs a painful operation on him. He is surely a brute, and not a rational creature, who has swallowed poison and would prefer it to take its course than take the necessary antidote in case his folly is exposed" (Lawson). Oh, for a teachable spirit to sit at the feet of our divine Master and learn from him.

2. A good man obtains favor from the LORD, but the LORD condemns a crafty man. Goodness is part of the fruit of the Spirit. **A good man** is a man filled with the Spirit. He reflects God's goodness.

The contrast to **a good man** is **a crafty man.** On the great day, the all-seeing Judge will take speedy action against him (Malachi 3:5; Psalm 50:16-21).

3. A man cannot be established through wickedness, but the righteous cannot be uprooted. Here we see that **a man** who lives by **wickedness** may prosper for a time, but he **cannot be established,** for only God can do that.

The condition of **the righteous** is firm and cannot be shaken. Their leaves may fall in the wind. Their branches may tremble in the storm. But they are rooted in God and cannot be moved. This is a bright prospect for the church, against whom not even the gates of hell can prevail (Matthew 16:18).

4. A wife of noble character is her husband's crown, but a disgrace-

ful wife is like decay in his bones. Faithful (31:11-12); chaste (Titus 2:5; 1 Peter 3:2); respectfully obedient (Ephesians 5:22-23; 1 Peter 3:4-6); immovable in affection (Titus 2:4); delighting to see her husband honored, respected, and loved; covering, as far as possible, his failings; prudent in the management of her family (14:1); conscientious in the carrying out of her domestic duties (31:27-28); kind and considerate to all around her (31:20, 26); and as the root of all, fearing the Lord (31:30)—such is **a wife of noble character.** Let a young woman, in contemplating this holy union, ponder in deep prayer its weighty responsibility. Will she be a **crown** to her husband or make him ashamed? Will she be what God made the woman ("a helper" [Genesis 2:18]) or what Satan made her (a tempter to her husband)? If she is not a **crown** to her husband, she will be a shame for herself. If she causes her husband's **bones** to **decay,** she will be a plague to herself.

5. The plans of the righteous are just, but the advice of the wicked is deceitful. The workings of good and evil are traced to their source. **The plans of the righteous** man, which are renewed in the spirit of his mind, **are just.** He learns to measure everything by God's unerring rule and to lean on his God rather than to trust in his own judgment.

6. Words are the natural expression of thoughts and plans. How murderous were the words of Ahithophel (2 Samuel 17:1-4). Yet even in the middle of a hail of words, **the speech of the upright rescues them.** The wisdom of our divine Master was an unfailing preservative (Matthew 22:34-35, 46).

7. We cannot but wonder at the divine patience that allows **wicked men** to fill the earth with such a mass of guilt and misery. Yet their triumph only lasts for a moment. In contrast to this, **the house of the righteous stands firm.** They will have a place in the Lord's house and in eternity (Revelation 3:12).

8. A man is praised according to his wisdom, but men with warped minds are despised. The normal judgment of this world is to replace light with darkness (Isaiah 5:20). What causes men to be **despised**? It is not their poverty, obscurity, or misfortune, but their **warped minds.** They are too proud to be taught. Perverse Nabal was **despised** by his own family (1 Samuel 25:17, 25). The prodigal son was **despised** by his former companions (Luke 15:15-16). All such people will live in shame here and in doom hereafter (Daniel 12:2).

9. Better to be a nobody and yet have a servant than pretend to be somebody and have no food. A man who can barely afford to **have a servant** may be despised by his rich neighbors. But his state is **better** than the proud show of rank or family where there is no means to sustain it. Nothing is so despicable as to be proud when there is nothing to be proud about. Yet it is hard, even for the Christian, as Bunyan reminds us, "to go down the Valley of Humiliation, and catch no slip by the way." We need our Master's unworldly, elevated spirit (John 6:15) to make a safe descent. Remember that the dazzling glare of man's esteem will fade away before the glory of our Lord's appearing!

10. A righteous man cares for the needs of his animal, but the kindest acts of the wicked are cruel. The details of Scripture are one of its most valuable properties. It shows the mind of God on many points that are apparently trivial. Here it tests us by the way we treat animals. They were given to man, as the lord of creation, for his use, comfort, and food (Genesis 1:28; 9:3), not for his wantonness. **A righteous man cares for the needs of his animal** (Genesis 24:32) and never forces it beyond its strength (Genesis 33:13-14). Therefore, the brutal habits, the coarse words, and inhuman blows done against animals are disgraceful. The delight of children inflicting pain on animals for their amusement, if not restrained, ends up with their growing into hard-hearted adults. For, as Mr. Locke has wisely observed, "They who delight in the sufferings and destruction of inferior creatures will not be apt to be very compassionate and benign to those of their own kind." Thus **the kindest acts of the wicked are cruel** and have no feeling.

But why is this humanity marked as a feature of **a righteous man?** Because it is the image of our heavenly Father, who spreads his cherishing wings over his whole creation (Psalm 33:5; 145:9, 16). Witness the sanctions of his law (Exodus 22:30; Deuteronomy 5:14; 25:4). So his children should reflect his whole image of love.

11. He who works his land will have abundant food, but he who chases fantasies lacks judgment. Special honor is given to the person who **works his land.** God assigned such a task to Adam in paradise. It was the work of Adam's eldest son. Its origin appears to have been under immediate divine teaching (Isaiah 28:23-29). In ancient times it was the business or relaxation of kings (2 Chronicles 26:10). "Of all the arts of civilized man, agriculture is transcendently the most essential and valuable. Other arts may contribute to the comfort, the convenience, and the embellishment of life. But the cultivation of the soil stands in immediate connection with our very existence. The life itself, to whose comfort and convenience and embellishment other arts contribute, is by this sustained; so that others without it can avail nothing" (Wardlaw).

Idleness is a blot on our royal name (2 Thessalonians 3:10-12). As an old writer observes, "The proud person is Satan's throne, and the idle man his pillow. He sits in the former and sleeps quietly on the latter" (Swinnock). The man therefore who **chases fantasies** instead of doing honest labor proves himself to **lack judgment,** and he will reap the fruits of his folly (13:20).

12. The wicked desire the plunder of evil men, but the root of the righteous flourishes. Man is always restless to press on to something that has yet to be enjoyed. The Christian reaches up to higher privileges and increasing holiness (Philippians 3:12-14). **Evil men** emulate each other in wickedness. **The root of the righteous** only **flourishes** when the righteous depend on Christ as the source of their blessings and so will forever remain fruitful (John 15:5). "As surely as the vine-branch can have no powers independent of the root, so surely cannot the Christian think, act, or live as such, but only so far as he derives his abilities from the stock, on which he is grafted" (William Jones). The spiritual branches "are nourished and increased by the living root of God's grace and blessing" (Diodati).

13. **An evil man is trapped by his sinful talk, but a righteous man escapes trouble.** We see that **an evil man** can trap himself. **His sinful talk** traps his own life (18:7; Psalm 64:8). "Many have felt the lash upon their backs for the lack of a chain on their tongues" (Henry).

On the other hand, the godly use of speech enables **a righteous man** to escape from **trouble,** into which the wicked rush headlong (Jeremiah 26:12-16).

14. **From the fruit of his lips a man is filled with good things as surely as the work of his hands rewards him.** We have seen the trap of the tongue. Here is its blessing, not to others only, but for ourselves as well. Here we have the characteristic of the saints of God who speak about the glory of God's kingdom (Psalm 145:10-11). We will be satisfied with good by the **fruit** of our consecrated **lips** (Proverbs 13:2; 15:23).

15. **The way of a fool seems right to him, but a wise man listens to advice.** The fool's conceit hinders his wisdom. He needs no guidance; he never asks for **advice.** He sticks to his own ways because they are his. He has no doubt about heaven. Instead of the way being so narrow that few people find it, in his view it is so easy to find that few people can miss it. Thus all his religion is self-delusion. *Oh, my God, save me from myself, from my own self-deceitfulness.*

What a proof of wisdom is a teachable spirit. Was not Moses wiser for listening to Jethro's advice, and David for listening to the restraining advice of Abigail? How precious, then, for the child of God is the work of the divine Counselor (Isaiah 9:6).

16. **A fool shows his annoyance at once, but a prudent man overlooks an insult.** Always discipline your tongue. An unbridled tongue is proof of an unrenewed heart. Never let it loose when you are angry. How easily the **fool** is known by his anger. He has no control over himself. The fool's anger is an even more painful sight in God's children. Self-control, which covers rising anger, is true Christian prudence. So when we feel that we are becoming angry, we must at once cry to him who stills the storm (Matthew 8:26; Psalm 65:7). We do well to keep before our eyes his blessed example who, when he was reviled, did not retaliate (1 Peter 2:23).

17. **A truthful witness gives honest testimony, but a false witness tells lies.** This proverb may seem to be so obvious that nothing needs to

be said about it. But Scripture not only teaches what is profound and searching, but stamps everyday truths with God's seal so that we may obey them.

A false witness does not always tell blatant **lies**, but he also lies when he misrepresents the truth and conceals the truth. Telling the truth and telling **lies** characterize two types of people in the world. Be sure that you are characterized by truth and righteousness.

18. Reckless words pierce like a sword, but the tongue of the wise brings healing. Who has not felt the piercings of false, unkind, inconsiderate **words**? How keenly have the servants of God suffered from this **sword**! Many will speak daggers without compunction who would be afraid to use them. Surely it was not without reason that our Lord accused an angry word or tongue with the guilt of murder (Matthew 5:21-22). Indeed, "a great and almost incredible calamity it is that man, who was created for humanity, should be so corrupted that no animal in the world is more ferocious and malignant" (Daille).

Wisdom is the guiding principle of the **tongue** that **brings healing**. It is full of discriminating tact, directing us, how, when, what, and to whom to speak. This is no negative responsibility. It is not enough that there is no poison in the tongue. It must bring **healing**.

19. Truthful lips endure forever, but a lying tongue lasts only a moment. How important it is to have our eye on eternity as we speak. The lasting value and permanent results of truth would then be seen. Speaking the truth may lead us into trouble in this world (Matthew 10:32-39). But who will speak against the martyr's testimony: "Be of good comfort, Master Ridley; play the man. We shall this day light such a candle by God's grace in England as, I trust, shall never be put out" (Foxe). The **lips** of the faithful minister of God also **endure forever**.

Truth then is eternal. **Lying**, even if it suits our purpose to escape from a difficulty, **lasts only a moment.** "None are so visibly blasted as those who make no conscience of a lie" (Matthew Henry).

20. The root of **deceit** is here traced to our **hearts.** How early it is found there. A lie quickly falls from a child's lips when he is tempted. **Deceit** takes many forms: falsehood, exaggeration, and deliberate perversion.

22. "One common but most responsible instance of this," observes Mr. Goode in his valuable sermon on this text, "is instructing servants to say: 'Not at home.' Great is their guilt who thus tempt a fellow creature to utter a palpable untruth for the paltry convenience of a master. No Christian servant will consent to defile his conscience by acquiescing in any such iniquity. 'It is a mater of common consent, and every one understands it.' Be it so, it is untruth still, and lying lips are an abomination to the Lord. Moreover, if it is so generally understood and admitted without offense, then how much more honorable and Christian it is to say at once, 'We are engaged. We wish to be alone!' Who that accepts one excuse will not readily accept the other?" No part of Christian education is more important than the training of children in the deepest reverence for the simplicity of the truth. Dr. Johnson has well observed that the prevalence of falsehood arises more from carelessness about truth than from intentional lying. If a child is saying what he has seen in the street, "do not," he advises, "allow him to say that he had seen it out of one window if he has seen it out of another." Let them know that every deliberate deviation from strict accuracy bears the stamp of **lying lips**.

23. A prudent man keeps his knowledge to himself, but the heart of fools blurts out folly. Here **knowledge** implies a talent to be wisely, not indiscriminately, passed on. As far as the knowledge found in Scripture is concerned, this must not be kept to oneself. It must be openly declared to suitable people at the right time. But much harm can be done by obtruding on the ungodly those interior matters of Christian experience that we are invited to tell to those who fear God. Every truth is not therefore suited for every person or for every occasion (Ecclesiastes 3:7; Amos 5:13). Our blessed Lord told his disciples to prudently conceal what he did until the appropriate time arrived (Matthew 16:20; 17:9). The apostle Paul kept some of his spiritual experiences to himself for fourteen years and then only mentioned them to validate his apostleship (2 Corinthians 12:1-6).

Fools, however, proclaim their **folly** everywhere. They are dogmatic in arguments when wiser men are cautious. They teach when they should be learning. Distrust of self and humility are most important if we are going to use God's gifts to his glory.

24. Diligent hands will rule, but laziness ends in slave labor. Diligence is the normal path along which to advance. The faithful steward is made to **rule** over his lord's household (Matthew 24:45-47).

A lazy spirit enslaves a person. "He is perpetually needing the counsel of others, and hangs on to it" (Dathe). We must be warned about being a useless servant (Matthew 25:26-30). Christians should beware of neglecting the responsibilities of living just to indulge themselves.

25. An anxious heart weighs a man down, but a kind word cheers him up. A heavy heart is a weighty sickness; it makes us stoop under its unbearable burden. But how **a kind word cheers [us] up**. "This maxim therefore points out an easy and cheerful way to being useful" (Scott). Here we realize the precious efficacy of the Gospel. It is full of **kind** words (Matthew 11:28; John 14:27).

Human sympathy may give temporary relief. But "that is the grace, softer than oil, sweeter than roses, that flows from the Savior's lips into the sinner's wounds; and being poured into the contrite heart, not only heals, but blesses it, yes, and marks it out for eternal blessedness. Oh, how sweet is the voice of pardon to a soul groaning under the burden of sin!" (Leighton).

26. A righteous man is cautious in friendship, but the way of the

wicked leads them astray. Although the **wicked** Balaam acknowledged the excellence of the **righteous,** he was still seduced by his own way, to his ruin (Numbers 31:8). Saul's testimony to David and Joash's respect for Elisha nevertheless allowed them to be led astray by their own corrupt deeds. So let me weigh my path most carefully. Who am I walking with? Am I walking in the right direction?

27. The lazy man does not roast his game, but the diligent man prizes his possessions. How miserable is the habit of sloth! It is a deadly disease. It can only be remedied by God's help and checked by early discipline and being constantly alert to it and always resisting it. Sometimes, however, a man rouses himself to the labor of hunting. But his fitful exertion is soon over, and he cannot even bring himself to prepare his supper.

Is this not a graphic picture of someone who claims to follow Christ but is lazy in his faith? He starts off very enthusiastic about being Christ's disciple, but if he has no root, he soon withers and shrivels (Matthew 13:20-21). What is the point of starting off with a flourish if you do not seek grace to persevere? Godliness without effort loses its full reward (2 John 8).

So, Christian, be **diligent.** Spend and be spent in Christ's service. Your privileges will be enlarged. Your God will be honored. Your crown will be secure.

28. In the way of righteousness there is life; along that path is immortality. Here **righteousness** is crowned with **life** and **immortality.** "In the path of righteousness is life; yes, the highway is immortality" (Dr. Good). **The way of righteousness** is the way of God's salvation, in which God's children come to him; and it is the way of his commands in which they walk. Enjoying the sense of God's love, confiding in his unimaginable, satisfying friendship, consecrating ourselves in spiritual devotion to his service, anticipating the fullness of his eternal joy—this is **life** and **immortality.** For where the life of grace is possessed, the life of glory is secured.

Proverbs
Chapter 13

1. **A wise son heeds his father's instruction, but a mocker does not listen to rebuke.** Such **a wise son** was Solomon himself. The link between **instruction** and **rebuke** points to the fact that **instruction** is obtained by discipline. Here we turn to our great Example. Was he not **a wise son** when his ears were opened to his Father's discipline? Remember how he descended to this painful school in order to learn obedience (Hebrews 5:8). How good it is in our daily practical walk to keep our eyes steadily fixed on him, following him closely in this childlike habit.

But the proud spirit does not easily bend. He never **heeds his father's instruction.** He soon sits with the **mocker.** When **rebuke** is necessary, he **does not listen** to it. Let me remember, if I am reluctant to heed the faithful **rebuke** of men, that I will also resist God's rebuke. How soon will this stubborn rebellion bring his patience to an end and my soul to destruction. "From hardness of heart, and contempt of thy word and commandment, Good Lord, deliver me" (Litany).

2. **From the fruit of his lips a man enjoys good things, but the unfaithful have a craving for violence.** If a Christian is walking with God, his mouth will be full of godly words. Whatever effect this has on others, at least his own soul will be warmed, refreshed, and edified. **From the fruit of his lips a man enjoys good things.** Never will we carry on our lips that beloved name to our fellow sinners in a base way, but its savor to our own souls will be like ointment poured out. We will feed ourselves in the Christian distribution of the heavenly manna.

The unfaithful man also enjoys **the fruit of his lips,** but they are not **good things.** His soul sets his tongue on fire. He loves **violence** and therefore eats to his own ruin. Let us make sure that our tongues are under the control of divine grace, restrained from evil, and disciplined for usefulness.

3. **He who guards his lips guards his life, but he who speaks rashly will come to ruin.** The last proverb contrasted a fruitful tongue with an

incautious tongue. We know that the heart guards this citadel. When we guard our **lips**, we set a watch at the gates of the city. If they are well guarded, then the city is safe. If they are unguarded, the city will become like Babylon and will be captured. "He who looks carefully to his tongue takes a safe route for preserving his life, which is often in danger by much and wild talking" (Bishop Hall). We must think before we speak. We must think about our words—their substance, manner, time, place, and audience. The unruly member needs a strong bridle and a strong hand to hold it.

"Set a guard over my mouth, O LORD; keep watch over the door of my lips" (Psalm 141:3) was the prayer of one who knew the danger of an unruly tongue and knew about the only way to control it. Will we not call on God's help so that our unguarded tongues never give place to the devil?

4. The sluggard craves and gets nothing, but the desires of the diligent are fully satisfied. Here is another vivid contrast between **the sluggard** and **the diligent** (see also 10:4; 12:24). **The sluggard craves** the fruit of diligence without the diligence that gains it. His religion has the same heartless character. He desires to overcome his bad habits and to enjoy the happiness of God's people. So far so good. **Desires** are part of religion. Nothing can be gained without them. Many people do not even have this desire. They ridicule it as enthusiasm. Yet **the sluggard . . . gets nothing** because he desires but puts forth no effort. "He always desires, but he takes no pains to get anything" (*Reformers' Notes*). He would like to go to heaven if a morning dream could carry him there.

If you are going to be industrious about anything, be industrious about religion. Eternity is at stake. Hours, days are lost. Soon they become years, and for lack of energy everything is lost. Heartless wishes do not give life. The halting step will not bring us to God. To expect the blessing without diligence is delusion.

5. The righteous hate what is false, but the wicked bring shame and disgrace. Observe the accuracy of Scripture. This does not mean that a **righteous** man never lies. David lied. Peter lied. But the child of God, although always a sinner, has a holy antipathy against sin (Romans 7:15, 19).

On the other hand, just because someone does not lie does not mean he is **righteous**. Selfish motives may dictate restraint without having any hate of sin as sin. But true religion brings in a new way of life—conformity to the mind of God. **The righteous hate what is false.** Such a man would prefer to suffer for the truth rather than sin by lying.

And yet how often, even in the church, is this feature of godliness obscured. Is not truth often sacrificed to courtesy? Is not lying sometimes acted, insinuated, or implied when we should be speaking in a straightforward way? We need to abstain from every appearance of evil (1 Thessalonians 5:22 [KJV]). This is the rule for the man of God. Commit the tongue to the restraint and guidance of the God of truth.

The wicked indeed take pleasure in deceit. Their base acts often bring **shame and disgrace** on this side of the grave. And **shame** will be their everlasting reward (Daniel 12:2; Revelation 21:8).

6. Righteousness guards the man of integrity, but wickedness overthrows the sinner. May this repetition of the aphorism (11:3, 5-6) deepen its impression on us. **Righteousness** is steady conformity to God's mind. We do not exalt it by any meritorious efficacy or put it in the place of simply looking to Jesus for life and salvation. When a Christian lives as a **man of integrity**, he never loses his sense of sin or forgets his needs of mercy. This **righteousness** is not perfection. Yet, blessed be God, the uprightness is accepted, and the fault is covered (2 Chronicles 15:17).

But while "saints are secured from ruin, sinners are secured for ruin" (Henry). The sinner's own **wickedness overthrows** him. He is bent on his own way, the sure road to destruction. "Let him not blame the Lord or any mortal man beside himself, inasmuch as he is the author of ruin to himself" (Muffet).

7. One man pretends to be rich, yet has nothing; another pretends to be poor, yet has great wealth. What bubbles are the world's riches! Yet some will ruin their lives in order to gain the respect usually linked with them. **One man pretends to be rich, yet has nothing.** Others pretend **to be poor** and live as if they were so, **yet** have **great wealth.** In all cases riches are more accurately judged by their use than by their possession. Both of these types of people are being deceitful before God. One pretends to have received what he has not received, and the other person virtually denies his gracious gifts. Both dishonor God's wisdom and goodness.

The true path of simplicity is to renounce all dependence on the flesh and to gladly welcome the Gospel of grace. Such disciples, rich in their holy poverty, are honored by the Lord. "O blessed Lord, who resists the proud and gives grace to the humble, give me more humility, that I may receive more grace from you. And as your gracious rain runs down from the steep mountains and sweetly drenches the humble valleys, depress my heart more and more with true lowliness of spirit, that the showers of your heavenly grace may sink into it and make it more fruitful in all good affection and all holy obedience" (Bishop Hall).

8. A man's riches may ransom his life, but a poor man hears no threat. The former proverb rebukes us for not being content with our lot, whether we are poor or rich. The wise man here strikes the balance between these two conditions. **A man's riches may ransom his life.** Extortion of money may prompt false accusation, and **riches** may be a **ransom** cheerfully paid. But what can a person give in exchange for his soul (Matthew 16:26)? It is too precious to be redeemed with corruptible silver and gold (1 Peter 1:18). When all the treasures of earth were insufficient for this ransom, the riches of heaven were poured out (1 Peter 1:19; Hebrews 10:5-8).

9. The light of the righteous shines brightly, but the lamp of the wicked is snuffed out. Who can evaluate the worth of a Christian's bright shining **light** (Matthew 5:14-16; Philippians 2:15; Proverbs 4:18)? Happy in his own soul, like his counterpart in the heavens, he sheds a joyful light around him.

Sin can bring a cloud to this **light**. Do we hope to shine in the heavenly firmament? Then we must shine with the present glory in the firmament of the church.

The wicked have their **lamp**, a cold profession of the name of religion. But as it has no oil, it quickly goes out (Matthew 25:8). But even while it lasts, they do not rejoice. Their **lamp** sheds no light on the soul. It guides no fellow pilgrim with its light. Its end will be dreadful.

10. Pride only breeds quarrels, but wisdom is found in those who take advice. Here **quarrels** are accurately traced to their correct source. All the evil things in the world, all the novel doctrines, produce **quarrels,** which originate in a proud mind (Colossians 2:18; 1 Timothy 6:3-5). Men scorn the beaten track. They feel they must strike out a new path. Individuality and extravagance are primary charms. They are ready to quarrel with everyone who does not value their opinions as highly as they do. Here **pride** takes over under the cover of giving glory to God. Truly "it is the inmost coat, which we put on first and put off last" (Bishop Hall).

This mischievous principle spreads in families and among friends. "Some point of honor must be maintained; some affront must be resented; some rival must be crushed and eclipsed, some renowned character emulated, or some superior equaled and surpassed" (Scott). Even in trifling disputes between relatives or neighbors, perhaps between Christians, each party argues vehemently for his rights instead of satisfying himself with the testimony of his conscience. He does not prefer to be misunderstood or misjudged rather than break the bond of the divine brotherhood (1 Corinthians 6:7).

The proud man thinks that he is wise enough. He does not ask for **advice** and so proves that he lacks **wisdom**. But Christian **wisdom** will keep us within our own limits. Whatever our gifts are, we will be humble, loving, and thankful.

11. Dishonest money [KJV: wealth gotten by vanity] dwindles away, but he who gathers money little by little makes it grow. This proverb does not imply the means by which wealth is acquired, but the impoverishing use to which it is applied. However large the wealth may be, it soon **dwindles away**. Frivolous and expensive pursuits, empty amusements, and the vain pomp and show of dress will soon show that riches have wings (23:5).

On the other hand, God blesses Christian industry. Only let us remember that the way to make **money . . . grow** is the dedication of oneself and one's substance to the Lord, readily acknowledging that one is not his own but is God's property for God's glory (1 Corinthians 6:19-20). "All that man can have, we have on this condition: to use it . . . to lay it out, to lay it down unto the honor of our Master, from whose bounty we received it" (Swinnock). May the Lord deliver us from the guilt of wasting on vanity what is due to him!

12. Hope deferred makes the heart sick, but a longing fulfilled is a tree of life. The first sign of **hope** is a pleasurable sensation, even though it is often mixed with pain. It is hunger that makes our food acceptable. But **hope deferred**, like hunger prolonged, brings a kind of torture. It **makes the heart sick.** Yet when **a longing** is **fulfilled,** that is so invigorating.

We must, however, limit this application to the spiritual world. Elsewhere the fulfillment of the desire, instead of **a tree of life,** is vanity (Ecclesiastes 2:11). In this world, the child of God is often tried in his faith but is never disappointed by his **hope.** We may have to wait a long time, but never let us despair. The patience of **hope** results in the full assurance of **hope.** What was it to Abraham that after long **deferred hope,** what he desired arrived, and he called the child of promise "Laughter" (Genesis 15:3; 21:3-6).

Time may seem to drag, trials may be heavy, and hearts may fail. But in a little while Christ will return (Hebrews 10:37-38; Revelation 22:7, 12, 20). The first moment of the glorious manifestation will blot out the memory of all the labors and trials.

13. He who scorns instruction will pay for it, but he who respects a command is rewarded. God as a God of holiness will not be trifled with. The one **who scorns instruction will pay for it.** He will not escape. The world before the Flood was the object of God's patience. A preacher of righteousness warned them of the danger, but those who despised God brought ruin on themselves.

May we hold God and his word in reverence, so that we may not be terrified by it. Because of our faith in Christ, we fear a Father, not a Judge.

14. The teaching of the wise is a fountain of life, turning a man from the snares of death. Reverence for God's commands have just been highlighted. Now the blessing of the law or instruction, **the teaching of the wise,** is shown. It is **a fountain of life** to a teachable and thirsty heart. There is no safe path to tread except God's way. The Word of God gives the necessary warning (Psalm 17:4; 119:9, 11). Let the young take care not to become entangled in **the snares of death.** Let the instruction of your God and his ministers be **the teaching of the wise** to keep your path safe. Where there is no actual law given, let the spirit of the law keep your heart and life. Do not do anything that is questionable in the law. Think of everything that upsets your praying and your communion with God as unlawful. Never go into any company, business, or situation in which the presence and blessing of God cannot be conscientiously asked and expected. "By the help of these . . . rules, I soon settle all my doubts and find that many things

I have hitherto indulged in are, if not utterly unlawful, at least inexpedient, and I can renounce them without many sighs" (Dr. Payson). Such rules are the spirit of the law and are well worth adopting.

15. Good understanding wins favor, but the way of the unfaithful is hard. This **good understanding** is not a cold and dry apprehension, but the glow of heavenly light and love in all the discipline of Christian habits. Natural conviction is often constrained to do homage to it, as the image of God is stamped on his servants. Joseph in this way acquired many of those valuable rules that won him **favor** and were essential for him in his various and important responsibilities. Being trained in this school of **understanding** benefited himself, his people, and the whole church of God.

Can we say this of **the way of the unfaithful?** They dream of a flowery path, but they make for themselves a **hard** way. "Wicked men live under a hard taskmaster" (Caryl). "I was held before conversion," said Augustine, "not with an iron chain, but with the obstinacy of my own will." Voltaire, judging from his own heart, pronounced, "In man is more wretchedness than in all other animals put together. Man lives life, yet knows he must die. I wish I had never been born." Wretch, indeed, must the person be who cannot endure to commune with himself and to whose peace it is necessary that he should rid himself of every thought of God and his soul.

In every shape and form, the service of the merciless tyrant is a hard way. Men fight their way to hell as well as to heaven (Acts 14:22)—through much tribulation. This happens through the perverse will and rebellion of the conscience. "The pain of wickedness is grievous, and, apart from all other consequences, the most painful" (Cicero). "Nothing makes a man so wretched as impiety and crime" (Cicero). "His own iniquity and inner dread, remorse, and agitation of conscience—these are the untiring furies of the guilty mind" (Cicero). This philosopher, utterly ignorant of the spiritual character of sin, probably only intended this to apply to heinous crimes. But the admission of the principle is important, as the path of sin is a present misery.

Which way will I then choose? *Lord, help me to choose for you. Help me, under your guidance, to choose the safe and pleasant path of wisdom, the rich portion of godliness for both worlds.* **The way of the unfaithful is hard,** for it ends in death (Romans 6:21).

16. Every prudent man acts out of knowledge, but a fool exposes his folly. How often is even valuable **knowledge** frittered away from lack of **prudent** application. We must ponder the time, measure, helps, and means of behaving prudently. In daily life this protects against unseen dangers (22:3) and provides a way of escape in trying difficulties. In the family it shows how children should be brought up (Judges 13:8-12).

Lacking this prudence, **a fool exposes his folly.** He pours out his wrath, vaunts his vanity, exposes his thoughtlessness, and exercises no judgment.

Let us study the minute details of our Master's life. He acted prudently as he confounded his enemies (Matthew 21:24-27; 22:42-46), and in tender sympathy he dealt with his afflicted people (Isaiah 50:4). How good it is to have our **knowledge** disciplined by his teaching and consecrated to his service.

17. A wicked messenger falls into trouble, but a trustworthy envoy brings healing. A messenger proves his character by his neglect or fulfillment of his trust. **A wicked messenger** betrays his trust and damages his master. But faithfulness is the servant's glory and his master's gain. He brings and receives a blessing. Gehazi's unfaithfulness was his downfall (2 Kings 5:26-27). Eliezer was faithful and was blessed himself and brought blessing to his master (Genesis 24:1-56).

18. He who ignores discipline comes to poverty and shame, but whoever heeds correction is honored. We see here that **discipline** is one of God's ordinances. Little do those who ignore it realize what a blessing they are discarding. **Poverty and shame** are often the Lord's rod for his wayward children. Young people, learn to dread the liberty of being left to your own choices. Dread the first step in the downward path of refusing to be disciplined. If godly **discipline** is slighted, all may end in **poverty and shame**.

But here honor is contrasted with **shame**. If we are humbled under God's reproof, we will be raised to his throne. Pleasant indeed are his words to his well-disciplined child. To have our ears open to receive **discipline** is to walk in the path of life and happiness. This is the honor of being conformed to our divine Savior.

19. A longing fulfilled is sweet to the soul, but fools detest turning from evil. Can everyone enjoy this sweetness? All may, but all will not be happy. Holiness makes heaven; sin makes hell. So which place are the ungodly suited for? Hating holiness means that you are fit for hell. Oh, what a great change there must be to kill the enmity and make it an abomination for the soul to commit evil.

20. He who walks with the wise grows wise, but a companion of fools suffers harm. Everyone wants to influence his companions. We are, therefore, naturally molded by them. It is not up to us to determine if there will be any influence, only what that influence will be. Walking **with the wise,** under their instruction, encouragement, and example, makes us become **wise.** Note, young people, the responsibility of the choice of friends. The world may allure, the ungodly may mock, the evil heart may consent to their voice. But you must seek strength from God and resolve to walk **with the wise.**

If we can live among the worldly without feeling out of our element, if we can breathe a tainted atmosphere without awareness of infection, if we can familiarize ourselves with the absence of religion in ordinary life, unsubdued worldliness has us in its grip. The first warning to sinners just rescued from the fire was to save themselves from this wicked generation (Acts 2:40).

21. Misfortune pursues the sinner, but prosperity is the reward of the righteous. "Sinners are sure to find evil at last; the righteous good" (Jermin). The lives of sinners—Cain, Achan, Abimelech, Ahab and his wicked wife—are solemn reminders that **misfortune pursues the sinner**, even when he seems to have found a refuge. The delay of centuries does not weaken the certainty of this (Exodus 17:14; 1 Samuel 15:3-7).

No less certain is the **prosperity** of **the righteous**. This is the **reward** of grace. Not the tiniest act of kindness, even the giving of a cup of cold water, will be without its **reward**.

22. A good man leaves an inheritance for his children's children, but a sinner's wealth is stored up for the righteous. Here we have a particular example of **the righteous** receiving a **reward** (verse 21). This should not, however, be taken as a universal statement. Many **a good man** has no **inheritance** to leave, and some have no **children** who survive them, let alone **children's children**.

Yet Scripture gives many examples of this dispensation of providence that show the blessing of personal godliness to unborn posterity. Caleb's children inherited their father's possession. And if there are no earthly possessions to pass on, yet a church in the home, a family altar, the record of a holy example and instruction, and above all, a store of believing prayer will be **an inheritance** to our children. The value of such an **inheritance** is inestimable.

23. A poor man's field may produce abundant food, but injustice sweeps it away. The produce of the soil is the fruit of industry. Indeed, for lack of prudent management the richest harvest can be wasted. Egypt with her abundant crops would have been destroyed but for Joseph's judgment in preserving the **abundant food** (Genesis 41:33-36). Solomon's prudent administration of his household restrained waste and extravagance.

What should we learn from this proverb? If talents lie inactive, or if their activity is not directed in a wise way, they will be swept away. The same ruin flows from the neglect of religious privileges. The harvest of grace withers into a famine. Slothful believer, rouse yourself and till the ground, or you will starve for lack of food.

24. He who spares the rod hates his son, but he who loves him is careful to discipline him. Among the many modern theories of education, how often is God's system overlooked! Yet this should be our pattern and standard. **The rod** of discipline is its main character—not harsh severity, but a wise, considerate, faithful application. Such discipline should always aim to subjugate the will and humble and purify the heart. Man often **spares the rod** and calls this love. But is not our Father's love of his children inconceivably stronger than that of any earthly parent? And yet he **spares** not **the rod**. What son is not punished (Hebrews 12:7)? Does **the**

rod demonstrate God's hatred? Certainly not! The Lord punishes the one he loves (Proverbs 3:11-12; Deuteronomy 8:5). Yet some say it is better for a child to be trained in the house of strangers than that he should be the unhappy victim of the cruelty of parental love!

The discipline of our children must, therefore, commence with self-discipline. Nature teaches us to love them a great deal. But we want a controlling principle to teach us to love them wisely. The indulgence of our children has its root in self-indulgence. We do not like inflicting pain on ourselves. Difficulties can only be known by experience. And even in this school one parent cannot measure the trials of another. But all our children are children of Adam. From the dawn of reason all choose the broad road of destruction. And can we bear the thought that they should walk in that road? We pray for their conversion. But prayer without teaching is mockery, and scriptural teaching implies discipline. Scripture combines discipline with instruction: Ephesians 6:4; Hebrews 12:5-6; compare with Psalm 94:12; 119:67, 71. So there must be discipline. All need **the rod,** some again and again. Yet it must be the father's rod, yearning over his disciplined child, even while he does not dare to spare him for his crying (19:18 [KJV]). **The rod** without affection is a dreadful tyranny.

Every vice commences in the nursery. The great secret is to establish authority in the dawn of life, to bend the tender twig before the knotty oak is beyond our power. A child who is trained by parental discipline will probably keep this wholesome influence to the end of his life.

25. The righteous eat to their hearts' content, but the stomach of the wicked goes hungry. Temporal blessings are assured, so far as they are really good for **the righteous**, whether they are many or few. They are enough to satisfy his needs, but not his lusts. Indeed, "he can never want [lack] a sufficiency, because his desires are moderate, and he makes a temperate use of God's blessings" (Bishop Patrick). Elijah was fed, first by ravens, afterwards by a widow, while the **wicked** country of Israel went **hungry**. And as for higher food and heavenly satisfaction, Christ is a substitute for everything, and nothing must be substituted for him. "If then," as the noble Luther declares, "we live here by begging our bread, is not this well recompensed, that we are nourished with the food of angels, with eternal life, and Christ himself?"

There is such a chaos of desires in the soul of **the wicked** that no abundance can satisfy his hunger. Ahab's crown could give him no rest without Naboth's vineyard. For the ungodly heart is full of insatiable cravings. But how intolerable will be this conscious lack throughout eternity, when a drop of water to cool the tormented tongue will be denied (Luke 16:24-26).

Proverbs
Chapter 14

1. The wise woman builds her house, but with her own hands the foolish one tears hers down. We have seen that the wife can be a blessing or a curse to her husband (12:4). Such is she to his **house** as well. Through her wisdom she may supply many of his defects, while all his care and prudence may be nullified by her folly. The godly woman is the very soul of the house. She instructs her children by her example no less than by her teaching. She educates them for God and for eternity—not to shine in the vain show of the world, but in the church of God. Her household order combines economy with generosity (31:13-27).

But note the **foolish** woman—her idleness, waste, love of pleasure, lack of all forethought and care. She allows her children to do just as they please; their souls are neglected, and their happiness is ruined. We see her house torn down in confusion. It would have been a sad result if this had been done by an enemy. But it is the doing, or rather undoing, of **her own hands.** Such was Jezebel, the destroyer of her house.

How important it is, then, to make the right choice when you marry. It is linked to the highest interests of unborn generations. If ever there was a matter for special prayer and consideration, this is it. To err in this matter may result in the ruin of ourselves and our future families. Of how little account are birth, fortune, and external accomplishments compared with godly wisdom.

2. He whose walk is upright fears the LORD, but he whose ways are devious despises him. Grace in the heart is the spring of those who **walk** in an **upright** way. The proof that we believe the reality of religion is that we walk in its power. The proof of the influence of the **fear of the LORD** is that we are in it all day long. Man may boast about his moral uprightness and that he would scorn to act in a mean way. But the Savior searches the heart, exposes the root of all worldly selfishness, and reveals that a man's ways are **devious** if he **despises** God.

**3. A fool's talk brings a rod to his back, but the lips of the wise pro-

tect them. How many illustrations does the wise man use to show the destructive evils of the tongue! Here it is **a rod** of pride. Sometimes it strikes against God and sometimes against men. It is always the **rod** for the **fool** himself. Yet when the heart is humbled and filled with wisdom, the **lips . . . protect** from imminent dangers, even from the threatened scourge of the **rod** of pride (Job 5:21; Psalm 31:20).

Were this iron **rod** to rule the earth, who could tolerate it? But adored be the grace that transforms the tongue, this unruly boasting member of unrighteousness, into an instrument of righteousness to God (Romans 6:13).

4. Where there are no oxen, the manger is empty, but from the strength of an ox comes an abundant harvest. We know **oxen** are used in husbandry (Deuteronomy 25:4; 1 Kings 19:19). **Where,** therefore, **there are no oxen** to till the ground, **the manger is empty** (Amos 4:6). Where there is no work, there can be no food that can be given to the **oxen**. God generally works by means, not by miracles. There must be good husbandry so there can be an abundant harvest. Let the ox be put to work, and his **strength** will achieve a great deal (Psalm 144:14). In spiritual husbandry where there are no laborers, all is barren and desolate. In all labor, both natural and supernatural, there will be **a profit** (Proverbs 14:23). But God will never acknowledge a lazy servant.

5. A truthful witness does not deceive, but a false witness pours out lies. This might seem to be obvious. But a closer look brings out a valuable maxim of practical wisdom. **A truthful witness** is moved neither by entreaties nor bribes, neither by promises nor threats to swerve from truth. He is a man to trust. He will not lie. **But a false witness** has lost all principles about truth. He will tell **lies** without any provocation, so long as they are to his advantage. You should run away from such people.

A truthful witness answers God's requirements (Psalm 51:6). He is therefore his delight (John 1:47). He is the citizen of the heavenly Zion.

The good and the corrupt tree each bring forth their own fruit. Let us remember that our principles, good and evil, are exemplified in the most trivial actions and gather strength from the slightest as well as from the most important deeds (Luke 16:10).

6. The mocker seeks wisdom and finds none, but knowledge comes easily to the discerning. Where does the promise that the seeker will find fit into this proverb? The failure lies at the mocker's own door. He **seeks** but without seriousness, without honesty, without delight, and solely for his own interest. He "finds therefore matter enough for his humor, but none for his instruction" (Lord Bacon). He accuses the Scripture of being dark, rather than admitting that the darkness is in his own heart. He feels that he understands the subject and so feels free to reject what he cannot understand or what he does not like. He scorns the humbling submission of faith, so that the glory even of the wisdom of God is foolishness with him. No wonder that while he makes an effort to seek, he does not find. He **seeks** his object but neglects the means and so perishes in the scornfulness of his own belief (1 Corinthians 3:19).

To another group of seekers, **knowledge comes easily.** The Ethiopian eunuch gathered his **knowledge** from simplicity. God gave him a ready will and a right taste. Obedience is the path of **knowledge.**

7. Stay away from a foolish man, for you will not find knowledge on his lips. Fellowship with the ungodly is absolutely forbidden, and it is never safe to contradict a plain command. Let us labor to win their souls to Christ. But the rule of providence directs us not to cast our pearls before swine. "Avoid," says the holy Leighton, "the mixture of an irreverent commonness and speaking of holy things indifferently in all companies." Therefore, when you perceive not in a foolish man the **lips** of **knowledge,** leave his presence. Some may be called to dispute with him. But take care that the call is clear. It is at least the safest path to dispatch your business with him as in a shower of rain, and not to loiter in his company.

Sweet indeed is the glow of the Savior's name upon the young Christian's lips. Its warmth may put older Christians to shame. But we must warn that young believer that harm can come from an imprudent endeavor to do good. Confess your Master wherever he may open your door and your mouth. But remember, there is a perpetual warfare with the old principles of corruption. No reliance can be placed on any habits that do not produce right behavior. The path of sin is much more easily avoided than relinquished. We can far more readily keep out of the course of the stream than stem the torrent. Walk closely with God. Under his cover and shield, make your protest against the ungodly. Commune much with his people. The very sight of a man of God is refreshing.

8. The wisdom of the prudent is to give thought to their ways, but the folly of fools is deception. This is not **the wisdom** of the learned, but **of the prudent.** This is not abstract speculation, but sound and practical learning. It is self-knowledge and self-control. It is looking upwards for divine guidance. How much this **wisdom** is needed so we can understand our way.

But while the attention of a truly wise man is occupied in understanding his way, "the arts of deceit engross the polluted minds of the wicked" (French and Skinner). Their wisdom of deceit is really **folly.** Gehazi's overreaching wisdom proved to be **folly** in the end. Ananias and Sapphira vainly endeavored to hide their covetousness under the cover of generosity. Who can deceive a heart-searching God? The attempt to do so is a fearful provocation and certain confusion.

9. Fools mock at making amends for sin, but goodwill is found among the upright. Do people exist who make fun of **sin?** Yes. They have never seen **sin** in its full horror or ever felt its weight. Look into eternity. **Sin** is thought to be a grave matter in heaven. It is felt so in hell. Why would **fools mock** it on earth? "It brought death into the world, and all our woe" (Milton). Is this a worthy matter to joke about? How does God feel about this? Go to Gethsemane. Go to Calvary. Learn from those places what **sin** is. Shall we **mock** what was a crushing burden to the Son of God? Ask converted souls, awakened consciences, dying sinners. Do they make light of **sin**? What will a wretched mocker call himself in eternity as God calls him a fool? This mockery cannot extend beyond the grave.

The upright cannot **mock** as the hardened fool does. While the latter "makes himself merry with his sin and scoffs at the reproof and judgment that pertains thereunto" (Bishop Hall), **the upright** have "the mark of those that sigh and cry for the abominations of the land." This is the sure seal of the Lord's favor. The mocking of the fool will soon come to an end. But in **the upright** is abundant **goodwill** that is unchangeable. Our God looks over us with compassion and love and saves us eternally. What crowns and kingdoms compared with such an earthly portion!

10. Each heart knows its own bitterness, and no one else can share its joy. This is a graphic illustration of the individuality of each person (see 1 Corinthians 2:11). The history of the soul is only fully known and felt by the conscious subject. **Each heart knows its own bitterness**, which is deep and interior. "Everyone is inwardly and the only true and faithful judge of his own joys and sorrows, and none else can truly perceive them" (Diodati). The most poignant sufferings often arise from reasons that cannot be told to our dearest friend. So each person must tread a solitary path, and in that path he must often be prepared to be misunderstood.

But think of Christ who made himself a man of sorrows, that he might be touched by weaknesses (Isaiah 53:3; Hebrews 4:15). None of us are too insignificant for his most endearing thoughts. Into his heart we may pour our distresses that no other ear listens to. We may not be able to understand this. But he will make us feel that his sympathy with our sorrow is not pretense but a precious reality. *My Savior, has my heart any* **bitterness** *that you do not know, that you do not feel with me, and for which you do not provide a support?*

No less personal is the heart's **joy**. It lies deep within. Michal could understand David's bravery, but not his **joy**. She knew him as a man of war, not as a man of God. This **joy** is the indwelling of the Comforter, which the world cannot receive (John 14:16-17 [KJV]). This is the highest **joy**. These are deep waters from the divine spring. Christ takes the believer to one side, feeds him hidden manna (Revelation 2:17), and makes him take part in his own joy.

11. The house of the wicked will be destroyed, but the tent of the upright will flourish. The feeblest state of **the upright** is more stable than the prosperity of **the wicked**. The latter build a **house**; the earth is their home, where they settle down and take their rest. But **the upright**, knowing the uncertainty of this world and seeking a better home, only set up a tent or tabernacle (Hebrews 11:9), which is weak and feeble. But the **house** is overthrown, while the **tent** flourishes. The strongest support of man totters. But God, who is omnipotent, gives his strength to the weakest. So we must walk by faith and not by sight (2 Corinthians 5:7). The great day will set everything in order before us and show that the Judge of the whole world acts in a right way (Psalm 58:11). Meanwhile, let us leave him to do his own work and to fulfill his own word in his own time.

12. There is a way that seems right to a man, but in the end it leads to death. No one can doubt the **end** of open ungodliness. But other paths in the broad road *seem* **right** but will also **end** in **death**. Vice passes under the cover of virtue. Covetousness is disguised under the name of prudence. Indeed, it is a dreadful characteristic of sin to hide its own nature. Our blindness to it increases in proportion with our familiarity with it. The self-deceiver has often been a backslider in heart. He lost his humility, relaxed his watchfulness, and neglected to diligently watch over his own heart. So sin soon found its way into his heart. When sin could not be completely covered, excuses were made for it. Appearances were kept up. Misgivings gradually vanished, and the fool took **death** for life by mistake.

"Take care then," as the godly Leighton warns us, "of sleeping unto death in carnal ease." Look to the foundation and soundness of your faith. Search carefully both the Bible and your heart. Go to the Lord in prayer and to his ministers to show you his way. May the Lord keep your eye steadily on the end and make sure that heaven is secure.

13. Even in laughter the heart may ache, and joy may end in grief. Many a sigh is heaved in the middle of loud **laughter** and folly. True joy is as unlikely to be found in hell as it is in the worldly heart. Just as it is impossible to gather grapes from thornbushes, so it is impossible to produce the fruit of the Spirit from nature's barren soil. It is far easier to drown conviction than to escape damnation. But to be merry for a day but to be in torment for eternity—who would not flee from such a situation?

14. The faithless will be fully repaid for their ways, and the good man rewarded for his. Every spot does not mean that you have leprosy. Every sin does not indicate that you are a backslider. A person may be overtaken in a fault (Galatians 6:1) or may sin in ignorance. **Faithless** implies a deliberate step. This may not always be obvious, but it is the more dangerous because it lies hidden. A man may be thought of as an eminent saint but may be a backslider in his heart. A secret cancer of unwatchfulness, conformity to the world, neglect, or indulgence has imperceptibly sapped his strength. He was once pressing forward. Now his prayers are formal and hurried. He is lukewarm about the means of grace. He reads his Bible to soothe his conscience rather than to feed his soul. His faithlessness was known to God long before it was known to the church. The foolishness of **the faithless** person is a merciful warning to the church.

God feeds **the good man** from a stream that flows from a higher spring, a living spring within himself (John 4:14). This is the witness of the Spirit, and the life and joy of the heavenly Comforter. This is not independence from God, but God living in the heart and filling it with his fullness. Let the sinner compare the satisfaction of sin and godliness, the curse and the blessing, and lift up his heart to make the right choice. Let **the faithless** person return to the Gospel and so reanimate his faith. Let **the good man** invigorate his soul daily from his well of consolation.

15. **A simple man believes anything, but a prudent man gives thought to his steps.** To believe every word of God is faith. To believe every word of man is credulity. Faith is a principle of infinite importance. Eternal life and eternal death hang on it. But it must be grounded on evidence, and it can only be exercised according to the character and measure of the evidence. An indiscriminate faith is, therefore, fraught with mischief. The world was ruined by this weakness (Genesis 3:1-6).

Look at the fruit of this folly in the church when our faith rests on man's wisdom instead of God's power. Men become loose in fundamental principles. So men are ready to drink from any cup that is offered to them, like children who think everything good that is sweet. Errors are built on partial, perverted truth.

But a prudent man gives thought to his steps. Cautious consideration should mark our general conduct. We should try everything before we trust it. In the church we should especially think about whom we should follow. Sift the most plausible pretensions. Never set a great name against the divine testimony. Ask for wisdom from God. Put feeling on the side, and under the direction of sound judgment.

16. **A wise man fears the LORD and shuns evil, but a fool is hotheaded and reckless.** Fear is sometimes thought to be an unmanly principle. But look at the dreadful extent of the **evil** that should be shunned. On the outside it is vanity and disappointment. On the inside it is the sting of guilt. So, to shun this **evil**—yes, to fear it—is true wisdom.

The **fool**, however, stout and stubborn in his mind, never fears until he falls. The voice of God is unheard in the middle of passion. He is "carried by his rash will and blind passion without understanding the end of things" (Diodati). He is **hotheaded and reckless.** Such a **fool** was Rehoboam when his self-willed confidence rejected the counsel of wisdom and experience (1 Kings 12:13-15).

17. **A quick-tempered man does foolish things, and a crafty man is hated.** Different types of sin are contrasted here. The sudden passion and the deliberate calculation; the gust and the long-lasting storm. A quick temper is foolishness, even in the eyes of men. What terrible damage can flow from an angry word! Who then, in light of the example, will relax the

watch on his lips? Are we sorrowful and made humble by these sins of temper? As we remember what they cost our crucified Friend, do they make us more watchful and prayerful? Is not our loving Father's rod sometimes necessary to bring conviction about the **foolish things** we do? "Let us give our hearts no rest until we have purged their gall and tempered them with the sweetness and gentleness of our Lord and Savior" (Diodati).

But sin grows from weakness to willfulness. "The first makes a man contemptible; the second, abominable" (Daille). Our dignity is our likeness to God. What shame and degradation there is when we do not bear his image.

18. The simple inherit folly, but the prudent are crowned with knowledge. Here **the simple** and **the prudent** are again contrasted. The child of Adam is born to **folly**. That is his inheritance. So long as he remains **simple**, he confirms this. Unlike an earthly inheritance, he cannot relinquish it. He holds in it life, he holds it in death, and he reaps its bitter fruits throughout eternity. There is no injustice here. There are no grounds for complaints. Sinner, is not wisdom offered to you freely? So, do you not continue to be **simple** by deliberate choice? "I confess," says Dr. South, "God has no need for any man's learning, but certainly then he has much less need of his ignorance."

The prudent, instructed in heavenly **knowledge,** are enabled to see divine objects in divine light. Is not this **knowledge** therefore their crown? It is not a laurel or gold crown, which perish, but the crown that adorns people with light, holiness, joy, and the glory of life eternal. Their glory in eternity will be sitting on God's throne, **crowned** with the hand of God himself.

19. Evil men will bow down in the presence of the good, and the wicked at the gates of the righteous. This is not the general rule of the present dispensation. Righteous Lazarus bowed at the wicked man's gate (Luke 16:20). Thus faith is tested, and the foundations of our heavenly hopes are more deeply grounded. And yet the letter of the proverb has often proved to be true. The Egyptians and Joseph's brothers bowed before Joseph. The proud Pharaoh and his people bowed before Moses. The saints will judge the world (1 Corinthians 6:2). Oh, let the sunshine of this glory irradiate every cloudy morning. If this is not enough to counterbalance the scorn of the ungodly, where is our faith? If we had a clear sight of this glory, would we have an eye for anything else? Would not everything else be an utter irrelevance?

20. The poor are shunned even by their neighbors, but the rich have many friends. This is a humbling but common illustration of natural selfishness. Sometimes, however, we hear of cheering exceptions. Ruth clung to Naomi in her poverty. Jonathan and David remained firm friends, even when this meant being stripped of royal favor. But all too often **the poor**, instead of being pitied and comforted, **are shunned even by their neighbors.** However, **the rich** could not be in a more enviable position. They **have many friends** because of their money and status. But Jesus was deliberately the poor man's friend. How endearing is Jesus' love!

21. He who despises his neighbor sins, but blessed is he who is kind to the needy. The previous proverb reflects the general standard of selfishness. This proverb reveals how sinful that is. Some men are so high that they cannot see their lower brothers. Yet the despised one is infinitely precious in the Savior's eyes. He was bought by Christ's blood.

We are clearly commanded to honor all people (1 Peter 2:17). We do not give exactly the same honor to different people, but as they deserve. We remember that everyone bears the image of God, no matter how much it may be defaced. Therefore, to look on the lowest as if he were to be despised reveals a lack of wisdom and a lack of heart. "Because we think we are superior to someone, we feel that we can overlook him" (Bishop Sanderson). So we do not have mercy on him.

But how happy is the man who is **kind to the needy.** "He shall be happy beyond expression" (Scott). Does not every act of love enlarge our own happiness? Do we not ourselves richly feed on the bread with which we feed the hungry? And will not the great day declare and honor every act of love that we have done for our divine Master?

22. Do not those who plot evil go astray? But those who plan what is good find love and faithfulness. Scripture traces actions to principles. Wicked as it is to do evil, it is far more wicked to **plot evil.** Children of God, do you show the same diligence and determination in planning to do **good? Love and faithfulness** are often seen as the reward of grace, the cheering encouragement of practical godliness. What can be more joyful than the glorious perfections of Jehovah pouring into the soul the quickening energy of divine blessing? **Love** is the fountainhead, **faithfulness** the pledge and fulfillment of unchangeable mercy. "Note," says an old expositor, "that Solomon here is no lawgiver, but an evangelist, leading us to Jesus Christ. For we can obtain no mercy but in him alone" (Cope).

23. All hard work brings a profit, but mere talk leads only to poverty. This is not universally true. How does the work of sin benefit anyone? Also the words of the lips can be fruitful (10:21; 15:7). But the contrast in this proverb is intended between what is solid on the one hand and what is shadowy on the other, between well-directed **work** and empty **talk.**

Enlarging the mind is also a benefit of mental work. But the **chattering fool** (10:8) "cut[s] himself off from all advantage, except that of being entertained by his own talk; his business in coming into company was not at all wanting to be informed, to hear, to listen, but to display himself, and to talk without any purpose whatsoever" (Bishop Butler).

Take care that religious conversation deserves the name. Let the burning theme of the Savior's love flow from the heart.

24. The wealth of the wise is their crown, but the folly of fools yields folly. The godly are made **wise** by being **crowned with knowledge** (verse 18). Then **the wealth of the wise is their crown.** For although no wise man desires wealth, yet as a gift from God it becomes his **crown.** It enhances his reputation and increases his usefulness as a consecrated talent for God. What a **crown** riches were to David and his wise son, to obtain the materials for building the temple, and for Job, who used them for the benefit of his fellow creatures. "It is necessary to distinguish between the thing itself and the abuse of it. Wealth is in fact a blessing when honestly acquired and conscientiously used. And when it is used in any other way, the man is to be blamed, and not his treasure" (Cowper).

Wealth is the crown . . . of the wise, but it cannot hide **fools.** It only makes their **folly** more apparent. Since it is wasted on their selfish gratification, it is not their **crown** but their **folly.** So whatever our talents are, let us use them for eternity; then they will be our everlasting **crown.**

25. A truthful witness saves lives, but a false witness is deceitful. How weighty is the responsibility of testimony. Every Christian has in him a principle of conscientious faithfulness. As **a truthful witness** he would deliver the innocent from oppression or ruin. But an ungodly man proves to be a **deceitful . . . witness,** an agent of Satan. He tells lies in order to destroy his neighbor. How much we need to walk before God in our words, being prepared to risk everything in the interests of truth as we consider our obligations to one another. "We must be mindful of that true and faithful witness that every man carries in his heart, whom no gift can blind, no power can silence" (Bishop Horne). We must remember that we will appear before the God of truth, and by our words we will be justified or condemned (Matthew 12:37). If the responsibility is so great for a witness in a court, how much more is the responsibility for the witness in a pulpit. "As they are the most profitable witnesses who preach to us Jesus Christ, even so, the most exquisite deceivers are those who under the shadow of religion set forth men's traditions" (Cope).

26. He who fears the LORD has a secure fortress, and for his children it will be a refuge. The true fear of God is a holy, happy, reverential principle. It is not the fear that throws out love, but that which brings love in. It is reverence tempered with love. We fear because we love. We fear, yet are not afraid. The holiest and the humblest is the most steady and trusting heart. The fear of man saps our strength; but the fear of God, such is the Christian paradox, makes us bold. Its childlike spirit shuts out all terrors of conscience, all forebodings of eternity.

27. The fear of the LORD is a fountain of life, turning a man from the snares of death. How bright is this divine principle. It is full of life—temporal life, spiritual life, and eternal life. It is the effect of the heavenly

Comforter who produces water welling up to eternal life (John 4:14). It is not only a refuge from **the snares of death,** but **a fountain of life.** Among the countless redeemed, no one finds cover from condemnation who has not been made alive with spiritual life. This invaluable grace flows with the full streams of gospel blessing.

28. A large population is a king's glory, but without subjects a prince is ruined. The Bible is a book for all. Even the king of Israel was commanded to treasure it (Deuteronomy 17:18). It describes him as a curse or a blessing to his people, as he is led by his own caprice or directed by divine wisdom. "He is not appointed for luxury or for pleasure, but that as a head he may preside over his members, as a shepherd he may care for his flock, as a tree he may nourish those under his shadow" (Geier).

Without subjects a prince is ruined. Here **subjects** are seen as the strength and stay of a ruler's kingdom. If his income fails, he is made feeble, and his enemies will take advantage of his weakness. His interests and his people's are one. In promoting their happiness, the **prince** secures his own honor. How great, then, is the honor of our heavenly King among the countless multitudes of his people.

29. A patient man has great understanding, but a quick-tempered man displays folly. The world does not care about someone being **quick-tempered,** except when it affects them directly. "It is a fit of passion, soon over and best forgotten," they conclude. But does God judge **a quick-tempered man** in this way? Note what God's Word says about this. Having a quick temper is giving way to the devil and grieving the Holy Spirit. It is contrary to the mind and example of Christ. It is degrading to human nature. It is a work of evil human nature, shutting us out from heaven and condemning us to hell. So to be **patient** shows that we have **great understanding.**

Let the children of God remember that a quick temper was condemned in the meekest of men (Psalm 106:32-33). Never was **folly** more clearly displayed than by the fretful selfishness of a prophet of the Lord (Jonah 4). The gentlest spirit needs to be in deep humility and love in order to have fellowship with God (Isaiah 57:15; 1 John 4:16). Has not God given us **understanding** to govern our tempers, and his Word and Spirit to crucify them?

30. A heart at peace gives life to the body, but envy rots the bones. Many agree that faith in God is good for the soul. But they do not think this can affect the body in any way. The wise man, however, teaches that **a heart at peace gives life to the body** (see 3:7-8). And surely **a heart at peace,** free from corroding passions and imbued with Christian habits, although this will not bring immortality, must be conducive to good health. Such **a heart** is free from selfishness and rejoices in the happiness of other people.

Envy, on the other hand, is wounded by our neighbor's prosperity. His ruin, or at least his injury, would give us pleasure. This evil is indeed the deadliest fruit of selfishness. Nothing flourishes under its shade. It **rots the bones**. "Truly," as Bishop Hall observes, "this vice is executioner enough to itself." This is the hell that such a man carries in his own heart.

31. He who oppresses the poor shows contempt for their Maker, but whoever is kind to the needy honors God. Are not the poor, no less than the rich, created in God's image? Both meet before their Maker. Both have the same nature in their hearts. Both sink to the same humiliating level in death. Both rise to the same eminence of immortality. Besides, do not the poor have a special interest in the Gospel? Was not the Gospel first spread by the poor? Has not the voluntary poverty of the Son of God for us elevated such a lowly condition to the highest level? So what grounds are left that we should oppress **the poor** as if they were inferior to us? If we do this, we are guilty of showing **contempt for their Maker** (see 17:5). We must not only refrain from oppressing **the poor**—we must have mercy on them.

32. When calamity comes, the wicked are brought down, but even in death the righteous have a refuge. We cannot judge men by their outward condition. Such judgments would most often be wrong. The standard of the world is most often erroneous. Most people think they are good enough for heaven. This hope is even entertained by criminals who believe they will receive mercy in the end. They think that little separates **the wicked** and **the righteous.**

But now let us turn to the striking picture before us, which sweeps away all human standards. Eternity is here set before us: **The wicked** and **the righteous** each go to their respective places (compare Acts 1:25). Let us ponder this with deep solemnity. Oh, my soul, make your calling sure.

The wicked include a wide range of people. Many are amiable, useful, and in many ways exemplary. Others are absorbed in vanity, or they wear themselves out in study or are given over to indulging themselves. But whatever their external state, they forget God and are traveling to hell.

But even in death the righteous have a refuge. Their death is full of hope. Job pierced his dark cloud of sorrow with this joyful hope. David rested his worn-out spirit on the Rock of salvation. And do we not daily hear the voice from heaven assuring us about the blessedness of those who die in the Lord (Revelation 14:13)? Praise to our Immanuel! "When thou hadst overcome the sharpness of death, thou didst open the kingdom of heaven to all believers" (*Te Deum*). Through Jesus Christ, as the way to the kingdom, we go freely, gladly out of life. We go to our natural home, to our Savior's heart, to our rest, to our crown, to our everlasting joy.

Does this text not clearly prove that while life and immortality were brought to light by the Gospel, the dawn of day beamed on the Old Testament saints? What could this hope of **the righteous** be but the consummating prospect of the Gospel? Solomon's sagacious mind could never have confounded two things so essentially distinct as hope in death and hope of escape from death. Satisfactory and beautiful is the comment of a learned German critic who notes "a splendid testimony of the knowledge of the Old Testament believer in a future life. The wicked in this calamity is agitated with the greatest terror. He knows not where to turn. But the godly in this last evil has no fear. He knows to whom to flee, and where he is going" (Dathe). Again, "The righteous dies in God's grace, and in an assured confidence of the salvation of his soul, and of the glorious resurrection of his body" (Diodati).

33. Wisdom reposes in the heart of the discerning and even among fools she lets herself be known. The wise man often speaks of the blessing of **wisdom** on the lips (10:11, 20-21; 15:2, 7). Here we trace it to its home. It flows from the head and **reposes in the heart**. Thus it did rest without measure in the humanity of Jesus (John 3:34). When it rests in our hearts, it is of incalculable value, as a fixed principle. It stops us from being tossed about by strange teachings. We see the vital difference between speculation and experience.

It is very different from worldly disputation. The latter, as Bishop Taylor observes, "covers no vices but ignites a great many. Though men esteem it learning, it is the most useless learning in the world." True **wisdom** sets its throne **in the heart**.

34. Righteousness exalts a nation, but sin is a disgrace to any people. If it is not beneath the dignity of statesmen to learn from the Bible, let them deeply ponder this sound political maxim, which commends itself to every instinct of the unsophisticated mind. Indeed, it would be a strange anomaly in God's order of the world if the link between godliness and prosperity, ungodliness and misery, established in individual cases, should not hold true in nations as well. Scripture clearly proves that this is as much a rule for nations as it is for individuals. The annals of the chosen people, depending on whether they were a righteous or a sinful nation, are marked by corresponding exaltation or reproach.

But sin is a disgrace to any people. No nation is so low as not to sink even lower under **sin**. The strongest nations are given an indelible blot if they are overcome by **sin**. What an enemy an ungodly man is to his country. He may talk eloquently about his patriotism, but even if God should elevate him in his work, he will only bring **disgrace** on his people. We need to pray and plead for our country's true prosperity with humility, faith, and constancy. Let us work for our country's exaltation with a completely united heart.

35. A king delights in a wise servant, but a shameful servant incurs his wrath. The work of **a wise servant** is often the reason for a nation being exalted. No wonder **a king delights** in such a person. In the same way it is hardly surprising that **a king** is so angry with **a shameful servant**.

It was like this with the great King. All of us are his servants, bound to him by the highest obligations. All of us have our responsibilities, our talents, and our work. Regarding the wise and faithful servant who has traded with his talents and who has been diligent in his work, the Lord will bless him with his favor. But the Lord's **wrath** rests on the servant who neglects his work and who is not prepared to give a good account of his talents. What will the solemn day of reckoning bring to me? May I, may we all be found to be **wise** servants to the best of Kings. We should be able to look with confidence to him for his wonderful welcome and for his "well done, good and faithful servant."

Proverbs
Chapter 15

1. A gentle answer turns away wrath, but a harsh word stirs up anger.
What a mine of practical wisdom the Book of God is! Let us ponder this
valuable rule for self-discipline, family peace, and church unity. Scripture
often illustrates the different effects of the tongue. The **gentle answer** is
water that quenches quarrels; **a harsh word** is oil that **stirs up** the fire.
Man's natural inclination is to give in to irritation, to justify oneself, and to
insist on having the last word. In an argument neither party is prepared to
give an inch. Pride and passion on both sides strike together like two flints.
We indulge in sarcasm as if we would rather lose a friend than miss scor-
ing a point in the argument. All this the world excuses. But the Gospel sets
before us our Savior's example and imbues us with his spirit; so we should
be careful not to provoke a chafed or wounded spirit. If others begin an
argument, let us not continue the strife. "Patience is the true peacemaker"
(Bishop Sanderson). **Gentle** and healing words gain a double victory—
over ourselves and our brother.

**2. The tongue of the wise commends knowledge, but the mouth of
the fool gushes folly.** In the previous proverb we had the tongue of love.
Here we have the **tongue** of wisdom. The tongue reveals the person. **The
wise** is in control of his tongue. **The fool** is controlled by his tongue. You
may possess a mass of **knowledge.** But because you do not know how to
use it in the right way, it runs to waste. Wisdom is shown, not by the quan-
tity of knowledge, but by applying it in the right way.

To judge the waters flowing from a fool's spring, listen to Baal's wor-
shipers, Rabshakeh's proud boasting, and the complaints of God's people
as they pour out their foolishness. Oh, for a large infusion of sound
knowledge in the inner treasure-house, that the tongue may be disciplined
and consecrated!

**3. The eyes of the LORD are everywhere, keeping watch on the
wicked and the good.** May this all-seeing God be adored! His inspection

of the universe is so minute, exact, and untiring. The first indication of apostasy is a dread of his presence. The ungodly try to forget it and often succeed in banishing him from their thoughts. Yet in spite of all their efforts to hide, the Lord does see them.

His **eyes . . . are everywhere.** Heaven, hell, and the secret places of the earth are all open to him. He sees evil, whether the king on his throne or in his palace, or the servant indulging his secret sin. Yes, it may be possible to shut out the sun from a house, but it is not possible to shut out God's **eyes.** Only a reckless person thinks he can hide from God. Thinking he can do this is the secret root of atheism.

The Lord's **eyes** also see **the good.** He sees them in outward destitution, in secret retirement, in deep affliction. He pierces the prison walls. He is with them in the furnace and in the storm. His eye guides them so they reach their home safely. "He fills hell with his severity, heaven with his glory, his people with his grace" (Charnock).

So how will I meet these **eyes?** Will I meet them as a rebel or as a child? Do they inspire me with terror or love? The overwhelming thought of this piercing eye is more than counterbalanced by the view of the great High Priest, who covers and cleanses all infirmities and defilements and pleads and maintains my acceptance, notwithstanding all discouragement (Hebrews 4:13-14).

4. The tongue that brings healing is a tree of life, but a deceitful tongue crushes the spirit. Wisdom is portrayed as **a tree of life** (see also 3:18). It is like salt that is thrown into a spring and cleanses polluted water (2 Kings 2:21). So when there is grace in the heart, there will be healing in **the tongue.** Words will be full of grace, seasoned with salt (Colossians 4:6).

Though the gracious **tongue brings healing,** the evil **tongue** wounds. The tongue of Job's friends broke the bruised reed that needed to be bound up. "Everlasting benediction be on that tongue that spoke as no other ever did or could speak pardon, peace, and comfort to lost mankind! This was a tree of life whose leaves were for the healing of the nations" (Bishop Horne).

5. A fool spurns his father's discipline, but whoever heeds correction shows prudence. Submission to parents is the law of nature and is recognized even by most uncivilized nations. Much more it is the law of God. The authority of parents is the authority of God. But pride must be broken down and the clothes of humility worn before the child will see that his parents know better than himself. Solomon's wisdom, though the special gift of God, was doubtless linked to his regard for **his father's discipline.** Will those who despise their earthly **father's discipline** listen to their heavenly Father? Therefore, this intractable spirit excludes people from the kingdom of God.

6. The house of the righteous contains great treasure, but the income of the wicked brings them trouble. The comparison between **the**

righteous and the wicked is always in favor of the righteous. Even when it comes to treasure, the world's idol, he comes out best. For although his house may have no money, it still has great treasure. "Drop millions of gold, boundless income, ample territories, crowns and scepters, and a poor contemptible worm lays his one God against all of them" (Bishop Hopkins). The wicked are too much concerned about their own worldly welfare and are unable to satisfy their souls. But is it not the crown of the Christian's crown and the glory of his glory that his portion is so full that he cannot desire more?

7. The lips of the wise spread knowledge; not so the hearts of fools. The correct use of knowledge is, first, to gather it in a barn, and then to distribute it from the barn. In this way our Lord spread the heavenly knowledge of his Gospel. He commanded his apostles to scatter the seed through the vast field of the world. The persecution of the church was overruled for this great purpose. The Reformers widely spread their treasures both by preaching and writing, and rich indeed was the fruit. Do we remember that our gifts and talents are the riches of the church? Like our father Abraham we are blessed, not for our own sakes, but to be a blessing. Be alert to small opportunities. The careful cultivation of the smallest field ensures an abundant harvest.

The sin of the wicked is not always that they pour out foolishness (verse 2); sometimes it is that they say nothing. They neglect to spread knowledge. If they do not misuse their talent, they neglect to improve it. If not blots, they are empty vessels in the church. If they do not harm, they do nothing. Indeed, they can dispense nothing from their empty barns.

8. Let the reader ponder this solemn question: "What am I, what is my service, when I am on my knees before God? Am I an abomination or a delight?" Man judges by deeds; God judges by principles.

The sacrifice of the wicked is performed while the heart is asleep. This is acting out a lie. This is an insulting provocation. This is not only vain but abominable. It is a "work, that doth not flow from a lively faith, and therefore hath in it the nature of sin" (Article Three, from the Thirty-nine Articles).

It is not that prayer itself is a sin. "It is," as Archbishop Ussher expounds, "a good duty, but spoiled in the carriage [the manner of carrying it out]." We do not want to discourage the wicked from praying. We only say that it must be done in God's way or it will not be accepted.

9. It is not only the sacrifice but the way of the wicked that God detests. It is not only his religion but his everyday life that is an abomination. His whole life is lived in rebellion against God. Everything he does flows from a polluted spring. It is a terrible thought that the wicked man's every step is detestable in God's sight.

10. Stern discipline awaits him who leaves the path; he who hates correction will die. But is not stern discipline also shunned by the child of

God? No. He knows his need of it; he kisses the rod, bows his will, and reaps a harvest of blessing. But he **who leaves the path** is only humbled by force, not in spirit. There is no surer step to ruin than to hate **correction**. Child of God, do you not still need **correction** so you can be more obedient? The Lord teaches you, when you have a thorn in your flesh, to pray for his grace to be in your heart (2 Corinthians 12:7). Seek your Father's favor more than your own ease. Desire sanctifying rather than the removal of his rod. Do not mock him with an empty show of repentance. *Lord, let me know the smart of your rod rather than the eclipse of your love. Show me your love, and then do with me as you wish.*

11. Death and Destruction lie open before the LORD—how much more the hearts of men! Once again we see an omniscient and omnipresent God. **Death and Destruction**, every recess of the vast Hades, the state of the dead and the place of the damned, **lie open before the LORD.** So **how much more** are **the hearts of men** open to him. Would men indulge in their vain thoughts, their trifles, their impurities if they really believed that the Lord searched their hearts? Your heart is open before God. He will never stoop to occupy a second place there. Your covering of deceit must be swept away.

The conscious sinner shrinks from this appalling sight. But the believer walks undismayed in the sight of this consuming fire. The sins that are known to the Father are covered from his justice.

12. A mocker resents correction; he will not consult the wise. The **mocker** has been flattering himself for so long that he cannot bear to be brought down to his correct level. So he thinks that a friend who tells him the truth is his enemy. He not only **resents correction**—he hates it.

13. A happy heart makes the face cheerful, but heartache crushes the spirit. A man's countenance is the index of his **spirit**. In experiencing joy "the heart sits smiling in the face and looks cheerfully out of the windows of the eyes" (Trapp). This cheerfulness, however, is very different from the noisy mirth of the ungodly. The word *cheerful* was often used by the old writers. It was Foxe's favorite description of the holy joy of the martyrs.

Sad, indeed, is the contrasting **heartache** that **crushes the spirit**. Too often a mischievous gloom worms itself into the hearts of God's children. The melancholy victim drags on through a weary, heavy-laden existence. His hands slacken, and his energies for God's work are paralyzed. He sinks into apathy and laziness as if he has no life left in him.

Every effort should be made to sweep away this dark, hovering cloud. Let sense and feeling be kept within their bounds. Listen to the Savior's encouraging voice. "I wonder many times," says Rutherford, "that ever a child of God should have a sad heart, considering what his Lord is preparing for him." The gleam of the present sunshine is the earnest of what it will be when, as he again beautifully observes, "we shall be on the sunny side of the Brae." Meanwhile, the first step in religion is not only beginning to be serious but to be happy. To maintain our Christian balance, even godly sorrow must be disciplined, so that it does not beat down the heart that it was only meant to humble.

14. The discerning heart seeks knowledge, but the mouth of a fool feeds on folly. Observe the man of natural understanding. Every apprehension quickens his thirst to **seek knowledge**. He is ready to learn from any quarter, even from a child. He is all eye, all ear, all heart for his object. Much more will spiritual understanding stimulate the desire. Repress the appetite to be wise above what is written. But make great efforts to be wise to the full extent of God's revelation in the Scriptures.

But while the **discerning heart** is never satisfied with its **knowledge**, the **fool** is completely satisfied with **folly**. His brutish taste **feeds on folly** as his meat and drink. Young people, be on your guard against this **folly**. Avoid trifling amusements, frivolous reading, profane merriment. In religion, beware of choosing empty speculations and arguments on indifferent matters rather than the rich pasture of the children of God. Let us all ponder the responsibility to go on to maturity (Hebrews 6:1; 5:14).

15. All the days of the oppressed are wretched, but the cheerful heart has a continual feast. Affliction, as the fruit and punishment of sin, is **wretched**. Hence **all the days of the oppressed are wretched**. Yet a solid principle of inner satisfaction will bring real comfort in most trying circumstances. Therefore, although the abounding consolation of Christian affliction does not blot out its penal character, the child of God is not so miserable as he seems to be. The darkest of all these **days** can never make God's consolations within him disappear. He can sing in a prison as much as in a palace. "Who is it," said the heavenly Martyn in a moment of weakness, "that makes my comforts to be a source of enjoyment? Cannot the same hand make cold, and hunger, and nakedness, and peril to be a train of ministering angels conducting me to glory?"

16-17. Here are the sources of the cheerful heart—**the fear of the LORD** and the love of man. And here also is the constant feast that so satisfies that the saint's little is better than everything the world has. "Riches and poverty are more in the heart than in the hand. He is wealthy who is contented. He is poor who wants more" (Bishop Hall). The universe will not fill a worldly person, while a little will suffice for a heavenly heart.

Few, alas, put this divine testimony into practice. Parents, do you seek the lasting happiness of your children? Then lead them to expect little from the world and everything from God.

18. A hot-tempered man stirs up dissension, but a patient man calms a quarrel. This proverb requires no explanation. But observe the principles of hatred and love. Some people make it their business to sit by the fire to feed and fan the flame in case it goes out. But when it is a harmful, consuming, and destructive element, it would be hard to fathom the motive of such people if we did not read that all that is evil comes from the heart (Mark 7:21-22).

What, then, should a Christian do? Instead of stirring up, he **calms a quarrel.** He should bring water, not fuel, to the fire (see verse 1). With a spirit that gives way he melts, subdues, and brings peace. Let me remember that I owe my very salvation to God's being slow to anger.

19. The way of the sluggard is blocked with thorns, but the path of the upright is a highway. Another picture of **the sluggard** is drawn here. He plants his own hedge of **thorns** and then complains that his way is **blocked.** He is always standing still. Every time he moves, it is like forcing his way through a hedge, because of which he cuts his flesh as he attempts to make forward progress. Indecision, delay, and sluggishness add to his difficulties and paralyze his exertion. So after a feeble struggle of conscience, but lacking the heart to do anything, he gives up trying.

This laziness brings ruin to our earthly life. But it brings even greater ruin in the Christian life. **The sluggard** in religion is never at ease. He knows that he needs to change. He makes an effort to pray or he takes up a book to read. But everything withers, for his heart is not in it. For him exertion is impossible. He sees no hope of victory; so he sinks into lethargy again.

Child of God, beware of such a sluggish spirit. Even morbid, scrupulous strife about your state may sometimes be slothful indulgence in direct opposition to the plainest declarations of God. Do not let unbelief rob your hand of God's promises or paralyze the hand that holds God's promises. If the way has been made clear to you, do not sit down and indulge your own comfort.

20. A wise son brings joy to his father, but a foolish man despises his mother. Do not the brightest joys and the bitterest sorrows in this world of tears flow from parents' hearts? The Christian **father** cannot rest until his son is **wise** and brings him **joy.** What is needed here is not any development of talent or superior attainment, but true wisdom. This wisdom is humble and docile and respects parents. Such a **son** does indeed bring **joy** to **his father** as the **father** watches, with pleasure and gratitude, the daily growth of his choice vine.

But what if **a foolish man despises his mother** and her tender love and her faithfulness? God's law commands us to honor and reverence our parents. If we break this law, that will not be forgotten. But what grace and wisdom are needed if parents are to be a blessing to their children and their highest interests. A single eye is the primary concern.

21. Folly delights a man who lacks judgment, but a man of understanding keeps a straight course. This book of instruction probes our Christian profession. What do we think about **folly?** It is not only practiced by the ungodly man; it is his joy. He sins without being tempted. He cannot sleep without it. He hates the Gospel because it saves him from it.

This appetite for sin shows that man is devoid of wisdom. **But a man of** understanding gives himself to the Word of God. He delights in wisdom, just as the sinner **delights** in **folly**. Even his painful discoveries of indwelling corruption ground him deeper in solid religion than those who know only the surface. He is taught by God, and he **keeps a straight course.** *Give me, oh, my God,* **understanding,** *that my joy may be in your wisdom, not in my own folly.*

22. Plans fail for lack of counsel, but with many advisers they succeed. The value of this proverb as a political truth is quite clear. A nation without **counsel** can never be established. A large number of counselors is an indispensable advantage to a ruler. In the church also, combined counsel has been a great help to our religious institutions.

In our individual perplexities we benefit from having **many advisers.** For how weak and ignorant we are! Were our judgment perfect, our first impressions would be infallibly right. But feeble and shaken as we are by the Fall, every dictate needs to be pondered. How much evil has been done by acting upon impulse in a hasty moment or by a few words or lines said or written without consideration. Our wisdom lies in self-distrust, or at least allowing for the possibility that we may often be wrong! So it is most expedient, especially in important matters, to seek experienced counsel. But even here the wisest counsel is fallible and often wrong. Most of all we should look to our heavenly Counselor. Blessed be God for this special privilege, for his counsel is always at hand.

23. A man finds joy in giving an apt reply—and how good is a timely word! This is a true proverb when the mouth is under divine discipline. A **word** for our great Master to our fellow sinner, he will condescend to bless. If we remember who made man's mouth (Exodus 4:11), pride will vanish. But the **word** that we speak must be **a timely word,** even though it comes from feeble lips. Thus Luther, following the example of the apostle Paul, gladly acknowledges his indebtedness: "The word of a brother, pronounced from Holy Scripture in a time of need, carries an inconceivable weight with it. The Holy Spirit accompanies it, and by it moves and animates the hearts of the people, as their circumstances require. Thus Timothy, and Titus, and Epaphroditus, and the brethren who met St. Paul from Rome cheered his spirit, however much they might be inferior to him in learning and skill in the Word of God. The greatest saints have their times of faintness, when others are stronger than they." But many a good word is lost by being given at an untimely moment. Obviously a moment of irritation is such a moment. We must wait for calmness and reason to return.

It is most important that our whole attitude bring conviction and that we yearn over the souls of those we have to reprove. The general rule is to give reproof in private (Matthew 18:15). Do not begin by taking the offensive, as this will immediately provoke resistance. Make sure your words apply to the person you are rebuking. A word spoken for everyone, like a coat made for everyone, fits no one. The wise heart knows the proper time and procedure for every matter (Ecclesiastes 8:5), and the word is then doubly effective.

24. The path of life leads upward for the wise to keep him from going down to the grave. Another beam of light and immortality shines here on the Old Testament dispensation. For if the **life** that **leads upward** is beyond animals, it must be the life eternal. **Going down to the grave**, which is contrasted with it, must stretch beyond **the grave** into eternity. But **the path of life**, the way in which alone **life** is found, the way to God, the way to glory, is but one. That way is Christ. If, therefore, I come to him, renouncing all other hope, throwing all my care on him, and every step of my way looking to him, am I not in this way?

The path of life leads upward. This **path** has a heavenly origin. It is the fruit of eternal councils. It displays the great wisdom of God. Fools never rise high enough to understand it, let alone to walk in its way. Their highest elevation is groveling. They cling to the dust of the earth, and they sink into hell beneath it. But the way of **the wise . . . leads upward**. They are born from above and taught from above, and so they walk above, even while they live on earth. **The wise** in their most favored moments cannot fully appreciate their present privileges. How much less will they be able to understand the glorious unfolding when all clouds vanish.

We would think less about the roughness of the way if we thought more about the future rest. But unless we know heaven as our present state, how can we hope to enjoy it as our everlasting home? "Grant, we beseech thee, that, like as we do believe thy only-begotten Son, our Lord Jesus Christ, to have ascended into the heavens; so we may also in heart and mind thither ascend, and with him continually dwell" (Collect for Ascension day, *Book of Common Prayer*).

25. The LORD tears down the proud man's house but he keeps the widow's boundaries intact. God's work is to humble **the proud** and to exalt the humble. The **proud** oppressor attempts to usurp God of his rights. Therefore he is a traitor, and God **tears down** not only his person but his **house**.

But **the widow**, whom most people do not care about and who is trampled underfoot, has a Friend and Protector. God condescends to link himself with widows in this special way, concentrating all his care and tenderness on their bereaved state. Did he not provide for the sorrowing Naomi and ultimately establish her **boundaries** in Israel?

26. The LORD detests the thoughts of the wicked, but those of the pure are pleasing to him. How little most people think they are responsible for their thoughts. They live as if they were on their own and so can indulge themselves without any restraints. But **thoughts** are the seminal principles of sin. Even the heathen accurately describe them as "the indigenous fountains of evil" (Plutarch). Plutarch also wrote, "If thou wouldest unlock the door of thine heart, thou wilt find a storehouse and treasury of evils diversified, and full of numberless passions." As a person thinks, so he is. Let the Christian give himself over to God, from whose sight nothing is hidden (Hebrews 4:13).

27. A greedy man brings trouble to his family, but he who hates bribes will live. What an awful stamp God has placed on covetousness. It is not only a curse to the sinner, but it **brings trouble to his family**. It did so in the cases of Lot, Achan, Saul, Ahab, Gehazi, and Jehoiakim. Whenever people do not seek to be enriched by God's blessing, we are hardly surprised that it is withheld.

The man of God is contrasted with the **greedy man**. The man of God is not corrupted by **bribes** since he always refuses them, for he knows to do otherwise would not honor God. Abraham refused the gifts of the king of Sodom, and Peter refused the enticement of Simon. "Let their money perish with them," was the noble confession of the Marquis of Vico, nephew to Paul V, "that prefer all the world's wealth before one day's communion with Jesus Christ and his despised people."

28. The heart of the righteous weighs its answers, but the mouth of the wicked gushes evil. Consideration is an important part of Christian character. It is nowhere more important than in the discipline of the tongue. We must think twice before we speak once. We must reflect and not speak in haste. Cultivate a pondering mind. If you are ever asked a question on an important subject, do not be quick with your reply, but seek it first from God. The only way to receive God's wisdom is through prayer.

The wicked have no such restraint. They do not care what they say. It does not bother them if what they say is badly timed, or if it is true, or if it wounds.

29. The LORD is far from the wicked but he hears the prayer of the righteous. The contrast between **the wicked** and **the righteous** is sharply drawn here. The Lord's favor is **far from the wicked,** and he rejects their prayer. But the Lord is near **the righteous,** and **he hears** their **prayer**.

However, the enemy will raise doubts in our mind. Does God hear us? **The righteous** is well aware what a shelter prayer is from Satan's assault. He knows that Satan seeks to stop us from praying. A second doubt that arises is: Am I **righteous?** No, you are not. But your Advocate is (1 John 2:1). So put your prayer in his hands. You cannot doubt his access to God. While God's ear may be deaf to you, it is open to your Advocate. Stammer out the prayer to your Friend. "O Lord, I am oppressed; undertake for me." "It would tire the hands of an angel to write down the pardons that God bestows on one penitent sinner" (Dr. Bates).

30. A cheerful look brings joy to the heart [KJV: the light of the eyes rejoiceth the heart], and good news gives health to the bones. The eye is the medium of the most rational enjoyment. Most elevating is the sight of the wonders of creation (Psalm 19:1; 111:2).

But let us look at the joy of hearing. How the patriarch's heart did leap at the good report of his beloved Joseph (Genesis 45:27-28). The absent minister seems to live again in the good news about his thriving people (1 Thessalonians 3:8). "How delightful must it be to the humbled sinner to hear the good news of salvation and to have his eyes enlightened to behold the glory of God in the face of Jesus Christ" (Scott).

31. By nature we are unteachable. But the Lord gives humility and self-knowledge. We become teachable, and light pours in. We learn the meaning of words that we had previously only known by name. The way we receive a **rebuke** tests our character. It reveals if we possess the graces of humility, sincerity, and self-knowledge.

32. Correction is indeed bitter to receive, but it is one of the most positive experiences in life. After a long time of reflection, we see the wisdom of honoring those who have dealt faithfully with our faults, even if it felt severe at the time. **Correction** is infinitely preferable to the poison of sweet flattery.

33. The fear of the LORD teaches a man wisdom, and humility comes before honor. As the child of God realizes the presence of a holy God, he will be full of **humility.** Indeed, no Christian grace can exist without it. Every dispensation of God strikes at the root of self-exultation.

Our Father's discipline is so wise: **Humility comes before honor.** Indeed, without **humility, honor** would be our temptation rather than our glory. True **humility,** which realizes our vileness, throws us onto the full resources of the Gospel, so that the most humble is the most triumphant believer. "The lower then any descend in humiliation, the higher they shall ascend in exaltation. The lower this foundation of humility is laid, the higher shall the roof of honor be overlaid" (Cope). Our Lord followed this same path. He endured the cross before he was rewarded with his crown.

Proverbs
Chapter 16

1. To man belong the plans of the heart, but from the LORD comes the reply of the tongue. [The preparations of the heart in man, and the answer of the tongue, is from the LORD, KJV]. The great question is decided here: Who is the first mover in the work of conversion? Can man prepare his own heart for the grace of God? This proverb teaches that the Lord takes the stone out of the heart so that it may feel; the Lord draws the heart, that it may follow; the Lord gives life to the heart, that it may live. The Lord opens the heart, that he may stamp it with his own law and mold it in his own image. This work begins with God. It is not that we come first and then are taught. We first of all learn, and then we come. God's grace both goes ahead of us and cooperates in our salvation.

Should we then idly wait until God works? Far from it! We must work, but in dependence on God. God does not work without us but with us, through us, in us, and by us. And we work in him. Ours is to obey; his is the strength. He gives life to our actions. His commands do not imply our power to obey, but our dependence on him for the grace of obedience. "The work, as it is a duty, is ours; but as a performance, it is God's. He gives what he requires, and his promises are the foundation of our performances" (Bishop Reynolds). Our works are not the cause but the effect of his grace. They could never come from us until God had first put them in us.

This habit of dependence must continue to the end of our lives. We can no more prepare ourselves after we have received grace than we could before we received it. "I beg," said Jerome, "that I may receive; and when I have received, I beg again." Dependence is not the excuse for indolence but the spring of active energy.

2. All a man's ways seem innocent to him, but motives are weighed by the LORD. If man were his own judge, who would be condemned? Man judges by acts; God judges by principles. God's eye, therefore, sees a mass of corruption in us, while a **man's ways seem innocent to him**. In fact, man will never believe his real character until some subtle temptation exposes his own evil. *O God, place the blood of your beloved Son in the scale of your justice, and we will give to you the glory of your wonderful work of grace.*

3. Commit to the LORD whatever you do, and your plans will succeed. An unsettled mind is a serious evil. It is a canker to Christian peace. Every faculty is upset. The memory is confused, and the will unsteady. Faith is the only principle that can establish us. This was our original happiness and security. Independence was the destruction of our well-being. To return to this humble simplicity is the privilege of the Gospel.

In all you do, seek the Lord's strength and guidance. Look to him for success in everything. Put your deeds, as you would put your children, with confidence into God's hands. Let your heart, as a matter of habit, turn to the throne of grace. Then in a time of crisis instant prayer will bring composure and resolution. This active faith will enable us to collect our thoughts, establish them in God's peace, and keep our souls safe. Indeed, a great part of our worship is to commit our deeds to him, not in a general dependence on his goodness or wisdom, but in a particular dependence for our special need. In this way, as we believe, we enter into his rest (Hebrews 4:3). We are solemnly warned that if we do not believe, we will not be established in this way. "Nothing can be more erroneous than for those who fear God to suppose that they are still liable to 'the changes and chances of this mortal life.' Change, if God sees fit, they may experience, but the sincerely religious have done with chance. Having once cordially committed themselves to God's paternal care, they can meet nothing in their course that is not the result of divine adjustment, of wisdom that cannot err, of love to which the tenderness of the tenderest parent bears no comparison. Under such a management what can we rationally fear? Let us, through divine grace, only keep within the circle where these movements are carried on, and we need not doubt that though we see nothing remarkable in our course, an unseen hand is directing every circumstance, so as, in the most effectual manner, to avert what might hurt us, to ensure what will benefit us, and to direct all our concerns to the best possible issue" (Alexander Knox).

4. The LORD works out everything for his own ends—even the wicked for a day of disaster. Every workman has some purpose in his work. God has the highest purpose in his work. Everything was made by God and for God (Colossians 1:16). This includes all the work of creation, all the events that take place in the nations, and all the dispensations of his providence. They all reveal his glory to his intelligent creatures.

Even the wicked, whose existence might seem hardly reconcilable with divine perfection, the Lord includes in the great purpose of setting out his name. "It is the greatest praise of his wisdom that he can turn the evil of men to his own glory" (Bishop Hall). And when men sin by their own free will, he ordains them to be punished, as monuments to his power, his justice, and his patience.

Clearly God is not the author of sin. He cannot impart what he has not and what is contrary to his nature. Infinite perfection cannot impart imperfection. Absolute holiness cannot be the cause of sin, although, like the law, it may be the innocent occasion of it. If he foreknows with "infinite knowledge," as Edwards profoundly observes, that "proves the necessity of the event foreknown; yet it may not be the thing that causes the necessity." The Lord can decree nothing but good. If he permits evil, so far as not to hinder it, he nevertheless hates it as evil and permits it only for the greater good, and for the greatest good of all—the fuller manifestation of his own glory in it and out of it. He will be glorified in, or on, all his creatures. His retributive justice, no less than the riches of his grace, sets out his glory (Romans 9:22-23). It would seem that the redeemed are allowed to see this and to participate with divine satisfaction. The flames of hell excite the reverential praises of heaven. "And again they shouted: 'Hallelujah! The smoke from her goes up for ever and ever'" (Revelation 19:3). "God made man neither to save nor damn him, but for his own glory. And it is secured, whether in his salvation or damnation. Nor did, nor does, God make man wicked. He made man upright. Man makes himself wicked; and being so, God may justly appoint him to damnation for his wickedness; in doing which he glorifies his justice" (Gill). Bishop Sanderson mentions "those two great acts of his most secret and unsearchable counsel, than the one whereof there is not any one act more gracious, the destination of those that persevere in faith and godliness to eternal happiness; nor any one act more full of terror and astonishment than the other, the designation of such as live and die in sin to eternal destruction; the Scriptures in the last resolution refer them wholly to his glory, as the last end. The glory of his rich mercy being most resplendent in the one, and the glory of his just severity in the other."

5. The LORD detests all the proud of heart. Be sure of this: They will not go unpunished. The hatred contained in a proud look has been mentioned (6:17). But the Searcher of hearts marks **the proud of heart** that may be disguised under a humble look (Matthew 6:16). Men do not detest this spirit. In their eyes, it brings no disgrace. Indeed, it is often thought to be noble. But in reality it keeps the **heart** from God. It lifts up the **heart** against God. It contends for supremacy with him. When it strikes out at God like this, it is no wonder that God **detests** it.

6. Through love and faithfulness sin is atoned for; through the fear of the LORD a man avoids evil. The correct exposition of this verse requires much care and consideration. We object to that false principle of theology that substitutes practical statements in place of the great doctrines of the Gospel. The **sin atoned for** here seems to point us in the direction of expiation. Therefore, to link this with man's **love and faithfulness** overturns the foundation of the Gospel. There are duties to be performed, but they do not atone for sin.

Man would atone for sin by repentance or external rituals. But God does this by sacrifice. He does not nullify the sanctions of the law by a simple deed of **love** but combines the manifestation of his **faithfulness** by fulfilling these sanctions on the surety that **love** provided (Isaiah 53:6). No display of **love** can be conceived of to compare with that awful moment when God did not spare his own Son (Romans 8:32) but allowed blameless **love** and purity to agonize on the cross. Yet, was this wonderful display of **love** no less a wonderful display of **faithfulness**? For it was the means by which inflexible justice could justify the guilty (Romans 3:23-26). How gloriously these two attributes harmonize! We do not ask to which we are most deeply indebted. **Love** engages; **faithfulness** fulfills. The ransom is provided by **love** and accepted by **faithfulness**. Both sat together in the eternal council. Both entered into the world together.

7. When a man's ways are pleasing to the LORD, he makes even his enemies live at peace with him. God's favor and man's favor are often linked for the man of God. Yet he will always have **his enemies**, even if they are only in his own home. "The best way for our enemies to be reconciled to us is for us to be reconciled to God" (Bishop Patrick). All our danger lies in his wrath, not in their anger. No creature can touch us without his permission.

Even if the **enemies** are let loose, if their harm is overruled for the more general good, is not the promise substantially fulfilled? "No wise man will tax him with breach of promise who, having promised a pound of silver, gives a talent of gold. Or who can truly say a man is not as good as his word who is apparently much better than his word?" (Bishop Sanderson). God will take care of his people. Either peace or war will turn to their everlasting good.

8. Better a little with righteousness than much gain with injustice. The substance of this proverb has been given to us previously (15:16). But here the treasures are more clearly seen to be **much gain with injustice**. It seems to be so obvious that it does not need to be explained. Yet the love of **gain** is so blind that it looks only at its own selfish end and to the present moment. It looks to things that can never bring true enjoyment or lasting security. Retributive justice is at hand.

Better is a little with righteousness. Was not the widow of Zarephath richer with her scanty fare than Jezebel in her royal attire? We learn this valuable lesson. The fewer desires we have, the more peaceful we will be. If godliness is great riches in this life, what will it be in eternity?

9. In his heart a man plans his course, but the LORD determines his steps. This is a good description of God's sovereign rule. It is an inscrutable mystery how God accomplishes his fixed purpose by free-willed agents. Man without his free will is a machine. God without his unchangeable purpose ceases to be God. As rational agents we think, consult, act freely. We are dependent agents, and the Lord exercises his own power in permitting, overruling, or furthering our actions. Thus man proposes, and God disposes. **A man plans his course, but the LORD determines his steps.** God orders our will without infringing our liberty or stopping us from being responsible creatures. For while we act as we please, we must be answerable.

The doctrine of providence is not like the doctrine of the Trinity, which has to be accepted by faith. Experience gives us evidence about God's providence, even in all the minute circumstances that form the parts of the divine plan. A matter of ordinary business, the indulgence of curiosity, the supply of a necessary need, a journey from home—all are connected with infinitely important results. And often when our purpose seems to be perfectly clear, we discover that our own plans are blocked by unexpected difficulties, and unexpected facilities open in a totally opposite way. Ultimately we acknowledge that the Lord has led us in a direct route. So we find our happiness and security in giving up our will to our heavenly Guide. He knows the complete route; he knows the end from the beginning.

10-13. Here is a manual for **kings**. It does not show them what they are but what God requires them to be. They should be a blessing to their people and benefactors to the world. Such a **king**, and this is the glory of royalty, will have no interest of his own apart from the public good. He remembers that **honest scales and balances** are the Lord's, and so he hands down even-handed **justice**. He will not only refrain from **wrongdoing** but detests wickedness. He is not only careful to remove all evil from himself, but he will surround himself with faithful counselors. Constantius, the father of Constantine, tested the character of his Christian servants by the imperative command to offer sacrifices to his gods. Some sank under the trial. But those who had really bought the truth would not sell it for any price (see 23:23). They were inflexible. Constantius banished from his service those Christians who did offer sacrifices to his gods. Of the remaining he said, "These men I can trust. I value them more than all my treasures." This was sound judgment. For who are so likely to be faithful to their king as those who have proved themselves faithful to their God? The righteous are the pillars of the earth, the lions around the king's throne, his glory and defense.

14. The vast power of a king is depicted in this graphic picture of eastern despotism. Life and **death** are in his hands. His will is law. The despot issues his order, and the executioner performs his warrant without delay or resistance. No ordinary wisdom could **appease** his wrath.

15. A king's . . . favor indicates the same absolute power. The restoration of Pharaoh's butler to his former place was like a dead man rising to life.

But think about the King of kings, before whom the mightiest monarch is as dust. One smile scatters the thickest cloud. And **his favor is like a rain cloud in spring.** "Christ lives," said the noble Luther, "or else I would not desire to live one moment." Yes, Christian, bitter and deep as your sorrow may be, fear above everything else displeasing your Lord. Look to that time when you will walk up and down in unclouded light. *Oh, my Lord, "let the splendor of that day irradiate my soul, even at this distance from it, and leave no space void of its light and comfort. Yes, let it eclipse all other joys, and by its glistening beauty make the small contentment of this world to be so many glow-worms, which shine only at night. Impress on my heart such a sense of yourself and your glory that I may prefer to forget myself rather than you and your appearing"* (Bishop Patrick).

16. How much better to get wisdom than gold, to choose understanding rather than silver! Even leaving inspiration on one side, this must be considered to be a sound judgment. It was made by someone who had the largest part of both blessings that ever fell to a man. If you put in the balances of the sanctuary the overwhelming interests of heaven and earth, of the soul and the body, of eternity and time, who will dispute the verdict? The spiritual understanding of this is like the sudden discovery of a rich treasure that can be used immediately.

17. The highway of the upright avoids evil; he who guards his way guards his life. Here **the highway of the upright** is the plain beaten path, the way of holiness, and it **avoids evil.**

We each have our own world of **evil.** Consider an inner circle where the conflict is sharpest. There the need for divine discipline is far more keenly felt than in public sins. Show great forbearance to others, but none to yourself. Admit no foibles or infirmities. Think of nothing that hinders your Christian life as small. The real injury is not from our living in the world, but from the world living in us.

18. What more vivid exposition of these proverbs (verses 18-19) is needed than our own ruined condition? Our father's **pride,** desiring to be as God, plunged his whole race into **destruction.** "O Adam," was the exclamation of a man of God, "what have you done!" "I think," said another holy man, "so far as any man is proud, he is kin to the devil, and a stranger to God and to himself" (Baxter). This most awful strength of divine eloquence seems to be concentrated to delineate the character and ruin of **pride.** Fearful indeed is our danger if we do not heed this warning, if we do not deeply feel our need.

A haughty spirit carries the head high. The man looks upward instead of to his steps. Little wonder, therefore, if he does not see what is in front of him and so falls. He loves to climb. The enemy is always at hand to assist him, and the greater the height, the greater the **fall.** For what is our **pride** is our danger.

19. But have we been preserved from open disgrace? Examine secret faults. Trace them to their source. Maybe we have a subtle confidence in gifts, attainments, and privileges. Then praise your God for his painful discipline, the preserving mercy from ruinous self-exaltation. Truly the way down the valley of humiliation is deep and rugged. Humility, therefore, is the great preserving grace. The contrite tax collector was safe, though the boasting Pharisee was confounded (Luke 18:14). **Better**—more happy, more honorable, more acceptable to God and man—are the **lowly in spirit** than the haughty who only end up by being destroyed. It is better to have a humble spirit than a lofty position in this world. But who believes this? Most men strive to rise; few desire to lie low. *May your example, blessed Savior, keep me low!* "When Majesty," said pious Bernard, "humbled himself, shall the worm swell with pride?"

20. Whoever gives heed to instruction prospers, and blessed is he who trusts in the LORD. If you are to prosper, you need two things: **instruction** and faith. One teaches us what to do for ourselves, the other what to expect from God. Let the young Christian earnestly study this wisdom. This **instruction** will be profitable for Christian humility and consistency.

God never intended us to create our happiness out of our own resources. To feel that we know nothing, that we can do nothing, contrive nothing, then to look up to him as our supreme Good, and to trust him as our only Friend—when was such reliance and expectation ever disappointed? To feel that we and all that we have are in his hands—this is our peaceful security. "I have had many things," said Luther, "in my hands, and I have lost them all. But whatever I have been able to place in God's, I still possess." In this quiet confidence we have nothing more to do with ourselves. A thousand perplexing thoughts are scattered to the winds. God now takes the place once filled by the most disturbing agitations. The soul is fixed on God. He reigns over all with an all-seeing eye and an all-loving hand. The eye of faith pierces through the darkest cloud and reads God's thoughts of peace and love. All the world cannot rob us of one word of God. Providence may seem to oppose his promises. But there is more reality in the smallest promise of God than in the greatest performance of man. "I will therefore ever trust him on his bare word—with hope, beside hope, above hope, against hope, for small matters of this life. For how shall I hope to trust him in impossibilities if I may not in likelihoods?" (Bishop Hall). This simple habit of faith enables us fearlessly to look an extremity in the face. Thus holding on, it is his honor to put his own seal to his word. Whoever trusts in the Lord will be blessed (Psalm 2:12; Jeremiah 17:7-8).

21. The wise in heart are called discerning, and pleasant words promote instruction. The **heart** is the center of wisdom. But intellectual wisdom without being applied in a prudent way achieves nothing. Lack of prudence makes the Gospel needlessly offensive.

Pleasant words promote instruction. Ambrose's engaging eloquence arrested and gradually convicted Augustine's mind.

22. Understanding is a fountain of life to those who have it, but folly brings punishment to fools. What is a religion of notions? It is a dream. All is death. There is nothing to stir the heart or move the emotions. But when **understanding** is enlightened so it can appreciate spiritual things in their spiritual glory, notions become principles. Feelings then flow from light and are filled with **life**. The book of God shines out with new glory. Every verse is a sunbeam. Every promise is irradiated with divine love. What had previously been meaningless noise now becomes spirit and **life**. This spiritual **understanding** is indeed **a fountain of life**. Even if it is not always bubbling, there is a supply of water flowing all the time from the spring.

Remember that if your **understanding** is not filled with heavenly light, it will be a polluted spring rather than a wellspring of **life**. What if your **understanding** is clear and your heart is dark? What if you are knowledgeable about the truth of Christ, yet you are not taught by him as the truth is in him? "Let us not think much of ourselves," says the excellent Bishop Reynolds, "though God should have adorned us with the most splendid natural gifts, with quickness of understanding, almost like that of angels; unless at the same time he adds to all the gift of his spiritual grace, by which we may attain to a knowledge and delight in the heavenly mystery."

23. A wise man's heart guides his mouth, and his lips promote instruction. The wellspring of life, however silently it may flow, cannot be concealed. Who does not know the difference between one who speaks about what he has read or heard and one who speaks about what he has felt and tasted? The one has the knowledge of the Gospel, dry and spiritless. The other has the "fragrance" of this knowledge (2 Corinthians 2:14), which invigorates. "Unbelievers," as Dr. Owen admirably observes, "may know more of God than many believers; but they know nothing as they ought; nothing in a right manner; nothing with a holy and heavenly light. The excellency of a believer is not that he has a large apprehension of things, but that what he does apprehend (which perhaps may be very little) he sees in the light of the Spirit of God, in a saving, soul-transforming light. And this is that which gives us communion with God." It is not, therefore, the intellectual knowledge of divine truth that makes the man of God. The only true divine is he who knows holy things in a holy manner, because he only is gifted with a spiritual taste and appetite for them. Divinity is not by rote. **A wise man's heart guides his mouth.**

In summary, man's religion begins with the head, but God's religion begins with the heart. Let me be careful in what atmosphere and under what teaching I live. Vivid theory merely brings me into the icy zone— cold and clear. "Going over the theory of virtue in one's thoughts, talking well, and drawing fine pictures about it—this is so far from necessarily or certainly conducting to form the habit of it in him who thus employs himself that it may harden the mind in a contrary course and form a habit of insensibility to all moral considerations" (Bishop Butler). Experiential application realizes the glow of evangelical light and warmth. Let me look mainly not to intellectual or theological attainments, but to heavenly teaching. Let me seek that my heart is taught first and foremost. Then let it teach my **mouth**, so that my **lips promote instruction** for the praise of my God and the edifying of his church.

24. Pleasant words are a honeycomb, sweet to the soul and healing to the bones. Pleasure and health flow from the words of man in the things of God. The eunuch was encouraged by Philip's exposition of precious Scripture (Acts 8:35-39). The two disciples were refreshed from their conversation with their divine Master on the road to Emmaus (Luke 24:32). When God is the subject and his Spirit the teacher, **pleasant** indeed will be the **words** spoken by Christians. This will exceed any earthly enjoyment.

25. There is a way that seems right to a man, but in the end it leads to death. Again we have this solemn, searching warning. For the danger of self-delusion is so dreadful that we are only kept safe if we are constantly given warnings. This is not because we do not understand, but because we love to sin. Our judgment is perverted because our heart is blind. It is no proof that **a way** is **right** because it **seems right**. All the ways of a man are **right** in his own eyes; yet, **in the end** they lead **to death**.

It seems as if we must travel along the road of disobedience. It appears to be only a slight deviation, but it is punished because in reality it is witchcraft and idolatry. The way of deceit often appears to be right, as if it is an easy way to escape from a difficulty.

It is madness to dream about heaven when every step is the way to hell. For **the end . . . leads to death**. It is the enemy's great purpose to stop us from seeing **the end**, so that our road **seems** to be **right**. The paths that lead **to death** are many. But there is only one way to life, and nobody can come to the Father except by Jesus Christ (John 14:6). Oh, the transcendent mercy of the eyes opened to see the awful danger of our own way, and our ears opened to hear the voice behind us saying, "This is the way; walk in it" (see Isaiah 30:21; Jeremiah 6:16).

26. The laborer's appetite works for him; his hunger drives him on. We must take care how we work. We must not strive for vanity, as this will bring ruin upon us. But even if we were spared physical toil, the spread of knowledge occupies us with mental activity until we are tired. But if this is under Christian discipline, it brings its own reward, as he who works in this way is not working for himself. Barrow handles the popular notion, "What is a gentleman, but his pleasure?" "If this is true," he remarks, "if a gentleman is nothing more than this, then surely he is a sad piece, the most despicable, the most pitiable and wretched creature in the world. But," he adds, "in truth it is quite different from this. To suppose that a gentleman is free from business is a great mistake. For indeed no man has more to do, no man lies under greater obligations to industry than he."

Yet all toil, whether physical or mental, is evil if it prevents concentration on the only satisfying object of labor. This is not for food that perishes but for food that lasts to everlasting life (John 6:27). Ponder this certain harvest—it is given by the Son of man. Look over the field of work—it is the Gospel of his grace. We do not annihilate our interests in this world, which have their due claims. But while our hands and our time are given to the world, our hearts are given to God. Everything is centered on God. The Christian's heart agrees with Augustine when he said, "All other plenty besides my God is mere beggary to me."

27. This proverb presents a vivid picture of the energy of sin. The **scoundrel** has broken away from restraint. Every part of his body, every part of his mind, has become a servant of sin. May we not learn from him in humility the true standard of concentration of mind and singleness of heart and the need for perseverance?

His speech is like a scorching fire. "His tongue is a burning firebrand, to set all the world in combustion" (Bishop Hall).

28. He sows **dissension** in every furrow. Where open disputes do not work, **gossip**, "a furnace of mischief" (Bishop Patrick), is used, and this **separates close friends**.

29. We note that this **violent man** is being used by his father, the tempter, to undertake the work that comes naturally to that master. He **entices his neighbor and leads him down a path that is not good.** His whole soul is filled with this satanic intent.

30. Sometimes we may see him, as he **winks with his eye . . . plotting perversity. He . . . purses his lips** as if he is engaged in deep thought, but he is all the time **bent on evil**. "This all expresses the profound study with which he contrives his neighbor's ruin" (Bishop Patrick).

31. Gray hair is a crown of splendor; it is attained by a righteous life. Here we see that **gray hair** is an old man's glory and his claim for respect. The elders are among those who should be honored (Isaiah 9:15). To despise them is sinful and will be severely punished. Wisdom and experience are rightly attributed to them.

But the diamond in the **crown** is when **it is attained by a righteous life**. "Truly is an old man's diadem that which not the art of man but the kingdom of God has fashioned and set on his head" (Muffet).

But if you separate heavenly virtue from **gray hair**, the **crown** falls and lies dishonored in the dust. "There is not on earth a more venerable and delightful spectacle than that of an aged pilgrim walking with God; and a more affecting and deeply melancholy sight can hardly, on the contrary, be imagined than that of a hoary-headed sinner who has lived his fourscore years 'without God in the world,' while all that time God was calling and he refused to listen to those calls. Now his body is bowed down beneath the weight of years; all his powers of action and of enjoyment decay; every hour is likely to be his last; time is behind him, and eternity all before him; and his soul is still dead in trespasses and sins. The hour of his departure has come, and he is not ready for the world for which he is bound. Oh, with what different emotions do we contemplate old age in this character and in the saint of God, who in approaching the close of his earthly pilgrimage is drawing near to what has been the goal of his hopes and desires; who, while outwardly decaying, is inwardly maturing for heaven; in whom every symptom of coming death is but a symptom of approaching life; and who, in the final exhaustion of nature, bids adieu to the world in the words of aged Simeon: 'Lord, now lettest thou thy servant depart in peace, for mine eyes have seen thy salvation'" (Wardlaw).

32. Better a patient man than a warrior, a man who controls his temper than one who takes a city. A great conflict and a glorious victory are set out here. The heart is the field of battle. All its evil and powerful passions are deadly foes. They must be met and triumphed over in God's strength. Those who are ignorant of God and of themselves make light of them. Instead of being **patient,** under provocation they think they are right to be angry. They justify themselves by thinking that it is wrong to put up with wrong. But a hasty **temper** is an infirmity. So not being able to control **his temper,** he is a captive, not a conqueror.

"To be our own master is far more glorious for us than if we were the masters of the world" (Lawson). "So old and not older," wrote Philip Henry in his *Diary* when he was thirty years old, "Alexander was when he conquered the great world: but I have not yet subdued the little world—myself." "Thou art a slave of slaves," said the proud philosopher Diogenes to a mighty conqueror, "for you are a slave to those appetites over which I rule." The complaint of Czar Peter—"I can govern my people, but how can I govern myself?"—was a practical acknowledgment of the difficulty. "Among all my conquests," said the dying Valentinian, "there is but one that now comforts me. I have overcome my worst enemy, my own haughty heart." This, then, is to subdue the enemy that has vanquished conquerors. This surely is what it means to be "more than conquerors." Christian, never forget that the source of victory comes through him who loved us (Romans 8:37).

This bloodless victory, so contrary to the turmoil of war, is the crown of Christian grace. No other grace of the Gospel can be exercised without its influence. Yet the daily conquest anticipates the final victory, the spoils of which will be reaped throughout eternity. "In all ages fewer men are found who conquer their own lusts than who conquer an army of enemies" (Cicero).

33. The lot is cast into the lap, but its every decision is from the LORD. The instructive lesson to learn from this proverb is that there is no waste in the most minute circumstances. Who can fail to see the hand of God, most wonderful in the most apparently casual contingencies, overruling all second causes to fulfill his will while they work their own? "When kingdoms are tossed up and down like a tennis ball, not one event can fly out of the bounds of God's providence. The smallest are not below it. Not a sparrow falls to the ground without it. Not a hair, but it is numbered by it" (Polhill).

Proverbs
Chapter 17

1. Better a dry crust with peace and quiet than a house full of feasting [KJV: sacrifices], with strife. The allusion is to the Jewish ordinance of feasting at home on the remains of the **sacrifices. A house full of feasting** was therefore a house with ample provisions. Yet when the spirit of love does not rule, self predominates, and this becomes a source of much **strife** and confusion.

Ponder every thought that may disturb contentment. If you have fewer comforts than you used to have, or fewer comforts than other people have, or fewer comforts than you desire, do you not still have more than you deserve? If you had more of them, would you not be tempted to forget God and to live in a worldly way? Does not the memory of the earthly lot that your Savior chose turn every thought about being discontented into adoration and gratitude? Do not forget that there is great gain in contentment.

2. A wise servant will rule over a disgraceful son, and will share the inheritance as one of the brothers. Folly leads to shame, while wisdom leads to honor. The **son,** the heir of the family, may bring shame on his family by his behavior, instead of bringing glory to his family. **A wise servant,** although he has only temporary interest in the home, may be promoted to **rule over a disgraceful son.**

Great wisdom, much prayer, and constant watchfulness are needed to promote humility and Christian consistency. Honor from man calls for abasement before God.

3. The crucible for silver and the furnace for gold, but the LORD tests the heart. The refiner's **crucible** and **furnace** test his metals. But Jehovah claims for himself the prerogative of testing **the heart.** His eyes are a flame of fire (Revelation 1:14). Nothing deceives him; nothing escapes his probing search.

The **gold** must be put into **the furnace.** It is so mixed with dross that the workman's eye can scarcely detect the **gold**. But for **the furnace**, the dross would cling to the **gold**. The refiner's process burns it out, and the pure metal is left behind. No burnishing is of any avail. The **gold** cannot be used until it has been through the fire.

Is it not necessary for every child of God to be put into **the furnace**? We do not know ourselves until our deeds are tested by fire (1 Corinthians 3:13).

But it is the Lord who cleanses the metal. We cannot do this ourselves. No ordinary power can separate the base alloy. No milder remedy will accomplish this purpose. Only by this process is the hidden evil brought out into the open so it may be humbled, while any hidden good may be honored. Deep personal affliction, the knowledge of the plague of our own hearts, and the discovery of secret sins are all discovered in the searching heat of **the furnace**.

This purifying process is painful. The flesh trembles at the fire. But will we not commit ourselves with well-grounded confidence to God's wisdom, tenderness, and love? Is not any **furnace** that purges away our dross (Isaiah 1:25) and brings us to know ourselves, our God, and his dealings with us a mighty blessing? The best materials for praise are brought out of this consecrated **furnace**. When the fire has done its work on the metal, we look for the results. Worldly idols will be displaced, stubborn wills melted, and **the heart** completely given over to God. "As gold cast in the furnace receives its new luster and shines brighter when it comes out than it did before, so are God's saints more glorious after their great afflictions, and their graces even more resplendent" (Bishop Sanderson).

The refiner's process may be slow, but its results are assured. Nothing but dross will perish. The vilest earth will be turned into the finest **gold**. No refiner ever watched **the furnace** with such exactness and care. Many glittering particles may be swept away. But the pure residue, the solid particles, comparatively few in number, will be delivered to the mold. Every hour of trial is greater than **gold** and produces a richer Christian character. A suffering Savior is realized and endeared.

Here, then, in **the furnace**, child of God, see the seal of your election, the ground of your confidence, the joyful anticipation that your faith that has been through the furnace will be made into a crown "of pure gold and be found to praise and honor the Lord" (Leighton).

4. A wicked man listens to evil lips; a liar pays attention to a malicious tongue. Here is a dark but true picture of human nature. **A wicked man** is not content with his own evil desires. He has such an appetite for sin that he seeks outside stimulants to increase his activities. "There would not be so many open mouths if there were not so many willing ears to entertain them" (Bishop Hall). Remember that the listening ear shares the responsibility of the **malicious tongue**. Both are involved in the treason and are directly or indirectly acquainted with the plot. *Oh, my God, fill my heart and tongue with your own gracious Spirit!*

5. He who mocks the poor shows contempt for their Maker; whoever gloats over disaster will not go unpunished. The sin against our **Maker** by oppressing the poor was previously noted (14:31). **The poor** are in their condition not by chance but by providence. So to mock **the poor** is to show **contempt** for **their Maker**, on him who made them and made them to be poor. This proverb states that **contempt** for **the poor** is a sin of the deepest dye.

All kinds of mocking of **the poor** is evidently rebuked here. "Why should I," asks Bishop Reynolds, "for a little difference in this one particular of worldly wealth despise my poor brother? When so many and great things unite us, shall wealth only disunite us? One sun shines on both; one blood bought us both; one heaven will receive us both; only he has not so much of earth as I, and possibly much more of Christ. And why should I disdain him on earth, whom perhaps the Lord will advance above me in heaven?"

6. Children's children are a crown to the aged, and parents are the pride of their children. This proverb has its limits. What a **crown** of thorns to each other are ungodly and graceless parents. But in the ordinary course of life gracious **children** and **parents** reflect honor on each other. Such parents rejoice in the number and growth of their **children**. Such **children** are proud of their **parents**. "A good root makes the branches flourish, by virtue of the living sap that it sends up. And flourishing branches win praise to the root, for the pleasant fruit that they bring forth" (Clever).

7. Arrogant lips are unsuited to a fool—how much worse lying lips to a ruler! The **lips** are the organ of the heart. Christ refused to accept even a sound profession of faith from the lips of demons, in case it should cause someone to stumble (Mark 1:34).

How much worse lying lips to a ruler, to a minister and guardian of truth! Yet in a world where the self reigns supreme, such inconsistencies are all too prevalent. The pure teaching of our divine Master alone secures Christian consistency in heart, lip, and life. We must never forget that if **arrogant lips** do not even suit **a fool**, how much less should they adorn the Gospel of Christ.

8. A bribe is a charm to the one who gives it; wherever he turns, he succeeds. "A gift is so tempting that it can no more be refused than a lovely jewel. It has such power that it usually effects whatever a man desires" (Bishop Patrick). "What a description," adds Mr. Scott, "of the mercenary selfishness of mankind." Even ungodly consciences seem to have a correct understanding about this evil. The saying of Philip of Macedon is well-known, that "there was no fortress so strong, but it might be taken if an ass laden with gold was brought to the gate." The poet Horace finely illustrates this remark, saying that "not Philip, but Philip's gold" conquered Greece. "Gold and silver pervert many things, especially right motives. Money has a great power with those who are in power. A golden key will open any prison door and cast the watchman into a deep sleep. Gold will break open gates of iron as well as silence the orator's voice and blind the judge's eyes. It will bind the strong man's hands and blunt the edge of the sword. It makes war, and it makes peace. What almost can it not do with corrupt minds?" (Caryl). Such is the affinity between an eye full of evil desire and a glittering gift.

Is not God's child also often attacked by this temptation? Does the influence of a gift never affect consistent godliness? Do no friendships lure us onto a crooked path? So be resolute in a strength that is better than your own as you resist sin. The battle is not against violent temptation or open sin, but against subtle and apparently harmless deviations from the straight path.

9. He who covers over an offense promotes love, but whoever repeats the matter separates close friends. Here **he who . . . promotes love** is a beautiful expression that we should constantly keep in mind. It shows a delight in the atmosphere of **love**, man's highest elevation in fellowship with God. It implies not the mere exercise of **love**, where it presents itself, but searching and making opportunity for it. But all too often it sits at the door of our lips instead of finding a home in our hearts. One step taken by our feet is better than a hundred words spoken by our tongue.

A forbearing spirit is a fine manifestation of this heavenly grace. Our motives are often misconstrued. We meet in a world of selfishness and cold reserve instead of glowing confidence. Prejudice builds a wall against Christian fellowship. Wounded pride seeks to return an unkindness with contempt. Resentment stirs up recrimination. Disappointment kindles morbid suspicion. But a disciplined tongue is a gracious mercy to the church.

10. A rebuke impresses a man of discernment more than a hundred lashes a fool. If we want to cover our offenses, we should not ignore **a rebuke**. A word is enough for the wise. But the discipline of **lashes** is necessary for **a fool**. Parents and teachers should especially study the character of children, that they may temper rebukes wisely. Many a fine spirit has been spoiled by unsuitable treatment.

Who will benefit from **a rebuke**? It is the person who has had his stony heart replaced by a heart of flesh (Ezekiel 36:26). A needle pierces deeper into flesh than a sword into stone. An attentive ear, a tender conscience, a soft heart, and a teachable spirit are the means through which a wise and loving father disciplines his children for his service, for his cross, and for his crown.

11-13. An evil man is bent only on rebellion; a merciless official will be sent against him. Better to meet a bear robbed of her cubs than a fool in his folly. If a man pays back evil for good, evil will never leave his

house. Some dreadful pictures of man are set out here. The person who is bent on **rebellion** resists all of God's and man's authority. This is no light sin. The **merciless official** who is sent against him is one who will not be deflected from his task. This **rebellion** is not the only sin, but it reveals a stubborn will. It may be hidden under a peaceful and amiable cover. But it is not dead—it sleeps. As Burke has remarked, "Those who do not love religion, hate it."

Look at the folly of this **evil man.** The strength and accuracy of the illustration can hardly be bettered. He is like **a bear robbed of her cubs.** He is like a savage beast that has been provoked to extreme anger. Do we not know of homes where uncontrolled anger breaks out every day? Does the self-willed man remember that "nothing is said or done in a passion, but may be better said or done afterwards" (Matthew Henry)? Do we never see the Christian, whom his Master's discipline and example should have transformed to a lamb, still behave like **a bear** that has been **robbed of her cubs?** It is no excuse to say, "It is my way." Is not this the very cause of grief to a contrite soul, calling for deep humility and increasing watchfulness?

Look again at man in his ingratitude. God forbids us to pay back evil for evil, and much more **evil for good.** This ingratitude is by no means uncommon, although the conscience is rarely troubled by it. What else is it when the ungodly resent an attempt to promote their best interests?

14. Starting a quarrel is like breaching a dam; so drop the matter before a dispute breaks out. Both destructive elements, fire and water, illustrate the danger of **starting a quarrel** (26:21; Judges 9:19-20). To neither element can we say, "This far and no further!" We might as well try to tell a raging storm to stop. The **dam** may hold back a large body of water, but if you open its sluices, the waters may form a flood. In this way the **starting** of a **quarrel** has ended in thousands of murders, and even in the destruction of kingdoms.

It is no less destructive in ordinary life. One provocative word leads to another. Every retort widens the breach. Seldom, when we have heard the first word, have we heard the last word. An inundation of evil overwhelms peace, comfort, and conscience. Does not Christian grace teach us to keep resentment at bay and to bear provocation rather than break the bond of unity?

Truly it is a wise rule to stop evil at its inception. The riverbank is much more easily preserved than repaired. Once the breach is made, even if it is only to let out a drop of water, that is the beginning of evil, the results of which are incalculable.

In being alert to quarrels and disputes, it must be remembered that the time to stop is not when things are at their worst but at the beginning. We must mortify our own proud tempers and cultivate our Master's meek and self-denying spirit. The following remarks by Mr. Burke are well worth consideration: "The arms with which the ill dispositions of the world are to be combated are moderation, gentleness, a little indulgence of others, and a great distrust of ourselves; which are not qualities of a mean spirit, as some may possibly think. They are virtues of a great and noble kind, such as dignify our nature, as much as they contribute to our rest and fortune. For nothing can be so unworthy of a well-composed soul as to pass away life in bickerings and litigations, in snarling and scuffling with everyone about us."

15. Acquitting the guilty and condemning the innocent—the LORD detests them both. Judicial iniquity is a dreadful abuse of God's authority. The judge or magistrate is God's minister (Romans 13:4). We appeal to him for justice, for he represents God (Deuteronomy 25:1).

But let us place ourselves before the Judge of everyone. We are accused by Satan, by our own conscience, and by the righteous law of God. We are convicted of every charge, yet we are justified. Does God then justify the ungodly? Far from it! If he justifies the guilty, it is because of righteousness. Nowhere in the whole world does the moral perfection of the Ruler of the world shine so gloriously as at the cross of Calvary. The satisfaction of the holy law and the manifestation of righteous mercy harmonize with the justification of the condemned sinner. And this combined glory is the tune of the song of everlasting praise.

16. Of what use is money in the hand of a fool, since he has no desire to get wisdom? We often find reckless infatuation in temporal things. A young man will spend a large amount of money at a university where he should be gaining wisdom, but he idles away all his time. The thoughtless dissolute person should be warned by his own friends. He is losing important opportunities and amassing great debts. This is how **a fool** handles **money.**

But it is more moving to see the picture of this folly in religion. The town where Jesus was brought up and the cities in which he performed miracles despised his wisdom. Such **a fool** considers what is more precious than rubies to be as valueless as a pebble. To him what is sweeter than honey is as tasteless as the white of an egg. He lives for himself, as if there were no God in the world. His heart is given to the world, as if the world could take the place of God in his life.

17. A friend loves at all times, and a brother is born for adversity. This beautiful picture of friendship has been drawn by moralists, sentimentalists, and poets. But the reality is only found where divine grace has transmuted natural selfishness into disinterested love. If virtue is the best basis of friendship, then this most heavenly virtue is the firmest ground of all.

We must look to our Lord for the best example in this matter. We see the Son of God taking on our nature so that he might be our friend and brother (Hebrews 2:14). The mystery of this friendship is beyond our imagination. His love is constant, even in death. "Here is a brother born for adversity. Trust him, oh, you trembling believers at all times and in all places. You will then possess the happy art of living beyond the reach of all disappointment" (Howell). "Though solitary and unsupported and oppressed by sorrows unknown and undivided, I am not without joyful expectations. There is one Friend who loves at all times: a Brother born for adversity; the help of the helpless; the hope of the hopeless; the strength of the weak; the riches of the poor; the peace of the disquieted; the companion of the desolate; the friend of the friendless. To him alone will I call, and he will raise me above my fears" (Hawkes).

The ancient Jews applied this proverb to Christ, adducing it as a testimony that the divine Messiah would by his incarnation become the Brother of man.

18. A man lacking in judgment strikes hands in pledge and puts up security for his neighbor. We may become popular through a thoughtless kindness. But the principle, closely examined, will be found to be another form of selfishness. There is no true benevolence in rash engagements that may involve our name and family in disgrace or ruin. It is true that if those hands that were nailed to the cross had not put up security for us, the accusations against us could never have been canceled (Colossians 2:14). But the eternal counsel is no pattern for our simple folly. Nor is infinite love combined with perfect wisdom a plea for our rash generosity.

19. He who loves a quarrel loves sin; he who builds a high gate invites destruction. We may all **quarrel** without loving it. But let us always look at it as a branch from the root of **sin** and the prolific source of **sin**. To love it is to love **sin**. Who will own up to such a charge? It comes from the root of pride.

He who builds a high gate invites destruction. The allusion to **a high gate** is to the gates of the splendid palaces of the East, which were generally elevated according to the vanity of their owner. The man who **builds a high gate** exalts himself above his neighbor and assumes a lifestyle beyond his rank. The sluggard sees his ruin in front of him and indolently waits for it, without making any effort to avert it. But the proud man **invites destruction.** He puts himself in the place where his honor will be swept away. *Watch over me, oh, my God, to preserve me from the first stirring of my proud heart. Or if I give in to it through weakness, keep me from the prevalence of this presumptuous sin.*

20. A man of perverse heart does not prosper; he whose tongue is deceitful falls into trouble. The history of God's ancient people is a picture of a **perverse heart,** with all its barren results. Whatever their patient God did, they were not satisfied (Psalm 78). And the best of us are too often gripped with the same perversity. Even when we seek to walk with God, how our perverse hearts struggle to walk with a will of their own. May the good Lord give us a mortified spirit, to restrain us from the guidance of our corrupt desires! Many erratic courses in the church can be traced to some unhelpful bias that was not disciplined by the divine Spirit and not molded by reverent faith. So should we not cry out and pray, "Not my will, O Lord. Let me have anything but my own way. Leave me not to my perverse heart"? As the **perverse heart** must be bridled, so the **deceitful . . . tongue** must be subdued.

21. To have a fool for a son brings grief; there is no joy for the father of a fool. The weeping parent not only finds **no joy** in the fondly cherished object of his expectation, but a cankering grief embitters all his joys and often brings him down with sorrow to the grave. Have not many afflicted parents felt the impassioned cry of Augustus, "Would that I had lived single or died childless"?

"None of you must think that you have sufficiently discharged your duty to those who are in your charge if you have instructed them, corrected them when they have done wrong, and rewarded them when they have done well, so long as your fervent prayers for them have been lacking. In vain will you wrestle with their stubbornness and other corruptions, even though you try with all your might, if it is only you who fight. You will only fight successfully when you do so in the strength of the Father of Spirits, as Jacob did. You must wrestle with him with your importunate prayers, and you must not give up until you have wrung a blessing from him, either for yourself or for them" (Bishop Sanderson).

Let the godly parent expect everything from prayer. In the deepest distress never let go of the covenant of grace. Let the determined faith of a praying mother encourage you to persevere (Matthew 15:22-28). God requires faith, but he never fails to honor it. He may delay in answering prayer, but every word, every sigh, is registered for acceptance in his best time.

22. A cheerful heart is good medicine, but a crushed spirit dries up the bones. Our Lord made **a cheerful heart** by his message of divine forgiveness (Matthew 9:2-7), and this was doubtless a greater **medicine** to the paralyzed man than the healing of his limbs. If I am a pardoned sinner, an accepted child of God, what earthly trouble can defeat me?

A broken spirit in an evangelical sense is God's precious gift. It is stamped with his special honor. But here **a crushed spirit** describes a brooding spirit of despondency that always looks on the dark side of things. If this is linked to religion, it flows from a narrow and perverted view and a spurious humility centered on the self. It has the effect of drying up **the bones.** The whole body is influenced. "It contracts and weakens the animal spirits, preys on our strength, and eats away at the vigor of our constitution. The unhappy person droops like a flower in the scorching heat of summer" (Bishop Horne). Our English proverb is, "Dry sorrow drinks the blood." This is a sorrow that cannot weep.

You must resist sinking into morbid depression. Gloom should not characterize Christians. Instead of the spirit drying up our **bones**, our spirits will be so high that we will need another body to contain them.

23. A wicked man accepts a bribe in secret to pervert the course of justice. We are again warned about how gifts can corrupt us (compare verse 8). No sin has a deeper stamp of wickedness. The temptation is a test of principle. According to his biographer, Sir M. Hale "had learned from Solomon that a gift perverts the ways of judgment."

Even a corrupt world is ashamed of this sin. The **bribe** is **secret** and concealed from the eye of man. But it does not escape God's scrutiny. God does not wink at any perversion of **justice**. One day he will "vindicate his omniscience from all the insults put upon it in the world by these foolish men, who were not ashamed to do those things in the face of God himself, in which they would not have wished the meanest of his creatures to detect them" (Lawson).

24. A discerning man keeps wisdom in view, but a fool's eyes wander to the ends of the earth. Let us trace our interest in **wisdom** from the beginning. It first enters the heart (2:10). There it stays with the person who has understanding (14:33) as his principle of conduct. Now in this proverb, wisdom is **in view** before his eyes, as his rule of faith and life. It is the center to which all his thoughts, motives, and pursuits tend. Everything is now in order. Every faculty, desire, and affection finds its proper place. "He who has understanding fixes his eyes on wisdom and is content with that object, whereas a fool's eyes are constantly wandering everywhere, and his thoughts settle on nothing that may avail to his good" (Bishop Hall). His **eyes** are on **the ends of the earth**, rolling and wandering from one object to another. His thoughts are scattered. He has no definite objective, no certain way of life. Talent, cultivation of mind, and improvement of opportunity are all frittered away. He cares about those things that are furthest from him and with which he has the least concern.

A writer vividly portrays this inconstancy in the following way: "Today he goes to the quay to be shipped for Rome. But before the tides come, his tide has turned. One party thinks him theirs, the adverse theirs; he is with both, with neither; not an hour with himself. Indifference is his ballast, and opinion his sail; he resolves not to resolve. He knows not what he holds. He opens his mind to receive ideas as one opens his palm to take a handful of water. He has lots of water, if only he could hold it. He is sure to die, but not certain which religion to die in. He demurs, like a lawyer, as if delay could remove some impediments. On controversial points he sides with the last opinion he has heard or read. The next opinion convinces him to change his mind, and a teaching stays with him so long as the teacher is in sight. He would prefer to take dross rather than gold. He does not want to test the metal in any furnace. He receives many judgments but retains none of them. He becomes fed up with manna after he had fed on it for two days. The best place for him to live would be his bedroom where he would trouble nothing but his pillow. He is full of business at church; a stranger at home; a skeptic abroad; an observer in the street; everywhere a fool" (Thomas Adams).

This diversion is a great friend to the enemy. Our enemy's great object is to turn the mind away from what is immediate to what is indefinite, from what is plain and important to what is unsearchable, from what is personal to what is irrelevant. Many trifles take the place of the one thing that is needful. And is not this waste of time often a temptation to the Christian also? We need to keep our eyes fixed on Jesus, to look to Jesus, on whom all heaven, all the redeemed, delight to gaze forever.

25. A foolish son brings grief to his father and bitterness to the one who bore him. Surely the divine Spirit did not repeat this proverb (see verse 21) for no reason. Was it not to deepen our sense of parental responsibility and filial obligation? Can parents be unmoved to the prospect of this **grief**? Can children be hardened into the unnatural selfishness of piercing a parent's heart with such **bitterness**? The mother's anguish is here added to the father's grief.

We should link our children when they are very young to the church. We should train their first years under God's yoke. Then instead of bringing us grief, they will restore life to us (Ruth 4:15). Instead of causing us **bitterness** because they are rebels against God, the Lord will own them and seal them so that they will declare his righteousness and set forth his praise (Psalm 22:31).

26. It is not good to punish an innocent man, or to flog officials for their integrity. Often the wise man's meaning goes far beyond his words. **To punish an innocent man** is not only **not good**—it is detestable in God's sight (see verse 15). If rulers are a terror to good works, they are ministers of God in authority, but ministers of Satan in how they fulfill their office. Such injustice will not be able to abide the coming day of the Lord.

Our duty is to pray. And who knows what God, who always hears our prayers, will send. He may send a righteous administration to bless the land.

27-28. A man of knowledge uses words with restraint, and a man of understanding is even-tempered. Even a fool is thought wise if he keeps silent, and discerning if he holds his tongue. The wisdom of these proverbs will be acknowledged by those who know the sins of the **tongue** and the immense difficulty of restraining the unruly member. **A man of knowledge uses words with restraint** when the likely outcome of speaking would harm him rather than benefit him. The good treasure is far too valuable to be unprofitably spent. Dr. Good gives this translation of an Arabic poetic proverb:

Keep silence then; nor speak, but when besought;
Who listens long, grows tired of what is told:
With tones of silver though thy tongue be fraught,
Know this—that silence of itself is gold.

Our Lord, careful as he was to make use of every opportunity to teach, sometimes held his words back (Matthew 16:4).

This restraint is most important under provocation. Passion demands immediate judgment. A cool, well-tempered understanding asks further time for reflection. The prophet wisely refrained from giving even a message from God to a king in a moment of passion (2 Chronicles 25:16). "A little spark blows up one of sulfurous temper; and many coals, greater injuries, and reproaches are quenched and lose their force, being thrown at another of a cool spirit" (Leighton). Indeed, a fool may acquire a reputation for wisdom just by keeping his mouth shut instead of exposing his folly to everyone. "He cannot be known for a fool who says nothing. He is a fool not who has unwise thoughts but who utters them. Even concealed folly is wisdom" (Bishop Hall).

Proverbs
Chapter 18

1-2. An unfriendly man pursues selfish ends; he defies all sound judgment. A fool finds no pleasure in understanding but delights in airing his own opinions. Desire is the wheel of the soul, the spring of energy and delight. The businessman or scientist is filled with the object of his desire. This one thing is everything to him. A Christian minister must give himself wholly to his office. There is much to be looked into and pondered. Men who live without doing this may be fluent speakers and accurate preachers; but the lack of unction paralyzes all spiritual impact. No intelligent Christian can fail to feel the immense importance of combining holy solitude with active life. He needs to nourish his faith as well as demonstrate every other Christian grace. Sir M. Hale left us this prayer: "I have endeavored to husband this short, uncertain, important talent [time] by dedicating and setting apart some part of it to prayer and the reading of your word; which I have constantly and peremptorily observed, whatever occasions interposed, or whatever importunity persuaded to the contrary."

Yet **a fool finds no pleasure in understanding.** His whole desire is to pour out his own frivolity.

3. When wickedness comes, so does contempt, and with shame comes disgrace. Selfishness is the characteristic of the wicked. "Wherever he comes, he is apt to cast contempt and reproach on every man's face" (Bishop Hall). His neighbor's circumstances or illnesses provide him with an opportunity to ridicule him. The word of God finds no favor in his sight. God's people are the object of his **contempt.** Their seriousness he calls gloom, their cheerfulness levity (Matthew 11:18-19).

A scornful spirit against the godly is never forgotten. Every bitter word is registered. But the Lord has declared that the rebuke of his people will someday be taken away from the whole earth (Isaiah 25:8).

4. The words of a man's mouth are deep waters, but the fountain of

151

wisdom is a bubbling brook. "This sentence expresses the depth, the abundance, the clearness, and the force of the counsels of the wise man" (Calmet). When a person has immersed himself in wisdom, his **words** are in themselves **deep waters,** and as they are spoken they become as fruitful as **a bubbling brook.** His **wisdom** is a **fountain** that "sends up full brooks that are ready to overflow their banks. So plentiful is he in good discourse and wholesome counsel" (Bishop Hall).

The **fountain** is especially invigorating when, as with Chrysostom, it gives a heavenly glow to outward eloquence. Consecrated mind and talent are gifts of God. May we improve in simplicity, not for the creature's honor, but for the glory of the great Giver.

5. It is not good to be partial to the wicked or to deprive the innocent of justice. "Whatever excuses man may make for its [partiality's/injustice's] course, it is an offense to God, an affront to justice, a wrong to mankind, and a real service done to the kingdom of sin and Satan" (Henry). For **justice** to happen, the *cause* must be heard, not the *person.* Let the person be punished for his wickedness, not the wickedness be covered for the person's sake. When one is **partial to the wicked,** the rights of God are despised, and the claims of his justice are thrown away.

6-7. A fool's lips bring him strife, and his mouth invites a beating. A fool's mouth is his undoing, and his lips are a snare to his soul. It is most remarkable that the apostle Paul, when analyzing man's depravity, focuses on the little member and all that is linked to it—the throat, the tongue, the lips, and the mouth (Romans 3:13-14). The tongue is such a world of iniquity that it defiles the whole body. We often see how it harms other people; here we note how it harms the man himself.

A fool's lips bring him strife. This is folly indeed. He makes a rod for his own back. There is no need to dig a pit for a fool, for he digs a pit for himself. The mouths of wild beasts devour each other. **A fool's mouth** is his own destruction. And he is not only the cause but the agent of his own destruction.

Will not the child of God watch in godly fear in case his own folly should call for his Father's rod?

8. The words of a gossip are like choice morsels; they go down to a man's inmost parts. Do men deny, question, or water down the depravity of our nature? Note again how the virulent poison of only one part of the body destroys practical godliness, social order, and mutual friendship. The man who spreads slander is condemned by the law (Leviticus 19:16). No character is more despicable, no influence more detestable.

The words of a gossip in an unguarded moment may inflict irreparable injury. This evil may be welcomed in certain circles that thrive on scandal. But that does not alter the real character of **a gossip,** who is detested by both God and man. Other than the power of holy love opening freely the channels of kindness and forbearance, what can overcome this mischievous propensity? And what can bring about this spirit of love other than a genuine interest in Christian privileges and a corresponding sense of Christian obligation (Colossians 3:12-14)?

9. One who is slack in his work is brother to one who destroys. Observe the affinity of the different principles and workings of corruption. The sluggard and the prodigal belong to the same family. The man who hid the Lord's talent was equally unfaithful as the person who squandered his goods (Matthew 25:25; Luke 16:1). The slothful has no heart for **his work**. Important opportunities slip by. His stock, instead of increasing by being traded, gradually dwindles into penury. God has filled the world with his abundant gifts. But unless we have a diligent hand to receive them, we will starve. "He who by the sloth of his hand disfurnisheth himself of the means of getting, he is as near of kin to a waster as may be" (Bishop Sanderson). He **is brother to one who destroys**. He is like the lord of a large estate who, instead of improving it and looking after it, **destroys** it with extravagance and folly.

It is the same in religion. One person is content with heartless orthodoxy. His family worship is a routine of formality that has no influence on the day itself. What is the big distinction between him who prays, reads, and does good deeds only in a formal way and the person who throws away these privileges? Both arrive at the same destination, though by different tracks. The one folds his arms in sloth; the other opens his hands in wastefulness. The one gets nothing; the other spends what he gets. Thus fearful is the guilt, solemn is the account, certain is the ruin of both. God gives talents not only to enrich, but to use. And whether those talents are selfishly neglected or carelessly thrown away, the wicked servant is condemned to outer darkness (Matthew 25:26-30).

Servant of Christ, let your Master's life be your pattern and standard. He was equally fervent in his daily work and in nightly prayer. Follow him in his work, and you will be honored with his reward (John 12:26).

10-11. The name of the LORD is a strong tower; the righteous run to it and are safe. The wealth of the rich is their fortified city; they imagine it an unscalable wall. Being aware of danger induces even the animal creation to seek a refuge. To man **a strong tower** is such a defense. But does man as a sinner realize his imminent death? Oh, may he accept his welcome into the **strong tower** set before him. Such is **the name of the LORD**—not the bare outward words, operating as a charm, but his character, that by which he is known, as a man is known by his name.

Think of the sinner as he becomes convicted of his evil condition. He trembles at the thought of eternal condemnation. He looks forward, and all is terror; he looks backwards, and all is remorse; he looks inward, and all is darkness. Until now he had no idea about his need of salvation. His soul's enemy now suggests that it is beyond his reach, that he has sinned for too long and in too many different ways. He has sinned against so much light and so much knowledge—how can he be saved? But the name of the Lord meets his eye. He spells out every letter and putting them together cries out, "Who is a God like you?" He runs to the Lord as to a **strong tower**. His burden of conscience is relieved, his soul is set free, and he enjoys his safety.

Think of the child of God who is feeble, distressed, and assaulted. "What if I should return to the world, look back, give up my Christian faith, give way to my own deceitful heart, and perish in the end with aggravated condemnation?" Perhaps you are walking outside the gates of the **tower**. No wonder that your imprudence exposes you to the arrows of the wicked one. Read again about **the name of the LORD**. Go back inside the walls. Look at the name on the **tower**: "I am the Lord; I do not change." Note how you are to trust in his name (Isaiah 50:10; Psalm 9:10).

Thus a sense of danger, knowledge of the way, and confidence in the strength of the **tower** all give a spring of life and earnestness to run into it. Here the righteous, the person justified by the grace and sanctified by the Spirit of God, runs every day, every hour. He is aware of both his serious danger and his perfect security. Within these walls, which of us needs to worry that the sharpest arrow can harm us? We realize our security from external trouble as we exercise our faith. We are safe from God's avenging justice, from the curse of the law, from sin, from condemnation, from the second death.

But only the righteous are found here. What do the ungodly know about this refuge? "Our God's mercy is holy mercy. He knows how to pardon sin, not to protect it. He is a sanctuary to the penitent, not to the presumptuous" (Bishop Reynolds). Yet how joyful it is that the gates of this city are always open. No time is a bad time to enter. No distance, no weakness, hinders the entrance. All who enter are protected by God's salvation. "Satan is raising batteries against the fort, using all means to take it, by strength and stratagem, unwearied in his assaults, and very skillful to know his advantages" (Leighton). But notwithstanding that enemy's disturbing power, the peace of God daily fortifies our hearts from fear of evil. Such is our **strong tower**. How much we owe to our gracious Savior who has made our way to it so free and so bright. We rest in the heart of God and are at peace.

But the **rich** man has his strong **city** and his high walls (compare 10:15). Well does the writer add that such a man is only wise in his own conceit. Little does he think that in a moment his walls may crumble to dust and leave him in a ruin and totally unprotected. "Trouble will find an entrance into his castle. Death will storm and take it. And judgment will sweep both him and it into perdition" (Scott).

Every man is as secure as his trust. A trust in God communicates a divine and lofty spirit. We feel that we are surrounded by God and living on high with him. Oh, the sweet security of the weakest believer, shut up in an impregnable fortress. But a vain trust brings a vain and proud heart, the immediate forerunner of ruin.

12. Before his downfall a man's heart is proud, but humility comes before honor. We have had both of these proverbs separately (16:18; 15:33). Surely this repetition was intended to deepen our sense of their importance. It is hard to persuade a man that he is **proud**. Everyone protests against this sin. Yet who does not cherish the viper in his own heart? Man so little understands that dependence upon his God constitutes the creature's happiness, and that the principle of independence is madness, and its end destruction. The **proud** walk on the edge of a fearful precipice. Only a miracle preserves them from instant ruin. The security of the child of God is when he lies prostrate in the dust. If he soars high, danger is imminent, even if he is on the edge of heaven (2 Corinthians 12:1-7).

There is danger here for a young Christian. The glow of his first love, the awakened awareness of the condition of his perishing fellow sinners, ignorance about the subtle working of inbred vanity, and the mistaken zeal of injudicious friends all tend to foster self-pleasing. Oh, let him know that **humility comes before honor.**

The spring of this **humility** is true self-knowledge. Whatever may be seen externally to a man's advantage, let him keep his eyes looking within. The true sight of himself must lay him low. When he compares his secret follies with his external decency, what appears to his fellow creatures with what he knows of himself, he can only cry out, "I am a vile sinner." The center of this precious grace is not in words, emotions, or tears but in the heart. No longer will he delude himself with a false conceit about what he has not, or with a vain conceit of what he has. There can be no true greatness without this deep-toned **humility.**

13. He who answers before listening—that is his folly and his shame. All too often this proverb is proved to be true in everyday life. Men will hardly hear out what is unacceptable to them. They will interrupt the speaker before they have fully heard him, and so give an injudicious answer.

This **folly** was specifically forbidden by God's law [in the context of the worship of false gods] (Deuteronomy 13:12-14). It was no less contrary to the Lord's own procedure. He examined Adam before he pronounced judgment [though he already knew what Adam had done]. He came down to see Babel and Sodom before they were destroyed, so that his justice would be clearly seen. While on earth, patient investigation marked his decisions (see Matthew 22:15-33). See also Deuteronomy 32:4.

14. A man's spirit sustains him in sickness, but a crushed spirit who can bear? Man is born in a world of trouble, and he has considerable powers of endurance. Natural courage and vivacity of spirit will bear us up even under the pressure of ponderous evils, poverty, pain, sickness, and need. Christian principle strengthens natural strength. Outward troubles are bearable, yes, more than bearable, if there is peace within.

A man's spirit sustains him in sickness. But what if his **spirit** is **crushed?** "If the strength that is in me is weakness, how great is that weakness" (Bishop Sanderson). The wound to the **spirit** pierces more deeply than a flesh wound, as the **spirit** is more vital than the body. Grief gains the victory and becomes intolerable.

The most powerful minds are quite vulnerable. Even the great Isaac Newton, "endowed with an intellectual strength that had unbarred the strongholds of the universe," who was distinguished by "unbroken equanimity," in the middle of his life was prey to mental oppression that, as he informs us, shook his "former consistency." Boyle describes his wounded spirit as so overpowering for many months that "although his looks did little to betray his thoughts, nothing but the forbiddenness of self-dispatch [suicide] hindered his committing it." So long as the evil is outside us, it is bearable. Natural courage can cope with it. **But a crushed spirit who can bear?**

In the spiritual realm the pressure is much worse. When he who made the spirit wounds or allows Satan to wound us, we might challenge the whole creation: **Who can bear it?** Spiritual wounds, like the balm that heals them, can never be known until they are felt. It is sometimes as if the arrows of the Almighty were dipped in the lake of fire and shot alight into the middle of the soul. The best joys of earth can never soothe the envenomed sting. Mirth is then madness and vexation.

There is also a hell for the wicked on this side of eternity. Man becomes a burden to himself. Cain's punishment was more than he could bear. Saul was filled with the darkness of despair. Ahithophel and Judas chose to strangle themselves rather than to live. Thus the torments of eternity are suffered beforehand. One hell is kindled within before entering into the other. Such is the foretaste of hell—only a few drops of wrath, for a few moments. What will its reality be like for all eternity!

However, this **crushed spirit** can be the Christian's first seal of mercy. It can be the preparation for all future and eternal mercy. Bitter indeed is the anguish when the mass of sin is raised from the grave of oblivion and set before our eyes. But is not this the sight that makes Jesus and his free salvation inexpressibly precious? And does not this **spirit** place us within the sphere of his healing commission? We ask now not, **who can bear,** but who can heal? Well did Luther say, and there is no better judge on such matters, "It is as easy to make a world as to ease a troubled conscience." Both are creation-work, requiring the almightiness of God. To him who wounded us we must return for healing. His remedy is the sight of himself wounded for us. And that sight, so healing, so reviving—

how it quickens the soul and animates faith, ending in a song of everlasting praise!

In these days of neglect of Christian teaching, when remedies other than the Gospel are applied to the **crushed spirit**, it is worth putting on record the way of healing in the British church back as far as the time of the Conquest, which, it will be seen, was not the baptism of tears, private confession, penance, or man's deeds, but the simple view of the great sacrifice as the one object of faith. In the form of a prayer for the Visitation of the Sick in the time of Anselm, Archbishop of Canterbury in 1080, the sick person was asked, "Dost thou believe to come to glory, not by thine own merits, but by the virtue and merit of the passion of the Lord Jesus Christ? Dost thou believe that our Lord Jesus Christ did die for our salvation, and that none can be saved by his own merits, or by any other means than by the merits of his passion?" The sick person answered, "All this I believe." Then the sick person was given the following instruction and comfort, as by a true physician of souls: "Give thou therefore as long as thy soul remaineth in this place, thy whole confidence in Christ's death only. Have confidence in no other thing. Commit thyself wholly to this death, with this alone comfort thyself. If he say, 'Thou deservest hell,' say, 'I put the death of our Lord Jesus Christ betwixt me and this judgment, and no otherwise do I contend with thee.' And if he say to thee, 'Thou art a sinner,' say, 'Lord, I put the death of our Lord Jesus Christ between thee and my sins.' If he say to thee, 'Thou hast deserved damnation,' say, 'Lord, I set the death of our Lord Jesus Christ between thee and my bad merits; and I offer his merits instead of my merits.' If he say, he is angry with thee, say, 'Lord, I interpose the death of our Lord Jesus Christ between me and thine anger.'" This is indeed the sovereign treatment for a case aggravated by the application of any other remedy of man's devising.

15. The heart of the discerning acquires knowledge; the ears of the wise seek it out. Here we see that **knowledge** shines its rays all around us. But everything that is intrinsically valuable centers in divine **knowledge.** "All arts," as Bishop Hall teaches, "are maids to divinity. Therefore they both adorn to her and do her service." For while we readily admit the importance of intellectual **knowledge**, the great objective is the salvation of the soul. And all **knowledge** that is not grounded on this primary conviction or that does not directly or indirectly subserve this great end is valueless. It is power for evil. It is a weapon of mighty influence that will ultimately turn against man himself. Never let us forget that unsanctified knowledge is still what it was at the beginning—gathering death, not life.

The young must remember how important it is to acquire this **knowledge.** You must grow in **knowledge** (2 Peter 3:18). Happiness and usefulness, light and glory are before you. While you sit at your Master's feet, you will enter more fully into the spirit of the saying of Ignatius: "I am now beginning to be a disciple."

16. A gift opens the way for the giver and ushers him into the presence of the great. We have seen how gifts can corrupt (17:8, 23). But we may justly apply this proverb and see how it can be legitimately used. The minister of the Gospel recognizes the value of gifts as they usher him into the presence of people, who perhaps will value his message also. Sympathy gives weight to his instruction when, after the example of his divine Master, he combines kindness to the body with love for the soul. A wise consideration may usher us into the presence of the great for the advancement of the Christian cause.

Blessed be God! We do not lack any gifts to bring before him. Our welcome is free. The door of access is forever open. Our treasure of grace in his unchanging favor is unfathomable.

17. The first to present his case seems right, till another comes forward and questions him. We have recently had a proverb about judging other people (verse 13). Here we are warned against justifying ourselves. Self-flattery is our cherished nature. We rate our supposed excellencies and are blind to our real imperfections. We are so ready to **present** our own cause in a good light and sometimes, almost unconsciously, to throw a shade over or even omit what might seem to balance it on the other side. It is so difficult to state facts and circumstances with perfect accuracy when our own name or credit is concerned. All the evidence must be sifted. Guard against a self-justifying spirit. Cultivate a spirit of self-distrust. Judge as if you are under God's eye. In sincere prayer lay yourself open to his searching out of your secret sins.

18. Casting the lot settles disputes and keeps strong opponents apart. The lot is here used as a way to settle **disputes** peacefully. Contending parties might agree to abide by the decision of **the lot**, especially when a legal appeal might have doubtful authority. Important matters of order under the divine theocracy were determined in this way (see 1 Chronicles 6:54). When Matthias became an apostle, his election by lot was hailed as if it were the voice of God. There seems, therefore, no scriptural prohibition against using this ordinance, so long as it is exercised in a reverential dependence on God and is not used for worldly purposes.

At the same time, the Word of God appears to be more fully recognized as the arbiter of the divine will. Sometimes it is easier to abide by the decision of the lot than that of the Word. The last requires more self-denial, humility, and patience and therefore is useful.

19. An offended brother is more unyielding than a fortified city, and disputes are like the barred gates of a citadel. A **brother,** not an enemy, **is more unyielding than a fortified city.** It is as if the closer the relationship, the wider the breach. The thread, once snapped, is not easily joined. "What a view does it give us of our corruption that the natural love implanted in us should degenerate into Satanic hatred" (Geier).

Nowhere is concord so important as in the church. She can never prosper unless, like Jerusalem, she is "closely compacted together" (Psalm 122:3). As we are born by the same Word, as we feed on the same food, as we are animated by the same life, should we not, with all our lesser differences, hold to the unity of the Spirit? Two reasons made the godly and learned Strigelius long to leave the world: "1. That I might enjoy the sweet sight of the Son of God and the Church of God. 2. That I may be delivered from the cruel and implacable hatred of theologians." Chrysostom gives this rule: "Have but one enemy, the devil. With him never be reconciled; with your brother never fall out."

20-21. From the fruit of his mouth a man's stomach is filled; with the harvest from his lips he is satisfied. The tongue has the power of life and death, and those who love it will eat its fruit. Who does not take care about what seeds he sows? The farmer knows that his harvest is dependent on which seeds he scatters. The **fruit** of our **lips**, the **power** of our **tongue**, can give one of two harvests. It can be poisonous or wholesome. It can lead to **life** or **death**. Evil words tend to **death**, good words to **life**. Good words bring comfort to the speaker as well as to the listener. There is no middle path. There are only extremes. It is either the worst of evils or the best of blessings.

Born as we are for eternity, no utterance of our **tongue** can be called trifling. A word, though light as air, may rise up as a witness at the throne of judgment for death or for eternal life. When I think of this dreadful power, shall I not, as Chrysostom warns, "guard this little member more than the pupil of the eye"? Are not the sins of **the tongue** an overwhelming manifestation of God's patience? In the inner man the heart is the main thing to guard, in the outer man **the tongue**. *Oh, my God, take them both into your own keeping, under your own discipline, as instruments for your service and glory.*

22. He who finds a wife finds what is good and receives favor from the LORD. This is obviously to be taken within certain limits. Manoah found a good thing in his wife (Judges 13:23), but Job did not (Job 2:9-10). To some their wives are a crown for their heads, while others find that their wives rot their bones (12:4).

What is **good** implies godliness. Godliness is found when the man marries in the Lord, and only one who is the Lord's. To be unequally yoked with an unbeliever (2 Corinthians 6:14), union for life between a child of God and a child of Satan, is a most dreadful anomaly. "I wish," said pious Bishop Hall, "that Manoah could speak so loud that all our Israelites could hear him: 'Is there never a woman among the daughters of thy brethren, or among all God's people, that thou goest to take a wife of the uncircumcised Philistines?' If religion be anything other than a cipher, how dare we not regard it in our most important choice? Is she a fair Philistine? Why is not the deformity of the soul more powerful to dissuade us than the beauty of the face to allure us?"

23. A poor man pleads for mercy, but a rich man answers harshly. It is natural for the **poor,** as they are so dependent on people, to plead **for mercy.** And this humiliation may be the discipline for that poverty of spirit that the Lord sealed with his first blessing (Matthew 5:3). But **a rich man** acts in a shameful way when he **answers harshly.** Instead of kind feelings flowing out, he seems to bind people in iron chains with his words. He listens with indifference to a tale of woe. As he himself has never experienced hard times, he has no sympathetic heart. The well-bred man of the world, who is all courtesy and refinement in his own circle, is often insufferably rude to those who are under him. His good breeding indeed is often only the polish of selfishness. The proud worm knows so little about the true use of power that when he exercises it, he is transformed into a tyrant. Would he but study the character of his divine Master, he would see the exercise of power brought to life with true greatness. Was Jesus not as considerate to blind Bartimaeus as to the nobleman of Capernaum? All classes of people alike shared in his tenderest sympathy.

And yet, as the **rich** in their conscious superiority may be overbearing, so the **poor,** by pleading **for mercy,** may show a servile spirit. They should not shrink from showing bold integrity that gives dignity to both the lowest and the highest of men. To all of us our providential circumstances bring their besetting temptations. Our only safeguard is to walk closely with God.

24. A man of many companions may come to ruin [KJV: a man that hath friends must show himself friendly], but there is a friend who sticks closer than a brother. To be without a friend indicates a state of painful desolation. On the other hand, a true friend is no common acquisition. Many people only pretend to be faithful friends. But the jewel itself is as rare as it is precious. Yet what is life without this cheering, enriching blessing? To Alexander, the conquered world without his Hephaestion would have been a desert. But if a man has friends and wants to keep them, he must **show himself** to be **friendly.** To throw them away through neglect, caprice, or needless offense is to show oneself utterly unworthy of the blessing. Love begets love and is accompanied with love. Not that this will show itself in extravagant words or lavish praise, which is only gratifying to the weak and repulsive to the intelligent. The true expression of friendship will be in unmistakable integrity.

The bond of real friendship is often closer than the natural tie. The friendship between David and Jonathan is such an example. **A friend who sticks closer than a brother.** Bishop Coverdale's version is very beautiful:

"a friend that delighteth in love, doth a man more friendship, and sticketh faster unto him than a brother."

Let the divine Friend be the first choice of youth, the tried and chosen Friend of middle age, and the Friend for eternity. Cultivate a closer acquaintance with him. Set the highest value on his friendship. Avoid whatever is displeasing to him. Be found in those places where he meets his people. Long to be with him forever. Is it not because men have no eyes to see him that they have no heart to love him? If their eyes were really open, they would soon affect the heart. Then everyone would be entirely devoted to his service.

Proverbs
Chapter 19

1. Better a poor man whose walk is blameless than a fool whose lips are perverse. Poverty is never a disgrace, except when it is the result of wrong behavior. But when it is adorned with **blameless** character, it is most honorable. **Better a poor man** than a person who is elevated in his own sight because of his riches and is given over to being **perverse.** Often men put under their feet those whom God carries in his heart. Man honors the **perverse** for their riches and despises the **poor** because of their poverty. But what does the rich man have if he does not have God? And what is a **poor** man lacking if he has God? It is better to be in a wilderness with God than in Canaan without him. Judge wisdom according to God's standard. God judges by character, not by status. Estimate the value of everything in the light of eternity. Death will strip the **poor** of his rags and the rich of his purple and bring them both naked to the earth, from which they came. Meanwhile, let us hear our Lord's voice to his despised people. He knows about our poverty, yet we are rich (Revelation 2:9). For those who honor God, he will reward with his seal, his smile, and his everlasting crown.

2. It is not good to have zeal without knowledge, nor to be hasty and miss the way. Let us note the evil of the lack of sound and disciplined **knowledge** in temporal matters. The uninstructed child or savage acts rashly. The impulsive person is impatient to finish his work and so always crowds too much into his days. He forgets that "things are not done by the effort of the moment, but by the preparation of past moments" (Cecil). Our wise moralist has well remarked, "He that is in a hurry proves that the work in which he is engaged is too much for him" (Dr. Johnson). Certainly **to be hasty** can be a sin when it comes from a lack of simple trust in God.

The right way to live is to do the thing of the day on that day. This is all that God requires to be done. The affairs of one day at a time is as much as can be quietly committed to God in the daily exercise of faith. This principle should be carried into all important responsibilities. Bishop Burnet's account of Sir M. Hale has a most valuable insight about this: "*Festina lente* [make haste slowly] was his beloved motto, which he ordered to be engraved on the head of his staff. He was often heard to say that he had observed many witty men run into great error because they did not give themselves time to think. But the heat of imagination made them make wrong decisions. Whereas calm men who made decisions in a measured way could search after truth and find it with greater certainty."

But this evil is far more serious in spiritual matters. "Where no discretion is, there the soul is not well" (Bishop Coverdale's translation). The man who is **without knowledge**, instead of pondering his path, is **hasty** and **miss[es] the way.** Eagerness, as opposed to sloth, is the energy of divine grace. But here it is compared with thoughtfulness, and to be **hasty** here leads to sin. This impatience shows that a person will only take notice of his own wishes and has no time for making carefully thought out decisions. Rash experiments, often the result of haste, often land the nation in serious trouble. The same spirit cuts the church in two with schism. Let us remember that without self-discipline there can be no Christian consistency. The best of intentions, without the will and Word of God, are only blind impulses. They should be checked and not followed. The real peace of faith is to stand or sit still and see how God will appear on our side, to make a way for us through many deep waters of perplexity.

3. A man's own folly ruins his life, yet his heart rages against the LORD. Such was the **folly** of Adam! First he ruined **his life,** then he accused God. As he caused his own miserable situation, it would have been reasonable to blame himself. But he was so proud that **his heart** raged against God, as if God, and not Adam himself, were responsible. This has been the foolishness of Adam's children ever since. God has linked moral and penal evil, sin and sorrow. The fool rushes into the sin and most unreasonably rages against the Lord. He blames his crosses not on his own perverseness, but on God's injustice. But God is free from all blame. He showed the better way, but man chose the worse way. God has issued warnings through his Word and through the conscience. But man, deaf to these warnings, plunges into misery and, while eating the fruit of his own ways, **rages against the LORD.** Such is the pride and blasphemy of a proud spirit. The criminal blames the judge for his righteous sentence.

We must study God's gracious dispensations carefully. "*O Lord, remove our ignorance that we may know you; our idleness, that we may seek you; our unbelief, that we may find and enjoy you*" (Bishop Hall).

4. Wealth brings many friends, but a poor man's friend deserts him. We have had the substance of this proverb previously (14:20). It is generally true that **wealth brings many friends.** "Riches have them," says Bishop Hall. But they are usually worth very little. The principle is to beware of selfishness. Few love at all times (17:17).

164

Lack of sympathy for the **poor** is a serious evil. It separates those whom God has linked by a mutual bond of reciprocal interest. The rich are the guardians and protectors of the **poor**, while the **poor** are the strength and support of the rich. But all too often the **poor** know their wealthier neighbors only as living in the most luxurious indulgence, while they themselves are left in their poverty, uncared for. This would never happen if the rich lived by the principle of divine love.

Poverty may separate a **poor** person from his neighbor, but who can separate him from his God (Romans 8:38-39)? "If it were possible for him to stand absolutely in need of the use and service of the whole creation, all the creatures in the world would surely wait on him and be appropriated to him" (Bishop Reynolds). With such an inheritance as this, why should he fret about a few years' poverty or neglect? Earth's short vision will soon be past, and then comes the eternal reality of unclouded joy.

5. A false witness will not go unpunished, and he who pours out lies will not go free. If **a truthful witness saves lives (14:25), a false witness** destroys them. This is an offense against the Ten Commandments.

The habit of lying, allowing an untruth to exist under the cover of a good motive, grows and results in more and more evil. There is much instruction in the wise reply of Solon on first seeing the rude theatricals of Thespis. Asking him how he dared to tell so many lies before the people, he received the answer that he only did it in play. "Yes," said the legislator, striking his staff with force into the ground, "but if we begin with telling lies in play, we shall end with telling them in earnest."

So careful attention to truth is vital in Christian education. The boundary line must never be trifled with. Not even a child can cross it with impunity. A child must never be allowed to play with a falsehood.

6-7. Many curry favor with a ruler, and everyone is the friend of a man who gives gifts. A poor man is shunned by all his relatives—how much more do his friends avoid him! Though he pursues them with pleading, they are nowhere to be found. Everyone loves, or professes to love, those from whom they expect something that will benefit them. If a person who is now fawned on for his gifts were by providence brought to poverty, the same friends would hate or neglect him. "Which of them," asks Bishop Hall, "would dare acknowledge him when he is going to prison?" As the winter brooks, filled with water from springs and from the torrents from heaven, are dried up and vanish in the summer heat, so these friends of the poor disappear in his day of calamity.

We need to consider how we should plead for the favor of our Prince. We need to reflect on the **gifts** he gives to his people. Should not those who are enriched by them show his rule of mercy to their poor brethren, especially to the heirs of the kingdom? *"Lord, in my greatest plenty help me to mind and feel others' poverty; and in my most prosperous condition keep me from forgetting the afflictions of your Joseph"* (Swinnock).

8. He who gets wisdom loves his own soul; he who cherishes understanding prospers. It might seem that self-interest could put us in a favorable position with God. Only a careless sinner could think that! Apply your heart diligently to seek **wisdom**, and then bring your heart to God for his light and teaching. Yet it requires as much care to *keep* the blessing as to *get* the blessing. It will quickly slip away from a negligent hand.

But no ordinary good is found here. To get **wisdom**, therefore, whatever the cost, is to love our **own soul**. One should be ashamed even to ask the question, will Christ or the world have our love, trust, time, and talents? It is like comparing pebbles with pearls, dust with diamonds, dross with gold. To follow our way is to destroy ourselves and not to love our souls.

9. A false witness will not go unpunished, and he who pours out lies will perish. The revealed character of Jehovah is that he is faithful and true. We should not be surprised at the repeated denunciations against deceit, for it greatly dishonors God's never-changing attribute. One addition is made to the previous sentence on this topic (verse 5). Not only will **he who pours out lies** not escape—he **will perish**. Lies and desolations are linked (Hosea 12:1; Malachi 3:5).

10. It is not fitting for a fool to live in luxury—how much worse for a slave to rule over princes! The **slave** has the same rational power as his sovereign. But lesser habits of mind make him unfit to rule. There are, however, exceptions to this, as in the case of Joseph. But God's order is seldom reversed without anarchy and confusion. Peace and happiness belong to godly contentment (1 Timothy 6:6). Those whom God has placed in a subordinate position should remember our Father's voice: "Should you then seek great things for yourself? Seek them not" (Jeremiah 45:5).

11. A man's wisdom gives him patience; it is to his glory to overlook an offense. What is anger but temporary madness? To give in, therefore, to its paroxysm, to act without deliberation under its impulse, is to do we know not what. But whatever we do will surely need to be repented over! A space between the inner rise and the outer manifestation of the anger is most important. **A man's wisdom gives him patience.** Mindful of his own infirmity, the wise man will guard against the indecent attacks of temper and take time to weigh the offense and not think of it in a worse light than it really is. Even heathen moralists acknowledge the value of this. "I would have beaten you, if I was not angry," said the philosopher to his offending servant. Augustus, when he was in a rage, was told to repeat the alphabet to give him time to calm down. "It is easier," as Seneca wisely observed, "not to give way to the passion than, when indulged in, to govern it." Justin Martyr, when asked which was Christ's greatest miracle, named his great **patience** in such great trials.

An affront, therefore, is a test. It will show whether we have **patience** or not. It will reveal if we are a slave to the passion of our own anger. The way of the world is to get even with people and to repay one insult with another insult. But the Christian way is not to trade insults but rather to repay an insult with a blessing (1 Peter 3:9).

It is to his glory to overlook an offense. Man is so warped in his judgment that **to overlook an offense** is thought to be an act of a fool or a weak person. But Solomon, a wise man and a king, declares that it is a weakness, not strength or greatness, to be able to bear nothing. **It is his glory to overlook an offense.** It must be so because it is acting in the same way as God acts. What a motive this gives us! "Let it pass for a kind of sheepishness to be meek. It is a likeness to him who was 'a sheep before the shearers, not opening his mouth' (Isaiah 53:7). It is a portion of his spirit" (Leighton).

12. A king's rage is like the roar of a lion, but his favor is like dew on the grass. The monarch of the forest is like the monarch of the land. Who would not fear a roaring **lion**? The rocks and hills echo the terrible cry. All the animals of the forest flee or, petrified, are rooted to the spot. Such is **a king's rage** in a land of despotism, where the king rules without law and acts above the law, as if there were no laws. This is a dreadful picture of cruelty and tyranny. Unlimited power is too much for the proud human nature to bear, unless endued with special grace from above. But the king's **favor** brings reviving blessing, **like dew on the grass**, when vegetation is nourished.

If **a king's rage** is so terrible, what, oh, my soul, must God's wrath be like! May this wrath be the great object of my reverential fear. Let me flee from it by the only way of escape, while escape is open to me, and seek God's favor, as the enriching **dew** to Israel, fertilizing my barren soil (Hosea 14:5-7; Psalm 72:6).

13. A foolish son is his father's ruin, and a quarrelsome wife is like a constant dripping. "Many," observes an old commentator, "are the miseries of a man's life; but none like that which comes from him who could be the stay of his life" (Jermin). As a wise son makes a glad father, so **a foolish son is his father's ruin**. The throne of grace to the Christian father will be the only refuge for his grief. There he will pour out the bitterness of his soul in humiliation for himself, and there he will pray for his child, and so find rest.

A quarrelsome wife is like a constant dripping. Another domestic calamity is now mentioned, but it is not as poignant as the first one. **A quarrelsome wife is like** rain coming through the roof of an old house. Such **dripping** utterly destroys a man's household comfort and wears away a heart previously firm as stone. But faith will seek strength to bear this meekly so that God may be honored. It is right to exact a solid blessing from a heavy trial. And who knows if the **quarrelsome wife** may not be won over through persevering prayer and patient forbearance and be a helper to her husband, and so both live a life of grace together.

14. Houses and wealth are inherited from parents, but a prudent wife is from the LORD. Every good gift comes from God. Some of these gifts come to us in daily life; others come in extraordinary ways. **Houses and wealth,** although they are God's gifts, **are inherited from parents.** The heir is known, and in the course of events he takes possession of his estate. But **a prudent wife** is totally unknown to the man and is not related to him. The account of Ruth's life beautifully illustrates God's providence in a marriage. The Moabitess married, contrary to all human expectation, an Israelite. In this way she was brought into Naomi's family. She had returned with Naomi to her land and then came to the attention of Boaz, who became Ruth's husband. Often the wheels of the Lord's working in this interesting matter constrain the admiration of men who are not used to observing spiritual matters (Genesis 24:50). And how much more endearing and secure is a special gift of God! The bread coming down from heaven was more valued than if it had been the fruit of labor. Thus **a prudent wife** is honored as "a special blessing of God's immediate choosing, and therefore to be obtained by our prayers at the hand of the giver" (Bishop Hall).

But is not the husband, no less than the wife, **from the LORD?** Let each person seek the blessing of God's ordinance. We must never trust our own judgment and affections without first seeking God's guidance. Let us realize the responsibility, as well as the comfort, of the union. Always count it as a gift from God, for his service and glory.

15. Laziness brings on deep sleep, and the shiftless man goes hungry. All experience and observation attest to the fact that **laziness** destroys mental energy, and idleness leads to hunger. What else could we expect from the sluggard lying in bed all day long? And if the sluggard does take a false step, he does not have enough energy to correct it. Marshall Turenne expressed his warm appreciation to a friend who had given him the following advice when first setting out in life: "When you have made a false step, spend not a moment in vexing yourself and moaning over it; but think how it may best be repaired, and instantly set about it." If there is any reward in perseverance, sloth will never find it. **The shiftless man goes hungry.**

Here is a word to the thoughtless sinner: Think how this applies to God's work. You persuade yourself that all is well because you will not trouble yourself to open your eyes to the truth, and you are content to let things run their course. You do not rebel against the Gospel openly. But has not our divine Master said that he who is not with him is against him (Matthew 12:30)? You like to think that you have done no harm. But have you done no harm if you have wasted every opportunity for eternity? Have you not wandered about in vanity from your cradle instead of living for God? You are determined to sleep. Although the two great treasures— the favor of God and your own soul—are in imminent danger, you still tell your soul to take its ease. Instead of weeping love, wrestling prayer, and working diligence, you turn over and go back to sleep. Wake up, or else you will sleep the sleep of eternal death.

16. He who obeys instructions guards his life, but he who is contemptuous of his ways will die. To fear God's **instructions** is to travel on the path of honor. To obey them is our security. If we keep the Word, the Word will keep us safe. Our duties are thus identified with our privileges. This is the first successful effort to shake ourselves from the deep sleep of laziness.

Yet, the power to obey God's **instructions** is not within a man. Is it not rather a matter of God working in us, through us, with us? Let the world know that we do not exercise obedience in a covenant of works, but that keeping the commandment evangelically is keeping our own souls. This is the way of present happiness, the seal of everlasting mercy, and the pathway to heaven.

17. He who is kind to the poor lends to the LORD, and he will reward him for what he has done. It is God's ordinance that there will always be poor in the land (Deuteronomy 15:11). Hence the universal obligation is to be **kind to the poor.** This is also taught in the New Testament, which inculcates the spirit no less than the act (Luke 6:30-36; Colossians 3:12). We must open our heart as much as our hand. For it is possible to give all our goods to the poor without having an atom of true love in our heart.

. . . lends to the LORD. Sir Thomas More used to say, "There was more rhetoric in this little sentence than in a whole library." The worldly philanthropist, however, has no conception of the divine honor of the principle involved in it. If your brother is the object of kindness, the majesty of heaven is concerned. The Lord considers it as a loan to himself. It is lending to the Lord. Selfishness would evade the obligation under the cover of prudence. But what we give is only a loan, to be repaid. The security we have for the loan we make will never fail.

The Lord of heaven condescends to be the Surety for **the poor.** He takes the debt on himself and gives us the bond of his word in promise of payment. Although he has a right to rule over everyone and is obligated to none, he becomes a debtor to his own. Many acts of kindness have been buried and forgotten. The witness of our conscience is the only fruit. But here is a safe deposit in the heart of God. It can never be lost or forgotten. "If then," as Bishop Hall writes, "we need to store our money, where should we put it other than in the Christian's treasury? The poor man's hand is the treasury of Christ. All my superfluity shall there be hoarded up, where I know it will be kept safe and surely returned to me."

And yet most people prefer to lend to a rich man of known integrity rather than to the Lord. It is indeed an act of faith, often of naked faith, when there seems no hope of return. But the King delights to honor this principle. And only on the resurrection day will most of this be brought to light. Meanwhile, let us admire God's wonderful grace. He puts the desire in the heart, disposes the heart, gives the opportunity, and after all accepts the act as if it had been his own work, without stain or any pollution.

18. Discipline your son, for in that there is hope; do not be a willing party to his death. Christian parents should study God's Word carefully. Note here too our Father's wise and loving discipline of his children. And which child has not blessed him for not withholding his discipline until it had accomplished its perfect work?

Is not this, then, our pattern and our standard, setting out the sound principle of Christian education? Fathers are not to embitter their children so that they become discouraged (Colossians 3:21). However, let the rule of discipline not be a hard saying. Is not so-called tenderness for the child a cover for the indulgence of weak and foolish affections? There is much more mercy in what seems to be harshness than in false tenderness. Let the child see that we are firm in our resolution. Let him realize that we will not be diverted from our duty by the cry of weakness or passion. It is far better that the child should cry under healthy correction than that parents should later cry under the bitter fruit to themselves and their children of neglected discipline. "Eli could not have devised which way to have plagued himself and his house so much as by his kindness to his children's sin. Parents need no other means to make themselves miserable than sparing the rod" (Bishop Hall). Yet much less of this would be needed if parents brought up their children as they ought to, through a firm decision or a word, a frown, or a look.

But the great force of the rule is its timely application, while **there is hope**. For hopeless the case may be if the remedy is delayed. The cure of the evil must be started in infancy. Not a moment is to be lost. The lesson of obedience should be learned at the first dawn. One struggle and victory in early life may, under God, set the tone for the rest of life. On the other hand, strong **discipline** may fail later on to accomplish what a slight rebuke might have produced much earlier.

Is there not all too often deliberate blindness here? We do not choose to see what is painful to correct. It is a false idea to say, "Children will be children." It only makes us pass over their faults and think that their tempers and waywardness are too trifling to require prompt correction. In this way, sin winked at in its beginning hardens and becomes deep-rooted corruption. For who would neglect their most trifling bodily ailment that might grow into a serious disease? Oh, what grace and wisdom are needed to discipline our minds, judgment, and affections so that we can train up our children to serve God, which will be their greatest happiness.

19. A hot-tempered man must pay the penalty; if you rescue him, you will have to do it again. How often the undisciplined child grows into **a hot-tempered man**. Friendly efforts to restrain this wrath must be repeated again and again (1 Samuel 19:1-11; 20:32-33), even though they are so often ineffective.

Meanwhile, the man **must pay the penalty.** He punishes himself. Wounded pride and resentment leave the wretched criminal brooding in his room. He suffers an intolerable burden of self-inflicted punishment.

What, then, is the radical cure? We must learn from the One who has a lowly heart (Matthew 11:29). The glory and encouragement of the Gospel is that trusting in God, despite difficulties, is possible and wise (2 Corinthians 12:9).

20. Listen to advice and accept instruction, and in the end you will be wise. We have just had a word for parents, telling them how to discipline their children (verse 18). Here the children and others are told to be humble. They need to be awake to **advice** and **instruction,** and so must **listen** to it and **accept** it. **Advice** and **instruction** are often at hand, but God's people so often pay no attention to this divine wisdom. But who, in view of the tragic sight of our present state of ungodliness, will not follow the advice of the godly man who cried, "If only they were wise and would understand this and discern what their end will be!" (Deuteronomy 32:29).

21. Many are the plans in a man's heart, but it is the LORD's purpose that prevails. Here is a fine contrast between man and God, showing the great distinction between the worm and his Maker. Man's most serious **plans** are nothing when compared to God's. And it is God's **purpose that prevails.** For man's **plans** are full of trouble and are eventually fruitless. But God's counsel is immutable, and it will stand forever.

It is a vain thing to attempt to fight against God. Our freedom does not interfere with his secret purpose. And we must be careful that we do not resist God's declared will. As his providence chooses our lot, let his Word discipline our desires as the best way to bring them to fruition. For everything is clear above, no matter how cloudy it may be below. All is calm in heaven, however stormy it may be on earth. There is no confusion there. One will alone reign. Every purpose reaches its appointed end.

22. What a man desires is unfailing love; better to be poor than a liar. The privilege of doing good is within reach of us all. If there is a willing mind, it is accepted according to what a man has, not according to what he has not (2 Corinthians 8:12). God's dealings with his people are grounded on this principle. David's desire to build the temple was as fully accepted and honored as the act itself, which was appointed for his son (2 Chronicles 6:8; 7:12-18).

This desire must be active and no mere wishful excitement. But be sure that your motive is pure. Men do not see our hearts, but the Lord weighs our motives (16:2), and fire will test every man's work to see what it is made of (1 Corinthians 3:13).

23. The fear of the LORD leads to life: Then one rests content,

untouched by trouble. Here the fear of the LORD as a legal principle is something that Christians are exempt from (Luke 1:74; Romans 8:15; 2 Timothy 1:7). But as a grace of the Gospel, men should cultivate such **fear** with consummate care. Its three fruits are set out for us here: **life**, contentment, and security.

It **leads to life**. This is not just natural life, which we have in common with the ungodly (although this blessing, insofar as it is good, is also included), but heavenly life, eternal life, life lived in the sunshine of God's smile. So far as we are under its influence, we speak, pray, think, and deal with man as if God were standing next to us.

Meanwhile, the contentment that it imparts is a precious privilege. God's service is now our great delight. The law is no taskmaster looming over our heads, but a principle of life and joyful energy. The hearts of the men of this world are torn with an aching void. But the cry of God's child reflects his contentment. *Lord, shine your light on me.*

We normally dread fear. But if you fear the Lord, that touch turns fear to gold. He who fears in this way does not fear. His mercy sweeps away the fear of terror. His holiness maintains the fear of reverence. Conscious of our security in God, we are even more fearful of ever leaving or being separated from his love.

24. The sluggard buries his hand in the dish; he will not even bring it back to his mouth! Here is another striking illustration of the disease of sloth (see 12:27; 26:15)! It so grows on its victim that he has no heart to do even necessary things for himself—as if he cannot take his **hand** out of his **dish**. He prefers the ravages of hunger to the exertion of putting food into his mouth! This is a melancholy picture of many good intentions and promises, and apparently good beginnings in religion, which all grind to a halt when the least effort is required. Every religious duty is a burden. The struggle necessary for prayer, the only means of receiving our spiritual food, is too hard. The soul that seemed to have been awakened sinks into its former lethargy. The effort to rouse it becomes fainter and more hopeless. The **hand** cannot reach out, even if a crown were within reach.

But remember this, Christian: He who has awakened you from the sleep of death will keep you awake until the Lord comes. But even with you, much drowsiness remains that the Lord will not tolerate. The Lord will make you feel that life is a solemn reality, that prayer is not a halfhearted work but close contact with the living God.

Look for rest only in the arms of victory. While the conflict lasts, there is no time for loitering or for slumber. Never forget to thank God for every victory. Thank him for his constant strength that enables you to continue fighting. Peace with God is our life, and the joy of the Lord is our strength, our health, our happiness, and so we will not be found in a listless state.

25. Flog a mocker, and the simple will learn prudence; rebuke a dis-

cerning man, and he will gain knowledge. There is a difference of opinion about the value of punishments. Some say that if the will does not give way to reason, enforcing obedience has little purpose. But God's Word and ordinance is our standard, although great wisdom is required in how we carry it out. Two things are mentioned in this proverb, both of which are linked to the character of the offender.

The mocker is a bold sinner. He needs to be flogged in order to learn prudence. This may be a timely warning to those who are led by him. Dealing with a ringleader can put an end to many troubles. Often when one person is made an example of, even though the sinner himself continues to be in a hardened state, it benefits a whole group of people. Thus "God strikes some, that he may warn all" (Bishop Hall).

A discerning man should be rebuked. He is not to be flogged. In the case of the mocker, his punishment is for the sake of others. In the case of the discerning man, his punishment is for his own sake. He will gain knowledge. Never let us forget the mercy of being kept from sin or being restored from it, even if it is by our Master's sharp and gracious rebuke. "Those whom I love I rebuke and discipline" (Revelation 3:19).

26. He who robs his father and drives out his mother is a son who brings shame and disgrace. This is a dreadful picture of recklessness. It is a picture of unrestrained depravity (Romans 1:30-31). Man is the debased slave of his selfish desires. The profligate may rob his father of his substance by extravagance, and his spirit and health by his evil behavior. Often a mother's tenderness has been repaid with crushing unkindness. The insolence of an ungrateful son virtually drives her out from her own home. Such monsters in human shape, polluting every principle of humanity, have been found in every generation. Yet seldom do they escape without some mark of retributive justice even in this life (30:11, 17).

27. Stop listening to instruction, my son, and you will stray from the words of knowledge. Our divine Master gave a similar warning when he told his disciples to beware of false prophets and to be careful about what they heard (Matthew 7:15; Mark 4:24). All instruction is not positive and does not always promote life. Teachers of evil, who are Satan's ministers, abound.

This instruction is not usually a clear departure from the truth. But, like the first temptation, it causes us to err gradually. We hardly notice that we are deviating from the straight and narrow route until the mischief has caught us. If Eve had at once stopped listening to the serpent, she would not have been led astray from the words of knowledge. But the success of the first attempt has made the seducer more bold to deal out his deadly poison to her weakened children.

But what if we are in a place where words of knowledge are not found? To start with, we would suggest that particular cases require particular action. There may be cases when the call is to stop listening. If the teaching is heretical or wholly unevangelical, if the teacher's life is immoral or scandalously worldly, if the children or servants of the family are clearly in danger of being led astray, it may be right to leave. In such a case you would be separating from the minister and not from the church. But in no circumstances should the ungodliness of the minister be an excuse to neglect Christian ordinances. At the same time, in many more cases than is usually supposed, the mature Christian will do well to stay where he is, continue to pray, abound in his labor of love, and be a consistent example. He may have the opportunity to administer a reproof. He definitely will have the opportunity to take up his appointed cross.

28-29. A corrupt witness mocks at justice, and the mouth of the wicked gulps down evil. Penalties are prepared for mockers, and beatings for the backs of fools. Here we are reminded that **fools** who make a mockery of sin often have their backs beaten by men who are God's instruments. If only thoughtless and careless young people would take such words to heart. When they join in scoffing, they should tremble in case they are standing in the company of sinners. Soon they will find themselves sitting with those who are scornful (Psalm 1:1). They may end up despising God's warnings even more than their companions.

Who is to blame when such **penalties** are handed out? "Our sin," says Bishop Hall," is our own, and the wages of sin is death. He who does the work earns the wages. So, then, the righteous God is cleared both of our sin and our death. Only his justice pays us what our evil deeds deserve. What a wretched thing is a willing sinner, as he will cause his own death." It would be a happy day indeed if he ever turned to God in repentance (Jeremiah 31:18-19).

Proverbs
Chapter 20

1. Wine is a mocker and beer a brawler; whoever is led astray by them is not wise. The history of the world from the days of Noah (Genesis 9:21) proves that the love of **wine . . . and beer** is a most insidious vice. The wretched victims are convinced too late that they have been mocked and **led astray.** Not only does it overcome them before they are aware, but it promises pleasures that it can never give. And yet so mighty is the spell that the overcome slave consents to be mocked again and again.

Its power turns humans into a level below the beasts as it turns each of its victims into **a brawler.** Reason surrenders to lust, appetite, or passion. Surely, then, **whoever is led astray by them is not wise.**

Human nature is humbled to see not only ignorant people but people with outstanding talents brutalized by this lust. Those who were once created in the image of God now sink into the dregs of shame. It is even more humbling to see God's own people wallowing in this mire. The examples of Noah and Lot are recorded, not as laughing-stocks to the ungodly, but as beacons to the saints. Anyone who thinks that he stands should take heed that he does not fall (1 Corinthians 10:12). The great apostle tells us not to be drunk on wine but to be filled with the Spirit (Ephesians 5:18).

2. A king's wrath is like the roar of a lion; he who angers him forfeits his life. Once before **a king's wrath** was mentioned in this way (19:12). Here the result of his **wrath** is described. Such was the power of the king, unknown in our happy land, that he was the sole, the uncontrolled, arbiter of life and death.

What, then, must be the wrath of the great King! "Armies of terrors and doubts are nothing to a look of his angry countenance. 'O Lord,' says that holy man (considering the frailty of poor man, and the power of God) 'who knows the power of your anger? According to your fear, so is your wrath'" (Leighton). "Miserable sinner, deprecate his wrath. Seek a Mediator. Beware of continuing to sin" (Geier).

3. It is to a man's honor to avoid strife, but every fool is quick to quarrel. The contrast between this precept and the maxim of the world shows that it is from God. A world of sin will always be a world of **strife**, because it is ruled by the wisdom that does not come from above (James 3:14-16). And yet an evil world is a fine theater in which the grace of God is displayed in the fruits of the wisdom that is from above, such as meekness and gentleness. Previously we have been reminded that it is man's **glory to overlook an offense** (19:11); here it is **a man's honor to avoid strife.** Many people are prepared to overlook an injury just so they can have a quiet life. But if they were involved in **strife**, they would feel that their **honor** was at stake; so they would make sure they struck the last blow. It is much more difficult to collect the waters once they have been freed than to restrain them within their proper bounds. To drop the matter in a dispute (17:14) is an honorable act (16:32; Romans 12:21); it is a triumph over the flesh. For how often is **strife** fed by the folly of man's pride rather than extinguished by a peaceful and loving spirit. But to put on meekness and patience and to let God's peace rule in our hearts are the characteristics of God's elect as we follow the example of our divine Master (Colossians 3:12-15).

4. A sluggard does not plow in season; so at harvest time he looks but finds nothing. We are taught again (see 19:15, 24) by a vivid picture about a most pernicious vice. **A sluggard** always has his excuses ready, so he can escape any work that might exert him. He **does not plow in season**, although there is nothing to prevent him from doing so except that his heart is not in the work. And does not the most trifling difficulty hinder us when our hearts are not given over to God's service?

But **a sluggard** will reap the fruit of his sin. If he **does not plow in season**, he cannot reap **at harvest time**. At that happy season, the reward for the laborer's toil, **he looks but finds nothing.** "Men's hearts are justly hardened against that man who by his own sloth and sinfulness has brought himself to want [lack]" (Poole).

And what else can a spiritual **sluggard** look for? He stays away from the house of God. His soul, therefore, perishes for lack of nourishment. If we only had to wish for heaven, who would miss it? But heartless wishes without the crucifixion of the flesh will stop short of the promise. Millions have perished in serious religion from a lack of diligence and self-sacrificing devotion.

It is no time to stand idle when we stand at the door of eternity. We cannot be slack when so great a salvation is so near. "Blessed are those who have sown much for God in their lifetime. Oh, the glorious harvest that they will have! The very angels shall help them take in their harvest at the great day. And, oh, the joy there will be in that harvest! The angels will help sing the harvest song . . . they will sing who have been sowers of righteousness!" (Burroughs).

5. The purposes of a man's heart are deep waters, but a man of understanding draws them out. We see that **a man's heart** is not easily fathomed. It is often full of subtle evil. And yet **a man of understanding** will often draw out the subtle **purposes** and set them in their true light. Paul drew out the secret counsel of selfishness in the schismatic preachers of the Gospel (Philippians 1:15-17).

But let us look on the bright side. Observe a man of God, who is taught by God. Natural intellectual wisdom is deepened and enlightened by spiritual light. His mind is enriched with the fruits of scriptural study and meditation. The **man of understanding** will discover and draw out valuable instruction.

But above all, familiarity with the deep waters of the counsel of God are to be prized. Do not say that you have nothing with which to draw water from the deep well. The habit of thinking in the exercise of prayer will enable you to draw water with joy from the wells of salvation. It will bring into your soul a well of water springing up to everlasting life (John 4:14).

6. Many a man claims to have unfailing love, but a faithful man who can find? The previous proverb showed the depth of the **heart**, and this proverb shows its deceitfulness and pride. Listen to a man's own estimate of himself, and we need no further proof of his lack of self-knowledge (16:2). Even the ungodly proclaim their own **unfailing love**. The Pharisee paraded his own goodness on the street corners. Such is the blindness of a self-deceiving heart. *Lord, teach me to remember that what is highly valued by men is detested in your sight.*

In contrast to this self-complacent goodness, Solomon, an accurate observer of human nature, exclaims almost in despondency, **but a faithful man who can find?** Who can find a guileless parent or adviser? Examine yourself closely. Look at yourself in the mirror of God's Word. Does your neighbor or your friend find that you are a **faithful** friend? Do you often speak what you know will be accepted rather than what is true? Never underrate the importance of moral integrity. Never does godliness shine more brightly than when we are **faithful** in all things (Titus 2:10).

7. The righteous man leads a blameless life; blessed are his children after him. The picture of the **faithful man** (verse 6) is enlarged on here. He is richly blessed by God. Take the account of the father of the faithful. Abraham was a **righteous man**; he was accepted by God, and he walked before God, leading **a blameless life**. The covenant God made with him extended to his children. In this way every child of Abraham can walk in integrity before the Lord. It is "not however for the merits of the parent that they deserve it: but such is the mercy of God to the root and the branches that, because the fathers are loved, their children also are embraced" (Muffet). "The branches fare better for the sap of grace in the root" (Swinnock). "When God says that he will be a God to the godly man and to his children, I believe he intended more in that promise for the comfort of godly parents than most of them think of (Acts 2:39; Genesis 17:7). The children of believers are heirs apparent to the covenant of grace in their parents' right" (Swinnock). But we must show our **blameless life,** as did our father Abraham, as we exercise our faith. We must not only take hold of the covenant on behalf of our children—we must bring them under the yoke of the covenant.

Christian parents, we must let blamelessness, as before God, be the general characteristic of our family religion. Do not live by the maxims of the world, and do not allow your children to walk in that way. Let us make God's Word, his whole Word, our universal rule. We must make his ways, no matter how much they may be despised, our daily guide. Let us seek first, for our children as well as for ourselves, God's kingdom and his righteousness. Then surely it will be true that your children will be **blessed** and their names found in the secret records of heaven, linked with the prayerful faith and love of their parents.

8. When a king sits on his throne to judge, he winnows out all evil with his eyes. This is the picture of a godly **king,** such as the wise man's father described and exemplified. He feared God as he ruled justly. In those days he sat **on his throne to judge** and made decisions as people were brought before him presenting their cases. Lapide mentions the custom of Louis of France, who sat twice a week on his throne to judge. His dying charge to his successor was not only to appoint the most upright judges but to oversee them as they carried out their work. Does not the Court of the Queen's Bench suppose the sovereign is sitting there as judgments are determined? The fairness of the king's judgment was so well-known that the wicked did not dare come into his presence. David, as a man of God and a ruler over his people, could not endure the wicked in his presence (Psalm 101:3-8).

So how can we stand before the great King who **winnows out all evil with his eyes?** May the High Priest always stand between the sinner and the holy God, so that we may walk reverently before the Lord.

9. Who can say, "I have kept my heart pure; I am clean and without sin"? The great King sits on his throne to judge and challenges every child of Adam: "Brace yourself like a man; I will question you, and you shall answer me" (Job 38:3). The question is confounding. The answer humbles us in the dust. **Who can say,** truly say, **"I have kept my heart pure . . ."?** A sinner in his self-delusion may conceive himself to be a saint. But it is impossible for a saint ever to consider himself in this way. **Who can say, . . . "I am clean and without sin"?** What? No vain thoughts, no sinful imagination dwelling within? No ignorance, no pride, no coldness, no worldliness, no unbelief indulged in? The more we search the heart, the more its impurity will confront us. Only vain people can boast that they have pure hearts. But the boast, far from showing their goodness, demonstrates their blindness. Man is so depraved that he cannot understand his own depravity. "Once I thought," said a holy man of God, "some humiliating expressions of the saints of God too low for me, proud, blind wretch as I was! Now I can say with Edwards, 'Infinite upon infinite only reaches to my sinfulness'" (Venn). There is not a conscious child of God who does not drink in this self-abased spirit. But for the clear manifestation of gospel grace, we would have good reason to tremble in case our sins should remain uncanceled. The pure heart, therefore, is not the heart **without sin**, but the heart cleansed and renewed by grace.

10. Differing weights and differing measures—the LORD detests them both. This probably refers to the iniquitous custom of having **differing weights and differing measures** for buying and selling. Such practices were common and brought down God's judgment on the people (Hosea 12:7; Amos 8:4-5; Micah 6:10-11). "A very grievous thing it is to think of the several kinds of frauds and deceits in which men have become experts, and shameless as well, that they think it does them credit and does not blemish their Christian characters" (Bishop Sanderson). But every man of moral integrity should scorn the flagrant breach of the golden rule. Let this, as every other temptation, be a matter of prayerful watchfulness. Do not be satisfied with merely abstaining from this dreadful vice. Blot out its darkness with the bright, steady shining light of love, self-forgetfulness, and active concern for your neighbor.

11. Even a child is known by his actions, by whether his conduct is pure and right. Parents should take note of their children's early habits. Generally the discerning eye will see something in the budding of the young tree that will indicate how the mature tree will grow. The child tells us what the man will be. No wise parent will pass over little faults, as if it is only a child doing childish things. If a child is deceitful, quarrelsome, obstinate, rebellious, and selfish, how can we but fear for his future as he grows up?

But we must never forget that we serve the God of hope. So we do not despair of his grace. We do not doubt his faithfulness. We hold on in patient hope. Tears of despondency will be exchanged for tears of joy. Augustine's mother experienced a severe test of her faith. But her patient wrestling was amply rewarded. And ever since then the judgment of the godly archbishop ("It is impossible that the child of so many prayers could ever perish") has been treasured in the church as an axiom of accredited warrant and cheering support.

12. Ears that hear and eyes that see—the LORD has made them both. Sight and hearing are the two senses by which instruction is conveyed to the mind. They are component parts of that divine structure that God so wonderfully made (Psalm 139:14). The celebrated Galen is said to have been converted from atheism by an attentive observation of the perfect structure of the eye. The natural senses are gifts common to everyone. The spiritual senses are the special gifts of sovereign power and grace. It was left to man to make the ear that cannot hear and the eye that cannot see. He then took leave of his senses and worshiped the work of his own hands. But **ears that hear and eyes that see—the LORD has made them both.**

Man is deaf and blind to the things of God (Matthew 13:13-14). The voice of mercy is ignored. To his need and to his remedy he is alike insensible. His ear is open to sound advice, to moral teaching, to the dictates of external decency. But as for the Gospel, he is a mere statue, without life. All his senses are blinded, deadened, and chained (2 Corinthians 4:3-4). His moral disabilities can only be removed by that almighty power that on earth gave hearing to the deaf and sight to the blind. We can as soon create our natural self as recreate our spiritual self.

"The hearing ear, which Solomon refers to, is the ear that believes and obeys what it hears. The seeing eye is that which observes in such a way that it follows the good things in its sight" (Caryl). So we rejoice that the Lord has opened our ears so that we **hear,** and our eyes so that we **see.**

13. Do not love sleep or you will grow poor; stay awake and you will have food to spare. Use "sleep as tired nature's sweet restorer" (Young). Man requires it, and God graciously gives it. Without it man could not go to a day's work.

But **do not love sleep** for its own sake. "Let your sleep be necessary and as required for a healthy life, not to idle time away" (Bishop Taylor). If you do not take care, it will become a habit and rob you of your talent and make you poor. Man is full of contradictions. He wants to live a long life but is willing to shorten it by sleeping it away. Nothing is done for God, for the soul, for his fellow creatures, or for heaven. He is rightly thrown out as a wicked, slothful servant.

It is beyond question that the Christian degrades himself from his proper level by needless indulgence. He chooses to live life as a brute beast rather than to elevate himself and have fellowship with the angels. Those of us who have an inclination to being drowsy should especially heed this warning—**do not love sleep.**

14. "It's no good, it's no good!" says the buyer; then off he goes and boasts about his purchase. The Bible gives abundant proof that man has been the same in every generation since the Fall. Where is the market in which this example of fraud is not mirrored? Commerce, the Lord's providential dispensation to bind man to man, is marred by his depravity. The wise man had previously detected the iniquity of the seller (verse 10). Here he exposes the evil ways of **the buyer.** He even uses the language of the market: **"It's no good, it's no good!"** "The article is of an inferior quality. I can get it cheaper elsewhere. It is worth so much, but it is not worth that to me. I have no use for it. I cannot think how it could ever be helpful." By these crafty falsehoods, he strikes a shrewd bargain. **Then he goes and boasts about his purchase.** He laughs at the simplicity of the seller and is highly commended for being so clever.

[words die in the air]

We are all engaged in pecuniary transactions. With many it is the main business of life. Yet such are the temptations from our own interest and the selfishness of others and the general example of the world to deviate from a straight line that we should be most grateful for this probing analysis of deceit. The man of God knows that he must do everything to the glory of God.

15. **Gold there is, and rubies in abundance, but lips that speak knowledge are a rare jewel.** This is not the standard of the world. There **gold . . . and rubies** are held in much higher esteem than **lips that speak knowledge.** Thus the young man made his choice and preferred his great possessions to following Christ. But when **gold** is our hope, it will also be our ruin. **Gold . . . and rubies** were plentiful in Solomon's day. Yet all these earthly treasures were as nothing in his eyes in comparison with heavenly teaching. **Lips that speak knowledge are a rare jewel.**

It is divine **knowledge** that is preeminent here. Human wisdom may captivate the imagination and furnish it with useful information. But the words for the most part die away on the ear. They do not feed the heart. They do not comfort the afflicted, bring hope to the despondent, or teach the ignorant. So while they may be pearls, they are not the pearl of great price, that **rare jewel** that dims the luster of earth's most splendid vanities (Matthew 13:45-46).

But lips that speak knowledge are a rare jewel. How precious is the sound of the messenger of the Gospel when he brings good tidings of great joy to a burdened conscience. Truly the sound of his coming is welcome on account of his message. Such was the delight of those who hung on the lips of the golden-mouthed Chrysostom that the common proverb was, "Rather let the sun not shine than Chrysostom not preach." So we are to spread this **knowledge** and so enrich our hearers.

16. **Take the garment of one who puts up security for a stranger; hold it in pledge if he does it for a wayward woman.** Again and again we are warned not to take a pledge for a stranger (see 11:15; 17:18). We should not do this for **a stranger,** no matter how enticing he may be, still less from **a wayward woman** (5:1-5), whose character has lost all credit. This is the sure road to ruin. If a person is so weak as to plunge into this folly, he is not fit to be trusted. Do not lend anything to him without good security. If necessary, take his **garment** as a pledge. The letter of the Mosaic law forbade this extremity (Exodus 22:26-27; Deuteronomy 24:12-13). But the spirit and intent of the law pointed to the protection of the poor and unfortunate, who were forced to borrow from necessity and therefore were to be treated compassionately. Here the command refers to the inconsiderate, who deserve to suffer for their folly as they deliberately plunge themselves into ruin. The love of our neighbor does not involve us in forgetting ourselves. The path of godly prudence is the safest for all parties. It can never be wise to help where such kindness will

only bring ruin. To refuse may be to exercise self-denial. It is right that this should be so.

17. Food gained by fraud tastes sweet to a man, but he ends up with a mouth full of gravel. "Holiness is sweet in the way and in the end too. Wickedness is sometimes sweet in the way, but always bitter in the end" (Caryl). With **fraud**, as with every other sin, Satan always holds out bait. He always promises gain or pleasure as the wages of his service but always disappoints the victims of his delusion. "The bread that a man obtains by fraud seems sweet and pleasant at the first taste, but by the time it has been chewed it is plain that it is full of gravel and wounds the tongue and offends the palate" (Bishop Hall). "Everything obtained in a wrong way is implied here" (Bishop Patrick).

Not a single step can be taken on the road of godliness without the complete renunciation of every evil practice. Not even the smallest violation of the law is allowed. The smallest sin breaks down the fence. And once it is broken down, the impulse is beyond restraint. Universal uprightness is the mark of the true servant of God. Let the man who teaches Christian doctrine exhibit holiness in his own life. Never let our religion be one thing and our business another.

18. Make plans by seeking advice; if you wage war, obtain guidance. Here is true wisdom. To deliberate before we act **by seeking advice** is the path of wisdom. Even the wisest of men valued this (1 Kings 12:6). God has placed us in society, so that we are more or less dependent on each other. So while it is most important to have clear judgment oneself, we must guard against an obstinate and exclusive adherence to our own opinions.

This rule especially applies to matters that affect the whole nation, such as when to **wage war**. Wars for the purpose of ambition and aggrandizement can never be wisely made.

Now ponder Bishop Hall's description of spiritual **war**: "It admits of no intermission. It knows no night, no winter. It abides no peace, no truce. It calls us not into garrison, where we may have ease and rest, but into pitched fields continually. We see our enemies in the face always, and are always seen and assaulted; ever resisting, ever defending, receiving and returning blows. If either we are negligent or weary, we die. What other hope is there, while one fights, and the other stands still? We can never have safety and peace but in victory. Then must our resistance be courageous and constant, when yielding is death, and all treaties of peace mortal." Does not this **war** bring the greatest need for **advice**?

19. A gossip betrays a confidence; so avoid a man who talks too much. Never let us forget that all our social life must be based on love. Any breach in this greatly displeases God. Think about the **gossip**. Unhappily, he has much time on his hands, which he uses in no helpful way. Hence he spends it on other people's business, ferreting out secrets or diving into family arrangements. All this is material for scandal. In his visits he talks about the business of the last family he saw. His present visit will give him material he can pass on to the next house he goes to.

This way of life is especially offensive to the God of truth. Even when **a gossip** has been told things in the strictest **confidence,** he tells everyone he meets about them. We must never think that this is a matter of little importance. We must never break any trust placed in us. We must resolutely determine to be faithful.

20. If a man curses his father or mother, his lamp will be snuffed out in pitch darkness. If **darkness** is the punishment, is it not also the cause of this atrocious sin? For surely even the light of nature must be extinguished if a child should curse those who under God have taught him to speak. Even a scowl, much more a word, breaks God's commandment. How great, then, is the guilt involved in a child cursing his parents! It is a visible sign of the last days (2 Timothy 3:2).

21. An inheritance quickly gained at the beginning will not be blessed at the end. The wise man obviously limits his observation to **an inheritance quickly gained** dishonestly. Joseph's advancement in Egypt happened **quickly,** in a moment, but it was under God's special providence. But the evil man, longing to be rich and great, may gain an inheritance but not be blessed by it (10:2-3). In our own history, Richard the Third ended his quickly gained crown in shame. Napoleon rose to prominence very quickly and, as it were, gained a magnificent inheritance. Yet he ended his days in disgraceful banishment. Less splendid possessions end in the same disappointment. Let the warnings to the rich in the Bible be heeded (1 Timothy 6:9-10). Place the cross and crown of Jesus in view. The world fades and selfishness dies at the sight of these. One object only, God's inheritance (Psalm 16:2, 5), attracts and satisfies. Here is blessing beyond our imagination, one that never ends.

22. Do not say, "I'll pay you back for this wrong!" Wait for the LORD, and he will deliver you. Vengeance belongs to God. Nobody else is fit to wield this. God is omniscient; our knowledge is at most partial. God's judgment is perfect, while we are blinded by our prejudices and evil desires. We so often long to take revenge on people. Even when we are restrained from doing this, we continue to burn with rage within ourselves. At best we are reluctantly obedient. We rarely display the victory demonstrated by godly people who overcome evil with good.

What is the remedy for this? In humility and faith we must lay this matter before the Lord. Put it in his hands. **Wait for the LORD, and he will deliver you.** Revenge rises in our hearts only because we have no faith. For if we believed that God would take up our cause, would we not leave everything in his hands? "Let it be sufficient for you that you possess your own soul patiently and know that all wrongs will be righted one day. God will set everything straight in the end, but that day has yet to come" (Bishop Sanderson).

23. The LORD detests differing weights, and dishonest scales do not please him. Here let us search God's mind. Three times he drives this point home (verses 10, 14, 23). Yet this is hardly vain repetition. There must be an important reason for this to be repeated. In the place of precept on precept and line upon line, he could have given an endless variety of instruction. For example, we are not amazed at the way the apostle Paul continually teaches about the justification of sinners before God in his letter to the Romans and in Galatians. From this repetition we understand how important this doctrine is.

The truth of this proverb should be especially taken note of in our evil commercial system. **Differing weights** are continually condemned as an abomination—yes, they are detested by God; yet how often are they ignored as if they were a necessity. But "the scant measure will fill up a full measure of guilt, and the light weights bring upon the soul a heavy weight of judgment" (Reynolds). Let the trader beware that his **differing weights, and dishonest scales** do not bear witness against him. We have great need to be watchful here. Man cannot even trust his fellowman. Oh, let me not forget that this deceit naturally grows in my heart. Only the cultivation of divine principles keeps down these poisonous weeds and nourishes in their place the fruits of righteousness. "The love of God constrains his servant. God is true to him; and he will not be false to others. God is merciful to him, and he will not be unjust to others" (Polhill). This is the practical effect of the Gospel.

24. A man's steps are directed by the LORD. How then can anyone understand his own way? Here are two basic principles: God's controllable power and sovereignty, and man's absolute dependence and helplessness. Here is no infringement of freedom on the one hand and no excuse for laziness on the other hand. Man often acts as if he is the master of his own situation, as if his **steps** are his own. Or else, having the warped idea of every event being predetermined, he sits still instead of working diligently, so the Lord's purposes may be fulfilled. But the humble Christian exercises his freedom in the spirit of dependence on God. His **steps are directed by the LORD**, who both inspires the effort and brings success.

We need to say to the Lord that we trust his wisdom, his goodness, and his faithful care. *O Lord, lead me, uphold me, do not forsake me.* Augustine mentions the weeping prayers of his godly mother when he traveled from Carthage to Italy. She was anxious that as he was no longer going to be under her influence, he would sink deeper into sin. But in the end this journey paved the way for his providential conversion. "In your deep and hidden counsel," Augustine wrote, "listening to the cardinal point of her desire, you did not grant what she then asked for, in order to accomplish in me what she always asked for."

25. It is a trap for a man to dedicate something rashly and only later

to consider his vows. Along every path the great fowler has laid his traps. Perhaps, however, the most subtle are reserved for us when we are serving God.

In such a hollow, halfhearted profession, "a man vows in distress to give something to God: but having obtained his desires, he wants to be freed from this obligation" (Bishop Patrick). Often in a moment of excitement, perhaps in the glow of a religious meeting, something has been pledged to God. "He entangles his soul in the snares of death who uses in a profane way what has been consecrated to God. If, after he has made a vow to the Lord, he later argues within himself about how he can change that holy promise, he is robbing God of his due" (Bishop Hall). Beware of a religion of temporary excitement. No matter what it costs you, truly consecrate yourself as a living sacrifice to God (Romans 12:1).

26. A wise king winnows out the wicked; he drives the threshing wheel over them. Solomon, as **a wise king**, was constantly keeping an eye on his own responsibilities. His standard was not to commit wickedness himself, nor to allow it in his people. He winnowed out **the wicked**; he did not encourage them. As the farmer's **threshing wheel** was driven over the grain, the straw was cut off, and so the chaff was separated (Isaiah 28:28-29). This is an obvious allusion to the way the harvest was threshed in the East. One method was to use a wain, which had wheels with iron teeth like a saw. The axle was fitted with serrated wheels. It moved on three rollers that were also fitted with iron teeth, or wheels, to cut the straw.

God often sifts his church by trial to make her purer. *Oh, my soul, how will you be found on that great day of judgment?*

27. The lamp of the LORD searches the spirit of a man; it searches out his inmost being. We are placed under a solemn dispensation of divine government. Every soul should, in some sense, acknowledge the judgment of the great Sovereign. For this reason conscience has aptly been called "God in man." God brings the searching light of his **lamp** into the darkness. Man would be happy indeed if all his ungodliness was put out by this **lamp**. Whatever man's mindless pleasures may have been, the time will come when he must leave them and live without them. And then, as the question has been framed in an unanswerable way, "What is all that a man can enjoy in this way for a week, a month, a year, compared with what he feels for one hour, when his conscience will take him to one side and accuse him?" (South).

This **lamp** is beyond value, as it throws God's light on the narrow path, so that we "are not scrupulous in small matters and negligent in big matters; and so that we do not tithe mint and cummin but forget about justice" (Bishop Hall).

When God makes his **lamp** shine brightly, will I be able to bear it? Do I welcome the horrible discoveries it makes? Do I value its light as it opens up the secret fellowship between a sinner and a holy, jealous God? Oh, let my **inmost being** be exposed to the Lord's **lamp,** that all the things I secretly indulge in may be searched out and mortified.

28. Love and faithfulness keep a king safe; through love his throne is made secure. Punishment is indeed a necessary security against breaking the law (verse 26). Yet a wise **king** will follow the example of the great Sovereign and delight in **love.** And as long as **faithfulness** is his inviolable guiding principle, the abuse of **love** need hardly be feared. **Love and faithfulness** are "the best guard of his body, and supporters of his throne" (Trapp).

29. The glory of young men is their strength, gray hair the splendor of the old. Every stage of life has special honor and privilege. "Youth is the glory of nature, and the glory of young men is their strength. Old age is the majestic beauty of nature, and the gray hair is the majestic splendor that nature has given to old age" (Jermin). These pictures describe the use, not the abuse. It is youth usefully exercised, especially consecrated to God, and used for his glory. The silver crown brings honor, reverence, and authority only in the way of righteousness.

Yet **gray hair[,] the splendor of the old** is most likely to be found where **the glory of young men** has been dedicated to God. The young plant, stunted and deformed in its youth, will generally remain crooked as it grows. But who can calculate the extent of fruitfulness where our early strength has been given to the Lord? Let youth and old age both beware of defacing their **glory.** Each takes the precedence in some things and gives way in others. Let them not, therefore, envy or despise each other's prerogatives. The world, the state, and the church needs them both, the **strength** of youth for energy and the maturity of **the old** for wisdom.

30. Blows and wounds cleanse away evil, and beatings purge the inmost being. Punishment is the Lord's ordinance. The pain of the flesh subjugates the spirit. Sometimes the flesh has even to be destroyed, so that the spirit may be saved (1 Corinthians 5:5). This does not describe gentle strokes but the severity of parental discipline. The diseased body needs medicine no less than food. The diseased soul needs punishment no less than consolation.

Child of God, think of your Father's character. He knows how you were made, and he never willingly afflicts you (Psalm 103:14; Lamentations 3:33). You will not be punished more than is necessary. But truly blessed are the **beatings** that humble and break the proud will. The fruits of righteousness are rich indeed that come from the conflict and sufferings of the flesh.

Proverbs
Chapter 21

1. The king's heart is in the hand of the LORD; he directs it like a watercourse wherever he pleases. Most people who reflect about life acknowledge that God is behind everything. In inert matter he acts by physical force; in wild animals, by instinct and appetite; in intelligent beings, by motives suited to their faculties; in his redeemed people, by the influence of grace. This proverb reminds us of one aspect of his providential care. The general truth, previously stated, that man is entirely dependent on God is illustrated by **the king's heart**, which is under God's sway.

A watercourse is an apt emblem of this agency. It starts as a single spring that is hardly able to turn a hand-mill to grind a day's corn. But as it is swollen by the confluence of other small and great streams, it is able to turn hundreds of mills and provide food for thousands of people. So the thoughts of **the king's heart** are at first a single idea for the good of his subjects. This then grows until it is fulfilled. For, after all, the great Sovereign **directs** the most despotic rule—all political projects—to his own ends, in the same way that **a watercourse** runs through its channel. The allusion is evidently to channels that were made to distribute water and so irrigate gardens or fields. The **watercourse** flows naturally in the direction of the channel. God directs **the king's heart** as his responsible agent, without interfering with the moral freedom of his will.

The history of our blessed, though now maligned, Reformation shows the same sovereign control of the royal heart. Henry VIII was used as an instrument, and his godly son as a willing agent, in furthering this great work. To recall this encourages us to refer all troubles in the life of the church to her great Head and to rejoice that in the place of kings, the King of king reigns.

2. All a man's ways seem right to him, but the LORD weighs the heart. May I be grateful for the repetition (16:2) of this weighty proverb. It is most valuable, as it probes my heart and tests my spirituality. The heart is so deceitful that it deceives not only others, but, even when Satan does not, itself. Every intelligent Christian bears witness to this self-deception. How differently do we judge the same action that we do when seen in the lives of other people. We often plead that there were extenuating circumstances for us to behave in a certain way, and so we justify ourselves, though we condemn this same action in other people. So we should always pray that God will search us, know us, test us, and reveal us to ourselves (Psalm 139:23). Nobody else in the world makes as many mistakes as we do ourselves. But to be approved of by God is no ordinary mercy!

3. **To do what is right and just is more acceptable to the LORD than sacrifice.** Did Solomon mean to undervalue **sacrifice?** Nobody ever valued it more highly than he did (see 1 Kings 3:4; 8:64). **Sacrifice** was appointed as a type of the great sacrifice for sin (Hebrews 10:11-12). But it was never intended to take the place of the universal moral obedience that God's law had from the beginning required. Yet how quickly man misunderstood the intention of the ordinance. How easily he substituted the offerings of bulls and goats for the self-denying service of the heart. The people of Israel abounded in the observance of their outward ceremonials while indulging in the sins of Sodom and Gomorrah.

No **sacrifice** can replace the love of God. We must ask ourselves if we are only worshiping superficially. Do you hear the voice calling you away from the dead form of religion to seek the living power of godliness? Cain brought a sacrifice, but not his heart. Remember that those externals stand in the place of a consecrated heart and are the delusion of the great deceiver. Let your heart be with God.

4. **Haughty eyes and a proud heart, the lamp of the wicked, are sin!** We cannot mistake God's mind that is so clearly declared here. Yet this sin assumes so many different forms that until God's Spirit reveals a man to himself, he does not think it applies to him. Indeed, he manages to be **proud** of his pride!

But such a man has not only **haughty eyes and a proud heart**, but even his natural actions are affected. **The lamp of the wicked** is full of **sin!** But how can an ordinary thing be sinful? The motive determines the action. The most natural actions are inculcated for Christian ends. They, therefore, become moral actions, good or bad according to their own motives. If you do not have a godly purpose in your actions, you sin. "Holy intention is to the actions of a man that which the soul is to the body, or form to its matter, or the root to the tree, or the sun to the world, or the spring to the river, or the base to the pillar. Without these, the body is a dead trunk, the matter is sluggish, the tree is a block, the world is darkness, the river is quickly dry, the pillar rushes into flatness and ruin, and the action is sinful or unprofitable and vain" (Bishop Taylor).

A person's idleness is **sin** in the face of a direct command (2 Thessalonians 3:10). His industry is the **sin** of ungodliness if he refuses God any room in his world. The substance of his work is good, but the corrupt principle defiles his best actions. If the spring is bitter, how can the waters be pure? **Sin** defiles every motive in the Christian's heart. But here it is the substance of **sin**. In one case it is the inability to keep walking along the path; in the other it is walking along a crooked path. With **the wicked,** "his eating as well as his gluttony; his drinking as well as his drunkenness; his business deals as well as his covetousness and his inordinate love of the world are all set down and reckoned by God as sins, and such sins as he must reckon for with God" (Hopkins). Fearful indeed is his condition. Would that he could see it! Whether he prays or neglects to pray, it is an abomination. He cannot but sin, and yet he is fully accountable for his sin. Should he not carry out his duties? "The impotency of man must not prejudice God's authority, nor diminish his duty" (Reynolds). What then should he do? Let him learn how vital it is for him to be born again. Let the wicked person seek the great Physician, whose word is sovereign healing (Matthew 8:3), and whose divine blood cleanses from every disease (1 John 1:7). Once the man's nature is cleansed, his deeds will be clean.

5. The plans of the diligent lead to profit as surely as haste leads to poverty. In Proverbs **the diligent** are usually contrasted with the slothful (10:4; 12:24, 27; 13:4); but here they are contrasted with the hasty person. **The plans** of each bear fruit. One leads to **profit**; the other **leads to poverty.** The patient, plodding, industrious man perseveres in spite of all difficulties. He is content to acquire wealth slowly. He never relaxes or gives way to discouragement. This diligence is profitable when it is blessed by God. "You may as well expect," says an old writer, "riches to rain down from heaven in silver showers as to provide for your family without industry in your calling" (Swinnock).

Those in **haste** may also be **diligent** to a certain extent. But as laziness is defective, so **haste** is undisciplined impulse. Actions are engaged in without thought. Hence our English philosopher wisely counsels us "not to measure dispatch by the times of sitting, but by the advancement of the business." A wise man, when observing people making a rushed conclusion to a job, said, "Stay a little, that we may make it complete quicker. To choose time is to save time, and unthinking action is just beating the air" (Lord Bacon).

The evil of **haste** under a worldly impulse is truly fearful. It often drives a person into doing rash projects. We are to run the race in front of us, not with **haste** or speed, but with patience (Hebrews 12:1). **Haste** is delusion and ends in disappointment. What is as important as cultivating a deep work of grace, which pervades the whole person and abounds with fruit to God's glory?

6-7. A fortune made by a lying tongue is a fleeting vapor and a deadly snare. The violence of the wicked will drag them away, for they refuse to do what is right. Here is a graphic picture of the hasty spirit showing how its own crooked ways lead to poverty. A treasure made by a **lying tongue** becomes a **snare**. Unrighteous gain is a bad bargain, for God's wrath mixes gall and bitterness with the wages of iniquity. Judas was eager to rid himself of his ill-gotten treasure, as it became an intolerable curse. But he was unable to run away from his conscience, which tortured him.

The ungodly seem to seek death as their reward. They seem to be in love with the way of eternal death. Meanwhile, their own sin is the seed of destruction.

8. The way of the guilty is devious, but the conduct of the innocent is upright. Observe the striking contrast between man as he is by nature and man as he is by grace. Who will say that man is now as he first came from his Maker's hand? He has turned away from God and follows his own will.

But once reborn by the grace of God, he carries out God's will. He now lives for God. He longs for heaven. *Oh, my God, show me myself, insofar as I can bear the sight, that I may be kept humble and always close to my Savior, always applying his precious blood, always covering myself in his pure and perfect work of righteousness.*

9. Better to live on a corner of the roof than share a house with a quarrelsome wife. "It cannot be but a miserable thing to behold that yet they are of necessity compelled to live together, which yet cannot be in quiet together" (*Homily on Matrimony*). But many bring this bitter trouble on themselves. They never seek God's help in their momentous choice. The wife is not asked for from the Lord, and so does not come from him, and so does not bring any of his favors with her. Illicit pleasure, avarice, or waywardness brings a calamity that no external advantages such as riches or rank can for a moment make up for.

The only safe way to enter this "honorable estate" is when both commit themselves to God. "Bestow me as you will, and on whom you will" (Chrysostom). The only way to be happy is when mutual love is grounded reverentially on God's ordinances. Each partner of the marriage should remember that passion is nothing, but patience is everything. The husband in his claim for submission will remember that he has found not a servant, but a wife. The wife will not forget "the unfading beauty of a gentle and quiet spirit, which is of great worth in God's sight" (1 Peter 3:4).

10. The wicked man craves evil; his neighbor gets no mercy from him. Here is a graphic picture of Satan himself! He not only does evil—he **craves evil**. Here we see that **evil** is natural to **the wicked**, for it is in their nature. They long to indulge their appetite, as this is their main delight.

His neighbor gets no mercy from him. His love does not extend beyond his own door. He takes no notice of anyone who stands in the way of his own selfish interests. Friend and brother have to give way to his selfish gratification.

Such is sin in its dreadful character and baneful fruits. But look at the man of God, with his heart enlarged and softened with the influence of the Gospel. Oh, for more of this gracious spirit in the church of God!

11. When a mocker is punished, the simple gain wisdom; when a wise man is instructed, he gets knowledge. The essence of this proverb has been given before (19:25) as an instructive illustration of the Lord's providential discipline. No stroke of his rod is without its effect. The same blow has two different results. The **mocker is punished** by it, but **the wise man is instructed** by it. To **a mocker,** the very idea of the grace of God is an object of scorn and contempt. So we are not surprised that the daring offender is marked out for punishment.

The **wise man,** though already taught by God, through his daily teaching gratefully receives increasing **knowledge.** Among his most fruitful lessons are the instructions of the rod. They are instructions, not punishment.

12. The Righteous One takes note of the house of the wicked and brings the wicked to ruin. The workings of providence are often puzzling. The prosperity of **the wicked** is an affront to faith and brings about harsh thoughts about God (Psalm 73:2-14). But when the man who trusts in the Lord looks with the eye of faith, he sees far beyond the dazzling glory of the present moment. When you take **note of the house of the wicked,** you will not just observe its splendor but will reflect on how it will end. Its prosperity will be short-lived, and its destruction is certain. All this is understood by faith.

13. If a man shuts his ears to the cry of the poor, he too will cry out and not be answered. If there were no **poor** people, much of the Word of God, which applies to their comfort and which teaches us about our obligations, would have been written in vain. The obligation implies not only a helping hand, but a feeling heart. Howard's rule, so nobly expounded by his own self-denying devotedness, is a fine comment on this example: "that our superfluities give way to other men's convenience; that our conveniences give way to other men's necessities; and that even our necessities give way to other men's extremities."

The deaf ear implies cruelty and insensibility and turning away from real and known distress. Count it a privilege, no less than an obligation, to minister to **the poor.** Think of it as a way of conforming to our divine Master's spirit and work (Matthew 14:14-21). Covetousness and sensuality harden the heart. And when the heart is hard, the ear is deaf.

14. A gift given in secret soothes anger, and a bribe concealed in the cloak pacifies great wrath. Here **a gift given in secret** implies a perversion. Both parties are involved in the guilt. The giver acts as the tempter. The receiver happily breaks God's law (Exodus 23:8). The passions of men are easily charmed. A greedy man is not angry when he is pacified with gifts, especially when they are given **in secret**, for they will tell no tales. Thus wounded pride is overcome by another ruling passion—avarice! How we need to keep a careful watch over our own hearts so that we keep walking closely with God.

15. When justice is done, it brings joy to the righteous but terror to evildoers. It is not just that **justice is done**, but **it brings joy** when it is done. Everything that **the righteous** man does centers in this. He has as much delight in **justice** as the wicked does in evil. But this **joy** is only for **the righteous.** For the person who only professes to believe in God finds that he offers God the service of a slave. He only knows God as a Master, and he thinks of him as a slave-master. He has never known him as a Father and therefore has never served him as a child. But when a Christian truly serves God, holiness is identified with happiness as naturally as heat accompanies fire and beams of light shine from the sun. This is how it was with our Lord, who delighted to do God's will. Oh, that we as God's servants might have the same spirit that our Lord had!

16. A man who strays from the path of understanding comes to rest in the company of the dead. This seems to describe the fearful and irretrievable ruin of apostates. God opens **the path of understanding.** So anyone who **strays** from this **path** implies that he once traveled along it. He was at least instructed about and professed to walk on this road. The end of deliberate wandering away from God is eternal death.

This state of death is often linked with the external observance of religion. The real reason for the death is that in the full blaze of religious knowledge, a living faith is absent. So there is no reality in prayer, and therefore there is no genuine desire to persevere with God. With all his light, knowledge, and privileges, this man still **strays from the path of understanding**.

Indeed, straying is the character of man's fallen nature. Beware of the first wandering step, whether in doctrine or in behavior. You may end up in a state of apostasy, like Bunyan's blind wanderers who left the straight path and were found among the tombs, **in the company of the dead.** Remember that to be found in such company reveals your character and your state. Will not everyone who deliberately turns away from opportunities to attain wisdom be found to have died in their sins eternally?

17. He who loves pleasure will become poor; whoever loves wine and oil will never be rich. Does this mean that we should have no pleasures? This would indeed stop people from believing in God. For **pleasure** is the characteristic of the ways of God (3:17). Should we not rejoice in our earthly comforts? God has provided us with everything for our enjoyment (1 Timothy 6:17). Yet, strange as it may seem, the way to enjoy **pleasure** is not to love it or to pursue it as if it is our goal in life. The person who gives his whole heart and all of his time to **pleasure** is on the road to becoming **poor.** As Rutherford observed, "Certainly the more a man drinks of the world, the more it intoxicates him." Our spiritual character is our glory. Personal holiness is indispensable to spiritual enjoyments. So always bear in mind how empty the pleasures of this world are.

18. The wicked become a ransom for the righteous, and the unfaithful for the upright. The **ransom** spoken about here is equivalent to a substitute (Psalm 49:7-8). Sometimes, for good reasons, God involves **the righteous** in the same judgment as **the wicked.** Sometimes the punishment of **the wicked** is the ordained way of averting calamity from a righteous nation (Joshua 7:24-26). Also often, in the Lord's retributive justice, **the wicked** are given over to the trouble they had planned for **the righteous** (compare 11:8). Sometimes God makes the enemies of the church fight among themselves as if they were a defeated nation. However poor the prospects of the church, we have no grounds to be faint and give up. So though the night may be dark, remember that the day is coming that will shine full of God's glory.

19. Better to live in a desert than with a quarrelsome and ill-tempered wife. Here is another (see verse 9), and perhaps even a stronger picture of the misery of domestic dissension! Let us remember that a choice made on the basis of beauty or intellect, with no reference to godliness, gives no promise of divine blessing or of individual happiness.

The matrimonial thorn in the flesh may be a necessary chastening that prevents us from being confident in ourselves (2 Corinthians 12:7). It is also an opportunity to exercise Christian grace. Hooker's meek endurance of the constant dripping (19:13) must have been seen by George Cranmer and others as a striking lesson on the influence of practical religion. Buxtorf quoted a Jewish saying: "How will a man prove his spirit? By enduring a bad wife." When Socrates was asked why he endured his wife, he replied, "By this means I have a schoolmaster at home, and an example how I should behave myself abroad. For I shall be the more quiet with others, being thus daily exercised and taught in the forbearing of her."

"The family," as Mr. Cecil rightly observes, "is sometimes a fierce fire. It is capable of becoming the most trying thing in the world to us." Yet much prayer and forbearance are required to avoid being upset by every trifle. This will keep us from being irritated needlessly. We must also bear in mind that we have divine support for all our heavy crosses. We also look forward with intense longing for the home of everlasting peace.

Here is a very serious question: Is it right to divorce or conveniently separate rather than endure and honor the cross? The supposition that it is **better to live in a desert** implies a worse alternative to living **with a quarrelsome and ill-tempered wife.** The latter was Job's lot, for he never divorced his wife. He lived with her even when she advised him to curse God (Job 2:9). "The devil," as M. Henry observed, "spared his wife to him, not only to be his tempter, but his tormentor." Enduring his matrimonial cross was part of the patience for which he was commended.

Our Lord restored the ordinance of marriage to its rightful place. He taught that there was only one ground for divorce and so excluded all other grounds (Matthew 5:32; 19:1-9). According to this rule an unfaithful wife can be put away because of sin, but **a quarrelsome and ill-tempered wife** should be endured as a cross.

20. In the house of the wise are stores of choice food and oil, but a foolish man devours all he has. The love of earthly treasure is the way to poverty (21:17). Yet we may thankfully enjoy it as the fruit of the Lord's blessing (10:22), for prudence is not worldliness. Further, indifference to impending trial is not faith but foolish simplicity (22:3).

Even the cottage of the godly poor often contains **stores of choice food and oil,** as they are the reward of Christian diligence. Yet poor indeed is the palace where the Bible with its stores of unsearchable riches is not the grand treasure and where the oil of gladness is not one's greatest comfort. Wherever this treasure is prized above everything else, we will find **the house of the wise,** whether it belongs to a prince or to a pauper. As Cecil, Queen Elizabeth's Secretary, said, on leaving Bernard Gilpin's house, "There dwells as much happiness as can be known on earth." We will never find such joy in the home of **a foolish man.**

21. He who pursues righteousness and love finds life, prosperity and honor. Holiness must be our way of life every day, as well as our religious duty. We are to pursue **righteousness,** not as a daily chore, but as a delight. It should flow from a heart filled with fearless **love.** "The will is in love with those charms that draw us to God. And as no man will complain that his temples are restrained and his head is a prisoner when it is encircled with a crown, so when the Son of God has made us free and has only subjected us to the service and dominion of the Spirit, we are as free as princes within the circle of their diadem. Our chains are bracelets, and the law is the law of freedom, and God's service is perfect freedom. So the better subjects we are, the more we reign as kings. The further we run, the easier the burden becomes. Christ's yoke is like feathers to a bird. They are not weights but the means for flight, and without them the body falls" (Bishop Taylor). We are to pursue this **righteousness** as our goal.

22. A wise man attacks the city of the mighty and pulls down the stronghold in which they trust. The art of war shows that wisdom is superior to strength (24:5-6). Prudent tactics, or the wise use of courage, triumphs over mere personal prowess. Joshua's strategy in taking Ai is an example of military wisdom (Joshua 8:3-22). Solomon seems to have known about **a wise man** who on his own delivered a city from the power of a mighty king.

So spiritual wisdom, a direct gift from God, overcomes formidable difficulties. Let us be like soldiers who are strong in the Lord and put on all of God's armor (Ephesians 6:10). The victory is assured. The **stronghold** will be pulled down.

23. He who guards his mouth and his tongue keeps himself from calamity. How frequently does the wise man remind us of the responsibility connected with the use of this little member (10:14; 12:13; 13:3; 14:3; 17:20; 18:6-7, 21). Yet as a test of the soundness or otherwise of our belief in God, we cannot have such exhortation in front of us too often (James 1:26). The soundness of the regenerate heart is nowhere more clearly seen than in its words. Conversely, the corruption of the heart may be the main source of evil; but its evil is dreadfully increased by the work of the lips. The **tongue** is the unbridled horse that brings his rider into jeopardy. If we open our mouth in a rash way and the **tongue** is allowed to speak as it wills, our neighbor will be harmed, and God will be dishonored.

How are we to avoid this? Walk closely with God. Cherish the tender spirit of his constraining obligations. Keep the **tongue** for his service. Ask for his grace at once, so you can both restrain it and use it.

24. The proud and arrogant man—"Mocker" is his name; he behaves with overweening pride. This is a vivid picture of Pharaoh, who in a **proud and arrogant** way asked who the Lord was that he should obey him (Exodus 5:2).

But this dreadful abomination may also be indulged in by God's own children. But God will not wink at their sin or spare his rod. The glory of their name will be darkened. They will see God's frown. Although Asa's heart was given over to God for most of his life, yet because of his sin, his sun went down in a cloud (1 Kings 15:14; 2 Chronicles 16:10-13). "For our God is a consuming fire" (Hebrews 12:29).

25-26. The sluggard's craving will be the death of him, because his hands refuse to work. All day long he craves for more, but the righteous give without sparing. We have often had the shame and wretchedness of the sluggard portrayed. Here is the final stroke. His **craving will be the death of him.** Where there is no effort, there will be no fruit. "What he longs for, he does not set his hand to gain. But he prefers to sit still and starve" (Bishop Hall). He lives by his wishes and not by working. "How can an object that stands at a fixed distance from its desire be procured by idle affections? Those affections must have life in them. Dead desires are deadly desires" (Dr. Reynold). Beware then of **the sluggard's** cry. His **craving,** instead of giving life, brings death in its wake. We must make use of all the means of grace. Sir Thomas More prayed the following excellent prayer: "Lord, make me to bestow pains in getting those things, for the obtaining of which I am used to pray to thee."

In order to continually serve the Lord, we must exercise faith. This is the spiritual power that God gave us to start with, and we must continue with it. Even if you are discouraged, or even if you become slothful, set your mind to praying that God will renew his strength in you. There is no time when the Lord will not give this to you. Consciously devote yourself to him. Make every necessary sacrifice. Seize every opportunity you have. For while the sluggard craves for himself, the righteous lives for God's church. He gives without sparing. He will be a blessing on the earth (Isaiah 19:24).

The following exhortations are well worth pondering. "Our heart is naturally distant from God. One single step will not bring us close to God. A few minutes of cold prayer are not enough to support our souls. Let us beware of laziness. We lose many hours and days on our road to heaven. These days soon become years, and we will be too late in the end for the marriage supper. We willingly exert ourselves to climb a mountain for the sake of the view at the top or for the pure air. Let us then use all our strength to climb the mountain of Zion, where we will breathe a truly vivifying atmosphere, and from whose heights we will behold the true Eden, the valley of peace, through which flow living waters, and where the tree of life flourishes. May the Lord bestow on us all the necessary will and energy!" (Felix Neff).

27. The sacrifice of the wicked is detestable—how much more so when brought with evil intent! This repeats a previous proverb (15:8) in an even more emphatic way. At no time, under no circumstances, can **the sacrifice of the wicked** be acceptable in God's sight. All the true requisites of holy worship are lacking. There is no heart. The worship is, therefore, only formality and hypocrisy (Matthew 15:7-9). There is no way of entering into God's presence. Therefore, all that kind of worship is full of self-righteousness.

How much more so when brought with evil intent! This makes the sin twice as bad. The mind that is dominated by the power of sin is like a pestilence that infests everything within its influence. And yet it sometimes *appears* that **the sacrifice of the wicked** is accepted. But the Lord sees into the center of men's hearts and never fails to punish them according to their motives.

28. A false witness will perish, and whoever listens to him will be destroyed forever. This is like rejoicing in iniquity rather than rejoicing in truth. Such **a false witness** will definitely be punished by God. And even "by man he will be confounded and silenced. No one in the future will take notice of or receive his testimony" (Poole).

29. A wicked man puts up a bold front, but an upright man gives thought to his ways. Here **a bold front**, which has no shame and does not blush in the presence of sin, is a dreadful manifestation of a hardened heart. Cain stood boldly in God's presence while his hands dripped with his brother's blood. The traitor had the effrontery to kiss the sacred cheeks of our Lord. What **a bold front** these evil men had! Their faces were implacably set to do evil. Truly "we have no stay and command of ourselves. So masterful are our wills and we are so headstrong that if God left us in our unruly nature, we would soon ruin ourselves" (Bishop Sanderson).

It is an encouragement to consider, in contrast to this, the tender spirit of the child of God. It is rest, indeed, to put ourselves in the Lord's hands, as we are fearful to take any step by ourselves. Godly simplicity greatly clears the eye of the soul. Where the heart is set on the duty, there is seldom any big difficulty in discovering the path. Here is the contrast: **A wicked man puts up a bold front** against God's ordinances, but **an upright man** is guided by them. Childlike confidence brings sunshine and acceptance, a brighter and more glorious privilege than the scepter of the universe.

30-31. There is no wisdom, no insight, no plan that can succeed against the LORD. The horse is made ready for the day of battle, but victory rests with the LORD. The history of the church proves the truth of these proverbs. "The decrees and counsels of God are firm and adamant; immovable, notwithstanding all human machinations. They can no more be resisted than the path of the sun" (Lavater). **Wisdom** and **insight** and man's best **plan,** when they are **against the LORD,** come to nothing. "They all signify nothing, if they oppose the counsels and decrees of heaven" (Bishop Patrick).

The horse may legitimately be used as a means of defense. But never let our confidence be in the material of warfare. Use the means, but do not idolize them. Those who put their trust in them will fall. Those who remember that their safety is in the Lord will stand upright. When it comes to spiritual warfare, it is even more important to exercise active faith and dependence on God. Salvation comes from the Lord. It is free, complete, and triumphant, an everlasting victory over all the powers of hell.

Proverbs
Chapter 22

1. A good name is more desirable than great riches; to be esteemed is better than silver or gold. What is this **good name** that is here said to be **more desirable than great riches**? It is not the name that the builders of the tower of Babel wanted to make for themselves. This **good name** is gained by godly consistency. Heathen understanding seemed to have some glimpses of this. Agesilaus, on being asked how a good name was to be obtained, replied, "By speaking the best, and doing the most upright things." To the same question Socrates answered, "By studying really to be what you wish to be accounted." The person who really does have this **good name** is either unconscious of the gift or is humbled by the conviction that it is wholly undeserved.

It is so valuable that it **is better than silver or gold.** Whereas **great riches** can fly away on eagles' wings (23:5), **a good name** will be remembered forever.

We must not overvalue man's estimation of our conduct. But, on the other hand, we must not indiscreetly underrate it. "I never thought," said the wise Sir M. Hale, "that reputation was the thing primarily to be looked after in the exercise of virtue (for that puts the substance for the shadow), but I looked at virtue and its worth as something to be desired, and reputation as a way to procure it."

Some, however, judge, "So long as my conscience is clear, I care not what the world thinks about me or says about me. Other people's consciences are not my judges." In resisting the efforts of the world to deflect us from our path of duty, "We may rightly comfort ourselves in our own innocency and flee for refuge from harmful words to our own consciences, as into a castle. There we can rest in safety, disregarding the reproaches of evil men" (Bishop Sanderson). But at the same time we should make great efforts to stop the mouths of those who make false accusations against us (1 Corinthians 4:3).

Yet as much as we want this, we must take care that it is not gained at the expense of conscience. It is far better that others should tarnish our name than that we should wound our consciences. "Two things there are," says St. Augustine, "about which everyone should be especially chary [vigilant] and tender: his conscience and his credit. But his conscience must be his first concern. His name and his credit must be content to come in the second place. Let him first be sure to guard his conscience well; then he may give attention to his name. Let his top priority be to secure everything inside him, by making peace with God and in his own heart. Once this is done, and not before this happens, he can look further afield if he wants to and strengthen his reputation with and before the world" (Bishop Sanderson).

While it is true that reputation and the affection of others are **more desirable than great riches,** we must not forget that they may be in themselves vanity and a snare. And since seeking them—or rather, when they are made into idols, the sin of a noble mind—is a weakness, more severe discipline is needed to preserve Christian simplicity and singleness. The only honor that is safe is that which comes from God.

2. Rich and poor have this in common: The LORD is the Maker of them all. There is great diversity in the circumstances of mankind. Yet the difference is mainly superficial, and the equality in all important matters is clear for all to see. The **rich and** the **poor,** apparently so remote from each other, have much **in common.** All are born into the world. All come into the world naked, helpless, unconscious beings. All stand before God. All are dependent on God for their birth. All are subject to the same sorrows, illnesses, and temptations. At the gate of the invisible world the distinction of riches and poverty is dropped.

We also all **have this in common:** We meet on the same level as sinners. All are tainted with the same original corruption. All are like sheep and have each gone astray (Isaiah 53:6). All need the same new birth to give them life. All need the same precious blood to cleanse them and the same robe of righteousness to cover them (Romans 3:21-22). In all these matters the **rich and poor** are as one.

3. A prudent man sees danger and takes refuge, but the simple keep going and suffer for it. A great part of wisdom is to see what God is doing or is about to do. When evil arrives, most men can see it. But **a prudent man sees danger** coming. This does not mean that God has given us knowledge about the future. This would only encourage us to be presumptuous. But God *has* given us prudence, so that we can see **danger.** If we know about the **danger,** that is the most effective way to escape from it. Even our divine Master acted in a prudent way (Mark 3:6-7) until his hour came (Matthew 26:46)

We can apply this to seeing spiritual dangers. Noah built his ark in order "to save his family" (Hebrews 11:7).

It is not that the **prudent man** has the gift of supernatural knowledge about the future. He only uses the discernment that God has given him. He takes notice of the signs of the times. He studies the Word of God in reference to God's coming judgments and acts accordingly. To walk carelessly in the middle of evil is reckless folly. We stand not by faith only, but by faith balanced with fear (Romans 11:20). Yet this is not the fear of slavery, but of care, watchfulness, and diligence (Hebrews 4:1, 11). Guilty, wandering, tempted, afflicted, dying as we are, prudence shows us our need of a **refuge**. Unless we seek one in time, we are lost in eternity. If we but realize the huge weight of guilt lying on us, can we rest in an unsheltered state? Would we not tread on everything that is in our way as we run to the shelter? There may be impending judgments. But let us set our face toward our hiding-place. God will look after us in danger. His own most loving voice points us to a shelter. "It is nature that teaches a wise man in fear to hide himself. But grace and faith teaches him where to hide. Where should the frightened child lay his head but in the arms of his heavenly Father? Where should a Christian lay himself but under the shadow of the wings of Christ his Savior?" (Hooker).

The simple act in a very different way. They are devoid of all prudence. They are unaware of any impending danger. So they fear nothing. They are absorbed in what they are doing and oblivious to the danger all around them. There are many who do not hear the distant thunder announcing the approaching storm. In their assumed security they laugh at those who are preparing for the evil day. Even when they are on the brink of destruction they continue to laugh, unless God sovereignly steps in.

4. Humility and the fear of the LORD bring wealth and honor and life. Who will then say that we serve God in vain (Malachi 3:14)? The enjoyment of **wealth and honor and life** belongs to those who serve God. But note the two characteristics of such people: **humility and the fear of the LORD.**

Humility is not mere meekness or modesty. While the latter is a lovely quality, it is not specifically a Christian grace. **Humility** is also not the servility of the hypocrite who is secretly seeking his own ends. It is easy to see genuine **humility**, as it will always be accompanied by **the fear of the LORD**. This **fear** is the blessed, holy reverence that only God's children experience. It represses presumption and establishes **humility**. An accurate understanding of who God is will always lay us in the lowest dust before him. Then **humility** is our greatest glory. The most humble is the most triumphant Christian. He may be depressed, but he is highly exalted. He has the **wealth** of grace and of glory. Nobody can deprive him of these.

5. In the paths of the wicked lie thorns and snares, but he who guards his soul stays far from them. This proverb teaches us that nothing stands in a man's way as much as his indulging his own unbridled will. The man who is most perversely bent on his own purposes is most likely to be thwarted in them. "He thinks to carry all before him, but this path is full of thorns and snares. His stubbornness causes him infinite perplexities, from which he can find no escape" (Bishop Hall).

Our happiness and safety lie in humble submission to the Lord. We should desire nothing but to do his will. We should fear nothing as much as being left to our own devices. This is how we are to guard our souls.

6. Train a child in the way he should go, and when he is old he will not turn from it. The hopes of at least two generations hang on this most important rule. Everything hangs on a child's training. Two paths beckon him. One path leads to ruin, the other to heaven. All training that is not based on the principles of the Bible must be harmful. To expand the mind without at the same time enlightening it is but to increase its power for evil. It would be far better to consign it to total ignorance, in that an uninstructed savage is less dangerous than a well-informed infidel.

Yet the religious training of **a child** must not be the edge of a garment that can easily be trimmed off. It must be the pervading substance of his life. Pray for your child. Teach your child to pray. Instruct him from childhood in the holy Scriptures as the sole rule of faith and way to behave.

If you do not give a child these principles, you leave him utterly helpless. And yet, all too often parents themselves have no established principles about how to educate children. They have children, and something has to be done about educating them, but the parents are ignorant about their own moral state and besetting evils. They are totally unable to **train** any children in God's ways. The child, therefore, becomes the victim of his parents' ignorance. The child concludes that greed is the only guide in life.

It was never more important than it is today that children be brought up by parents who teach the principles of the Scriptures. Otherwise later on in a child's life, when an attempt is made to set them right, we find that we are "building where there is no foundation, or rather where there is not even any ground to build on" (South). The primary object of a child's upbringing must be the salvation of his soul. But most people in the world deal with their children as if they were born only for this world, with nothing to look for after death. They totally ignore such questions as: How will this or that matter affect their soul? Their only thought is: They must be like everyone else if they are to make their way in the world. And so in all important matters parents educate them for time and not for eternity. We hardly need to point out that this is an education without God, without his promise, and without rest. The parents of such children, and the children of such parents, are both in need of compassion.

7. The rich rule over the poor, and the borrower is servant to the lender. Too often **the rich rule over the poor** in a harsh way. Indeed, without submitting to God's rule over us, we can hardly be trusted with power over our fellowmen. Man becomes alienated from his brother. He becomes the victim of the other's gratification, not the object of his sympathy. "Sell not your liberty to gratify your luxury" (Henry). If it is possible, owe nobody anything except love (Romans 13:8). "Guard against that poverty which is the result of carelessness or extravagance. Pray earnestly; work diligently. If you should become poor, bear poverty with patience. Throw yourself in childlike dependence on your God" (Geier).

8. He who sows wickedness reaps trouble, and the rod of his fury will be destroyed. Scripture often draws practical lessons from seedtime and harvest (Psalm 126:5-6; Hosea 10:12; Matthew 13:3, 24-30). They are linked together in the spiritual, as well as in the natural, world. The harvest is determined by the seed (Galatians 6:7-9). Every thought is a seed for eternity, resulting in a harvest of eternal joy or desperate sorrow. The wise man concentrates here on the latter. All experience and observation testify to the fact that the diligence of the ungodly sower can only end in **trouble** and in utter disappointment. But the harvest from God's seed is totally different. God's harvest brings an assured reward of everlasting joy. So we must sow generously (2 Corinthians 9:6, 9).

9. A generous man will himself be blessed, for he shares his food with the poor. Nehemiah, instead of using his own considerable power for his own ends, spent his wealth on feeding people at his own table. He is a good example of someone sharing **his food with the poor**. Nehemiah's work required a large heart, and God had given him such a heart. Every Christian must remember that God's standard is sacrifice, not convenience. We are only stewards of God's bounty. "Beneficence is the most exquisite luxury; and the good man is the genuine epicure" (Bishop Horne). As Luther put it, "One good work done for God will be seen to show more glory than the whole frame of heaven and earth." We must continue to be partners with God and reflect his image.

10. Drive out the mocker, and out goes strife; quarrels and insults are ended. Here is a word for rulers. **The mocker** stirs up **strife** in the church (3 John 10). He must be restrained. If restraint is to be effective, he must, if possible, be thrown out (Titus 3:10-11). He must not be argued with (Proverbs 26:4). We must have no dealings with him. We must openly rebuke him in case his influence upsets the faith of the simple. If God scorns the scorner, how can we but banish him from our fellowship? But if we do cast him out, we must not cast him off. Pray for him. Remember that you were once like him (1 Corinthians 6:11). While abhorring the sin, pity the sinner.

But what are we to do if we are unable to throw him out? He may be a husband or a child. We must at least object to what he is doing. Turn away from his mockery. This will mortify, if not silence, him. Turn from him to your God. This will bring peace. Honor your divine Master by enduring as he did, year after year, the opposition of sinful people (Hebrews 12:3).

Perhaps this meek and silent endurance, with a loving, bleeding heart, might have the power to throw out the scorning and to humble the mocker so he sits at the foot of the cross.

11. He who loves a pure heart and whose speech is gracious will have the king for his friend. Here **a pure heart** does not describe the natural but the renewed person. It is no external varnish, no affectation of holiness. It is sincerity, humility, turning from sin, conforming to God's image. Anyone who has attained this purity is before God's throne. He who **loves** this is God's child on earth. Such a person is welcomed by the King into his heavenly kingdom. As our Lord said, "Blessed are the pure in heart, for they will see God" (Matthew 5:8).

12. The eyes of the LORD keep watch over knowledge, but he frustrates the words of the unfaithful. In Scripture the phrase **the eyes of the LORD** often describes his searching omniscience (see 5:21 [KJV]; 15:3). Here it describes his fatherly care.

This proverb illustrates God's faithful watch over truth in the world. Indeed, it may be thought of as a prophecy that will be fulfilled at the end of time. For how wonderfully has the **knowledge** of God been preserved from age to age. All the malignant schemes to blot it out have been frustrated by God. The Scriptures, as the words of **knowledge,** have been preserved in a far more accurate state than any other book of comparable age. When the church herself supported the Arian heresy, the same watchful eye raised up the champion Athanasius. All **the words of the unfaithful** have been overthrown.

13. The sluggard says, "There is a lion outside!" or, "I will be murdered in the streets!" "This sentence belongs to those who flinch from the cross" (Melanchthon). Real difficulties in the way of heaven exercise faith. And these are far too great for those who have never counted the cost of following Christ. But indulging in sloth introduces imagined difficulties. **The sluggard** is a coward. He has no love for his work, and therefore he is always ready to invent some flimsy excuse that will prevent him from doing his duty. He shrinks back from any work that is likely to involve him in any trouble. Imagined dangers frighten him from real and present duties. **"There is a lion outside!" or, "I will be murdered in the streets!"** What absurd excuses! As if public **streets,** except in special cases, were the haunts of wild beasts. We need courage from God. We must stand equipped with all of God's armor (Ephesians 6:11, 13). We all need this. Each day, each hour we need to seek this, whether we are in the front line of the battle or are the most ordinary soldier of the cross.

14. The mouth of an adulteress is a deep pit; he who is under the LORD's wrath will fall into it. This dreadful temptation has often been touched on (2:16-19; 5:3; 6:24-29; 7:5; 9:16-18). But in a book that is intended especially for the young, who is to say that such a fresh warning is superfluous? Is it not the voice of mercy? For what but endless compassion could stand, as it were, on the edge of the **deep pit** and alert the unwary to the danger.

Adultery is indeed **a deep pit**. It is easy to fall into but hard, next to impossible, to get out of. For this sin overwhelms the body, the mind, and the conscience. There is no more humbling proof of the total depravity of human nature than the fact that those affections that were originally given for the purest enjoyments of life can become the corrupt spring of such a defilement. The sin and snare seem to be inflicted on those who willfully reject God. They have turned away from instruction; they have hated reproof; they have given themselves over to their wicked desires. They have clearly abandoned God. Must not God's holiness and justice be against those who deliberately choose evil and reject both God's warnings and love? They are **under the LORD's wrath**.

15. Folly is bound up in the heart of a child, but the rod of discipline will drive it far from him. What parent, what teacher will not agree that **folly is bound up in the heart of a child? Folly** is the birthright of everyone. Children show their inclination to evil even before they can speak. Augustine mentions a good example of the Fall. He describes how a baby, before it could speak, revealed on its face envy and anger toward another infant who was about to share his food. Augustine adds, referring to himself, "When, I beseech thee, oh, my God, in what places, when or where, was I innocent?" So education should begin in the cradle.

Note that what is being spoken about is foolishness, not childishness. "A child is to be punished," as Mr. Scott wisely observed, "not for being a child, but for being a wicked child." Comparative ignorance, the imperfect and gradual opening of the faculties, constitute the nature, not the sinfulness, of the child. As a holy child, Jesus increased in wisdom (Luke 2:52). But **folly** is the strong propensity toward evil. It imbibes wrong principles, forms bad habits, and joins in with ungodly company. It is the root and essence of sin in a fallen nature. It is the **folly** of being in revolt against a God of love.

16. He who oppresses the poor to increase his wealth and he who gives gifts to the rich—both come to poverty. These two ideas seem to contradict each other. But both of the people described are devoid of God's love and love for their brother. Both seek to please themselves. The one **who gives gifts to the rich** hopes to receive something in return. Both actions, paradoxical as it may seem, lead to the road of **poverty**. "Sin pays its servants very bad wages; for it gives the very reverse of what is promised. While the sin of oppression promises mountains of gold, it brings them poverty and ruin (Jeremiah 12:13-15). Injuries done to the poor are sorely resented by the God of mercy, who is the poor man's friend and will break in pieces his oppressor" (Lawson).

But if oppression is the road to poverty, is not generosity the way to **wealth**? This is so, if our actions are engaged in on behalf of God. But here the man is pretending to be generous, hoping for a huge reward, while at the same time he grinds the poor into the dust with impunity. To give **to the rich** is bad stewardship and does not serve the poor well. Oh, let the Christian always hear his Father's voice: "Walk before me; be perfect."

17-21. Pay attention and listen to the sayings of the wise; apply your heart to what I teach, for it is pleasing when you keep them in your heart and have all of them ready on your lips. So that your trust may be in the LORD, I teach you today, even you. Have I not written thirty sayings for you, sayings of counsel and knowledge, teaching you true and reliable words, so that you can give sound answers to him who sent you? Solomon changes his way of writing here. From chapter 10 he has mainly given aphorisms in an antithetical form, contrasting right and wrong principles with their respective results. Now his observations become more personal and are more closely linked to each other.

The wise man here shows the power and the use of the Word of God. He begins by telling his readers to pay attention to what he says. He was not talking about ordinary things but about the sayings of the wise.

Observe the attractiveness of wisdom. It is both pleasing and profitable. But worldly people do not understand how anything linked to religion can be pleasurable. For such people, religion spoils all their pleasure. But heart-religion always conveys vital happiness. The fruit comes from the tree of life and is sweeter than honey and the honeycomb.

Note also the link between the religion of the **heart** and of the **lips**. Our words should be "like a string of rich and precious pearls" (Diodati). For the lips of the righteous feed many people (10:21). We must never allow our mouths to attempt to speak wisdom until our hearts have been given over to meditation and understanding (Psalm 49:3).

But even the words of wisdom are powerless unless they are applied to us personally. Each person should separate himself from other people and be alone with God, under the clear, searching light of his Word. Let us not forget that the great purpose of this revelation is that we may be sure about eternal things. The Gospels themselves were written for this reason (Luke 1:1-4). Our confidence in the sure foundations of the Christian faith should not be shaken. This does not mean that we still need to know more in order to have faith. For we should always be humble enough to depend on God about what we do not know. Paley has given us a golden maxim of Christian philosophy in which he defines true and firm understanding to consist "in not suffering what we do know to be disturbed and shaken by what we do not know." We should never delay to have faith just because we have not solved all the 10,000 objections of a proud unbeliever. We know whom we have believed (2 Timothy 1:12), and we should continually support our weaker brethren.

22-23. Do not exploit the poor because they are poor and do not crush the needy in court, for the LORD will take up their case and will

plunder those who plunder them. Perhaps after so solemn an exhortation we might have expected something more important. Yet what can be more important than the law of love, and to rebuke those who break that law? Robbery and oppression, under any circumstances, break God's commandment (Exodus 20:15). But to exploit the **poor** because he is **poor** and so has no means of protection is a cowardly aggravation of the sin. To crush the needy in court perverts God's sacred authority that was given to protect **the needy.** God is most resisted in wronging those who cannot resist and defend themselves. "The threatenings of God against the robbers of the poor are sometimes laughed at by the rich and great. But they will find them in due time to be awful realities" (Lawson). "Weak though they [the poor] are, they have a strong one to take their part" (Sanderson). God will plead their case. And woe to the man against whom he pleads. The accumulation of divine vengeance is heaped upon this sin.

24-25. Do not make friends with a hot-tempered man, do not associate with one easily angered, or you may learn his ways and get yourself ensnared. Sin is contagious. Alas, our corrupt constitution predisposes us to receive it in any form in which it may be presented to us. The base passions of the **hot-tempered man** repel rather than attract. But sin never loses its infectious character.

Friendship blinds the eye. When there is no light in the mind, no true tenderness in the conscience, we see evil things done by those we love who have blunted sensibilities. Being **friends** of a **hot-tempered man** is like living in a house that is on fire. How quickly does a young person, living with a proud man, become like him and turn into an overbearing person. Evil **ways,** especially those that our temperaments incline toward, are more quickly learned than good ways. We learn to be angry more easily than to be meek. We pass on disease, not health. So it is a rule of self-preservation, no less than the rule of God, not to make **friends** with **hot-tempered** people.

26-27. Do not be a man who strikes hands in pledge or puts up security for debts; if you lack the means to pay, your very bed will be snatched from under you. Avoid being involved with not only the **hot-tempered,** but also with the imprudent. Do not put up **security for debts** without forethought. Repeated warnings have been given about this danger (11:15; 17:18). If you accept a bill on behalf of somebody else, it may be almost like signing a warrant for your own execution. The creditor may justly act against not the debtor, whom he knows is worth nothing, but you, because you have put up **security** for the debtor's debts. The wise man points out how rash such behavior is and that it will end up with you having your **bed** taken away from you as you sleep.

There is, however, so much danger of being overcautious and of indulging in selfishness under the cover of prudence that these warnings must be heeded thoughtfully.

28. Do not move an ancient boundary stone set up by your forefathers. Everyone has a right to what is his own. He must, therefore, have a way of knowing and securing his right. The **ancient boundary stone** was protected by the wise laws of Israel. God himself set the bounds to the respective parts of his own world, restricting each part within its proper limits. The **ancient boundary stone** stood as the witness and memorial of each man's rights, which had been **set up by** their **forefathers**. It was forbidden to remove it. Such action was a selfish and unjust invasion of property. This proverb also teaches us to respect well-established principles.

29. Do you see a man skilled in his work? He will serve before kings; he will not serve before obscure men. Here **a man skilled in his work** is one who is improving his talents all the time and is making the most of his opportunities. He is like Henry Martyn, who was known in his college "as the man who had not lost an hour." "Nobleness of condition is not essential . . . for nobleness of character. It is delightful to think that humble life may be just as rich in moral race and moral grandeur as the loftier places in society; that as true a dignity of principle may be earned by him who in homeliest drudgery plies his conscientious task as by him who stands entrusted with the fortunes of an empire" (Chalmers).

Diligence, even without godliness, is often the way to advance in the world. But when we serve the Lord, we will have the honor of standing before the King of kings. Our whole life should be spent so that we will hear his words, "Well done, good and faithful servant!" (Matthew 25:21-23).

Proverbs
Chapter 23

1-3. When you sit to dine with a ruler, note well what is before you, and put a knife to your throat if you are given to gluttony. Do not crave his delicacies, for that food is deceptive. God's Book tells us how to behave, not just what to believe. It gives directions about the details of our daily lives. Suppose we are invited to a meal with **a ruler**. We are given this wise warning: **Note well what is before you**. Think about where you are. What besetting temptation may attack you? What impression is your behavior likely to make? If your appetite is out of control, ungodly people may criticize you, and you may be a stumbling-block to the weak (1 Corinthians 8:9; Romans 14:21).

We ourselves are also in danger. The luxuries on the table may encourage us to overindulge our appetite. You may have to **put a knife to your throat**. That is, be stern with yourself. If an unbeliever can say, "I am greater and born to greater things than to be the servant of my body" (Seneca), is it not a shame for a Christian, born as he is, the heir of an everlasting crown, to be the slave of his carnal indulgences?

It is exceedingly dangerous to go to the limits of intemperance. "He who takes his full liberty in what he may, shall repent him" (Bishop Hall). "If I see any dish to tempt my palate, I fear a serpent in that apple and would please myself in a willful denial" (Bishop Hall). Temptation is hard to resist. So be on guard at your weakest point. "Curb your desires, though they be somewhat importunate, and you will find in time incredible benefit by it" (Bishop Sanderson). Pray the following prayer, for the first Sunday in Lent: "Grant unto us such abstinence, that our flesh being subdued unto the spirit, we may ever obey thy godly motions." To knowledge, add self-control (2 Peter 1:5-6).

4-5. Do not wear yourself out to get rich; have the wisdom to show restraint. Cast but a glance at riches, and they are gone, for they will surely sprout wings and fly off to the sky like an eagle. Here we are warned about covetousness. If **riches** come as a result of God's blessing, receive them thankfully, and consecrate them wisely and freely to him. But to **wear yourself out** trying to become **rich** is to follow earthly wisdom, not the **wisdom** from above.

We need to recall the intrinsic value of **riches**. Luther declared that "the whole Turkish empire in all its vastness was only a crust, which the great Father of the family cast to the dogs." The person who has devoted his every waking hour to amassing a fortune is often deprived of all his wealth at a stroke. In a moment his financial empire can crash as a result of divine judgment, laziness, extravagance, or theft. It is much wiser to lay up treasure in heaven (Matthew 6:20).

This is where the contrast lies. The world sees realities only in the objects before their eyes; the Christian only sees reality in invisible things. So, Christian, think about your heavenly birth, your eternal expectations. With this glory in mind, how dreadful it is to focus on everything that is passing (1 Corinthians 7:29-31). The philosopher Longin has remarked, "Nothing can be called great which to despise is great. Thus riches, honors, dignities, authorities, and whatever besides may have the outward pomp of this world's theater cannot be to a wise man preeminent blessings, since the contempt of them is a blessing of no mean order. Indeed, those who enjoy them are not so much entitled to admiration as those who can look down on them with a noble superiority of mind."

6-8. Do not eat the food of a stingy man, do not crave his delicacies; for he is the kind of man who is always thinking about the cost. "Eat and drink," he says to you, but his heart is not with you. You will vomit up the little you have eaten and will have wasted your compliments. It is best to decline an invitation to **eat** with **a stingy man** when his offer of friendship is a cloak for some selfish action. We do not judge him by his words, but by his heart. But there are no such dangers linked to the invitations of the Gospel. The table is ready, and the invitations have been sent out. The only qualification is our own hunger to accept the invitation and eat the heavenly food. Then we discover that our appetite increases with every mouthful we consume.

9. Do not speak to a fool, for he will scorn the wisdom of your words. Our Lord gave similar teaching when he spoke about not casting pearls before swine (Matthew 7:6). Don't throw away your good counsels on incorrigible sinners. But so long as there is any hope for reclaiming the **fool**, make every effort for his precious soul. In the spirit of our Master we must present the Gospel to the worst and most unwilling listeners. We must never allow prudence to be an excuse for laziness. But there is the right time to speak and the right time not to speak (Ecclesiastes 3:7).

10-11. Do not move an ancient boundary stone or encroach on the fields of the fatherless, for their Defender is strong; he will take up their case against you. The general prohibition against moving **an ancient**

boundary stone has already been given (22:28). Now a special warning and a specific reason for this is given. Many people who do not dare to touch the rich are quite prepared to oppress the poor. But **the fields of the fatherless** are under the Almighty's protection. As **the fatherless** are powerless, God will accuse anyone who wrongs them. So beware of being at the receiving end of divine vengeance.

12. Apply your heart to instruction and your ears to words of knowledge. This counsel is repeatedly given in the Book of Proverbs. This only goes to show how men rebel against divine **instruction** and how careless they are about paying attention **to words of knowledge.** The best-taught Christian and the most advanced Christian will be the most earnest in seeking more **instruction.** He will gladly sit at the feet of the Lord's ministers to hear the **words of knowledge.** This is where the value of the Bible lies, as the one source of **instruction** and the only storehouse of **words of knowledge.**

Observe the link between the **heart** and **ears.** The **heart** that is otherwise open to sound advice may be shut against Christ and his teaching. It may be closed up in unbelief, prejudice, indifference, and the love of pleasure. A listless **heart** can, therefore, produce a careless ear. But when the **heart** is graciously opened and enlightened, the **ears** instantly become attentive. Awakened spiritual desire brings prayer, and prayer brings blessing. And every work of knowledge is more precious than thousands of pieces of gold and silver (Psalm 119:72, 127).

13-14. Do not withhold discipline from a child; if you punish him with the rod, he will not die. Punish him with the rod and save his soul from death. Christian parents do not always recognize the scriptural standard of discipline. Parents, no less than children, are foolish. They, too, need correcting. The rule for parents concerning disciplining their children, notwithstanding all the pleas for pity, is: do not withhold it. Do it wisely, firmly, lovingly. Persevere with it, even when the results look unpromising. Link this discipline with prayer, faith, and careful instruction.

We agree that it is revolting to inflict pain and to make those we love tenderly, cry. But while our hearts are what our hearts are, it is not possible to train without discipline. If it is asked, will not a gentle approach be more effective? The reply is that if this had been God's wish, since he is a God of mercy, he would not have provided a different way.

But some parents use nothing but **discipline.** They indulge their own passions at the expense of their less guilty children. Unlike our heavenly Father, they willingly inflict pain on their children. They vent their own anger on them, and they are not really interested in subduing the sins of their children. We need to ask ourselves the question: "Am I about to discipline my child for his good?" An intemperate use of this scriptural ordinance brings discredit on its efficacy and sows the seed of much bitter fruit. Children become hardened under an iron rod. Sternness and severity close up their hearts. It is very dangerous to make our children afraid of us. "If parents," said a wise and godly father, "would not correct their children except in a prayerful frame of mind, when they can 'lift up their hands without wrath,' it would neither provoke God nor them" (Henry).

We must learn not to expect too much from our children. We must not be too depressed by their naughtiness. However, we must not overlook their sinful follies. We must not love them less, but more. And because we love them, we must not withhold, when needed, discipline from them. That would be more painful to us than to them. This is most humbling. For since the corrupt root produces the poisoned sap in the bud, what is it other than the correction of our own sin? "Lord, be pleased to strike with every stroke, that the rod of correction may be a rod of instruction" (Swinnock). "It is a rare soul," said Bishop Hall, "that can be kept in constant order without smarting remedies. I confess, mine cannot. How wild I would have run if the rod had not been over me! Every man can say he thanks God for his ease. For me, I bless God for my trouble."

15-16. My son, if your heart is wise, then my heart will be glad; my inmost being will rejoice when your lips speak what is right. The wise man now turns from parents and addresses himself most tenderly to children, perhaps to his own child. What Christian parent does not respond in this way? But would we be happy if our child was honored by this world because of his talent or wealth, if he lacked godliness? The spring of parental joy is the **wise . . . heart** of the child. His health, his comfort, his welfare are unimaginably dear to us. The love of our child's soul is the life and soul of parental love. None but a parent knows the heart of a parent. None but a Christian parent knows the yearning anxiety, the many tears and prayers for the soul of a beloved child.

17-18. Do not let your heart envy sinners, but always be zealous for the fear of the LORD. There is surely a future hope for you, and your hope will not be cut off. The Christian's **hope** is to be continually with God. God is to be our guide now, and after this life he will receive us into glory (Psalm 73:24). With this hope for the present and for the future, how can we possibly **envy sinners?** The Lord will show us the path of life, and we will have everlasting joy (Psalm 16:8-11). What more could we want? So our hearts, instead of **envy[ing] sinners**, should be full of compassion for them, for they have nothing to look forward to but death.

19-21. Listen, my son, and be wise, and keep your heart on the right path. Do not join those who drink too much wine or gorge themselves on meat, for drunkards and gluttons become poor, and drowsiness clothes them in rags. The repeated exhortations in the Book of Proverbs to **listen** remind us of our Lord's earnest and affectionate call to use our ears (Matthew 11:15; 13:9). They show the great importance of listening as the first step to becoming wise. For wisdom, no less than faith, comes from what is heard (Romans 10:17).

But this call especially warns against a besetting temptation. God's creatures abuse his gifts. **Wine** becomes the occasion of excess. Gluttonous eating degrades the soul and enslaves the body. We are warned not only not to be one of them, but not to **join** them. Can we be among lepers, figuratively speaking, without catching the disease? The best way to show love is not to sit down with them but to work for their conversion. And if this is not effective, then avoid them. Young people, remember, "Tinder is not better at receiving fire, or wax the impression of a seal, or paper ink, than youth to receive the impression of wickedness" (Greenhill). Do not think that the enemy wants even your present happiness. His malice holds out a poisoned bait. Poverty and shame are temporal fruits. But the eternal ruin of his deluded victims is his far more deadly design.

Noah, as a drunkard, and the Corinthian converts, polluting their sacred feast with drunkenness and gluttony, warn the man of God to "watch and pray" in case he himself is tempted (Matthew 26:41). Always combine these parental warnings with the principles of the Gospel. Do not walk as drunkards, but put on the Lord Jesus Christ (Romans 13:13-14).

22. Listen to your father, who gave you life, and do not despise your mother when she is old. "A thing comely and pleasant to see," says Bishop Hall, "and worthy of honor from the beholder, is a child understanding the eye of his parent." Scripture is full of beautiful examples for us to imitate. There is Isaac with Abraham, Jacob with both his parents, Joseph's deference to his elderly father, asking him to bless his children, Moses with his father-in-law, Ruth with her mother-in-law, and most of all, the Savior's tender care for his mother as he died in agony. Dr. Taylor's "godly exhortation to his son," as Foxe writes in his biography, "is worthy of all youth to be noted": "When thy mother is waxed old, forsake her not; but provide for her with thy power, and see that she lack nothing; for so will God bless thee, give thee long life upon earth, and prosperity, which I pray God to grant thee."

23-25. Buy the truth and do not sell it; get wisdom, discipline and understanding. The father of a righteous man has great joy; he who has a wise son delights in him. May your father and mother be glad; may she who gave you birth rejoice! This is the merchant who sold everything in order to buy the pearl of great price (Matthew 13:45-46). This is a gift from God that cannot be bought with money, no matter how much is offered (Isaiah 55:1). It is free, and it is precious. But this proverb says it is important to gain it at any cost. Let us first of all be satisfied that the seller is no deceiver. Are we sure that he is upright in his dealings? The Savior says that we should buy from him (Revelation 3:18). This settles the matter. If we do not really want the goods, we will not pay much attention to the proverb. For we only buy what we eagerly desire.

Note also that this purchase is of inestimable value. It is **the truth**, the only means of salvation, the only deliverance from sin, the only way of holiness. It is the one thing that is necessary (Luke 10:42). Put this blessing fully in your sights. We cannot be defrauded in such a purchase. It is cheap at any price. Those who love pleasure value highly the baubles of Vanity Fair. But Bunyan beautifully describes the pilgrims answering the sneering reproach. "What will you buy?" They lifted up their eyes to heaven and said, "We will buy the truth."

But like the seasoned merchant, we must buy the genuine article. Many counterfeits are offered for sale. We must measure everything by God's standard. What brings wisdom, instruction, and understanding is **the truth** of God.

26-28. My son, give me your heart and let your eyes keep to my ways, for a prostitute is a deep pit and a wayward wife is a narrow well. Like a bandit she lies in wait, and multiplies the unfaithful among men. Solomon now speaks in the name and person of divine Wisdom (see 1:20; 8:1). Who else could claim your heart? Jesus Christ has bought it with his own blood.

All the blessings of the Gospel are yours; but if you refuse them, you trample them under your feet. You live a life of rebellion against your best friend. This is cruel madness against your soul. If you live without Christ, you will die without hope, accursed, lost forever. The command is an invitation of love. Think about that. Think about how right, how reasonable, how attractive it is, how much it is beyond everything else. How much more than any other joy is the delight of giving your **heart** to the tender, compassionate love of your dying Savior! And then, having made him the object of your desires, be determined to be resolute in rejecting every temptation. "Our heart given, gives all the rest. This makes eyes, ears, tongue, hands, and all to be holy and special in God's sight" (Leighton). His Word will be our rule, his providence our interpreter. The **heart** will no longer be divided. The **eyes** will no longer wander.

Here also is our power to resist the strong seductions of the enemy (see 2:10-11, 16). God has my **heart**, and he will keep it. But as long as we live according to our sinful nature, we will die. But we will live if by the power of the Spirit we put to death the misdeeds of the body (Romans 8:13). In our new atmosphere of heavenly light, the mask falls off from the allurements of sin. The **prostitute** appears as frightening as a **deep pit** or a **narrow well**, from which it is impossible to escape. Mighty and strong men have fallen into it. "Samson broke the bonds of his enemies, but he could not break the bonds of his own lusts. He choked the lion, but he could not choke his own wanton love" (Ambrose). The temptress hides the danger while she lays in wait for the prey. Blessed be God if though the lusts of the body have destroyed their thousands and tens of thousands, we have, by giving our heart to our divine Lord, been enabled to abhor the temptation and to ascribe to our faithful God the glory of our deliverance.

29-35. Here is a drunkard looking at himself in the mirror. Let him see his own face. Let this be hung up in his own cottage. Hang it in the alehouse. Every sin brings its own sorrow. Wisdom's voice is: Avoid the allurements of sin. Often a seemingly harmless look leads into a fatal temptation.

Rarely does any sensual temptation come on its own. One evil desire prepares the way for another. The first step is sure to lead to further steps. Drunkenness opens the door for impurity.

Though we see the whole nature so depraved in taste, so steeped in pollution, we ask, is anything too hard for the Lord? May his name be praised for a full deliverance from the enslavement to sin—to all sins and to every individual sin—and even from the chains of this giant sin. The drunkard becomes sober, the unclean holy, the glutton temperate. The love of Christ overpowers the love of sin. Pleasures are then enjoyed without a sting, for no serpent or adder can live in his presence, and the newly planted principle transforms the whole man into the original likeness to God. See 1 John 3:9; 5:18.

Proverbs
Chapter 24

1-2. Do not envy wicked men, do not desire their company; for their hearts plot violence, and their lips talk about making trouble. This counsel has been given recently (23:17). But it is very difficult in the false glare of this world's glory to walk by faith as evidence of what is not seen. In the confined atmosphere of impatience and unbelief, the spirit that lives in us envies intensely (James 4:5). This evil spirit, if it does not bring the scandal of open sin, curses our blessings, withers our virtues, destroys our peace, clouds our confidence, and stains our Christian profession. The full cup in the house of evil men stirs up the desire to be with them. Take away the delusive veil and who would **envy** them? Let me only desire to be with the man of God. The Christian is the only person in the world who should be envied. The apparent blessings that **wicked men** receive are God's heavy curses. If we stand right with heaven, every cross is a blessing, and every blessing is a pledge of future happiness. If we are not in God's favor, all his benefits are judgments, and every judgment prepares the way for perdition.

3-6. Why should we envy the prosperity of the wicked? Even if they build **a house**, it cannot be **established** because it is built on iniquity. "It is only the snow-palace built in the winter, and melting away under the power of the summer's sun" (Geier). The wise woman builds her house on piety and prudence, which is a far more solid structure.

Heresy is restrained by conceding supreme authority to the Bible. Anyone who is not enlightened by divine truth has but a feeble grip on God's teaching as he imbibes evil opinions. Growth in spiritual, as distinct from speculative, knowledge will always be accompanied by growth in grace.

We should also note how God has laid the foundations of the spiritual **house**, shaped and framed the materials by his own divine **wisdom**, and **filled . . . its rooms . . . with rare and beautiful treasures.** "Oh, the transcendent glory," exclaimed Martyn, "of this temple of souls; living stones, perfect in all its parts, the purchase and work of God."

Another advantage of **wisdom** is that a wise man is strong. He has great power. Every view confirms Lord Bacon's far-famed aphorism that "knowledge is power." The discovery of the mechanical forces and the power of steam has increased the strength of machinery over 100 times. Intellectual **knowledge**, wisely applied, has immense moral ascendancy. It restrains the king from entering into foolish wars. The man of spiritual **knowledge** is a giant in **strength**. Conscious ignorance is the first principle of **knowledge**. "I am but a little child," said the wisest of men. This humility of wisdom was the foundation of establishing his kingdom. For the people who know their God will be strong.

7. Wisdom is too high for a fool; in the assembly at the gate he has nothing to say. The commendation of **wisdom** continues. The person who is richly endowed with **wisdom** comes with authority and speaks **at the gate** among the wise. The **fool**, destitute of **wisdom**, is barred from such an honor. The simple and diligent prove that the treasure is not really out of reach; but it **is too high for a fool**. His groveling mind can never rise to so lofty a matter. He has no understanding of it, no heart to desire it, no energy to hold it. Its holy spirituality is **too high** for his reach. Nobody seeks his counsel. His opinion, if given, is of no account. While he may have a babbling tongue in the street, **at the gate he has nothing to say.** He is totally unfit to give judgment in the presence of wise and judicious men. This is not the result of any natural defect, but the result of deliberate perverseness. His Lord had committed at least one talent to him, but he frittered it away and did not trade with it. Let **wisdom** be sought while it is still within reach, as it is so freely promised.

8-9. What a picture of human depravity is given here. We see its active working, its corrupt source, and its fearful end! Talent, imagination, and an active mind are so debased as to be all concentrated on Satan's own work.

The **plots** and the **schemes** of **evil** people are sinful. "But what guilt," it is asked, "can there be in a thought? It is but an idea; it is next to nothing. It can do nothing. A malicious thought does not hurt anyone. A covetous thought cannot rob. What guilt or danger belongs to such an insignificant being?" If it were left to us to judge man, all this might possibly be thought of as mere trifles. But as the thought is the source of the action, God judges the thoughts as well as the actions and holds us responsible for them. The smallest sin involves us in breaking the whole law (James 2:10-11).

10. If you falter in times of trouble, how small is your strength! May this word strengthen and encourage us. The marvel is that those who do not know where to look for a refuge when the storm is breaking over their heads do not always **falter**. Natural courage, or a deeper involvement in the world as a diversion from sorrow, may raise them above their troubles for a time, but it drives them further from God.

Every Christian's heart responds to the confession that he tends to **falter**. "The strongest and holiest saint on earth is subject to some qualms of fear" (Bishop Hall). This arises not from the greatness of the danger but from the weakness of his faith. Remember that when we seek **strength** from our own resources, when faith gives way to distrust, praise to complaining, hope to despondency, then we **falter in times of trouble**.

A Christian may be tired with his burden, but he will soon be at rest eternally in his Father's arms. He will never be called to a martyr's trial without a martyr's faith. "Be of good heart," said Ridley to his brother Latimer with a wonderfully cheerful look, running to him, embracing him, kissing him, "for God will either assuage the fury of the flame, or else strengthen us to abide it." The rod of punishment is the seal of everlasting love. The temporal cross comes from the same hand as his everlasting crown. "Never believe," Christian, "that your tender-hearted Savior, who knows the weakness of your constitution, will mix the cup of affliction with one drachma weight of poison" (Rutherford). Commit yourself daily to him, for his supply of grace is sufficient for you. So go forward, weak and strong at the same time—weak in order to be strong, strong in your weakness.

11-12. Imagine a fellow creature who is in imminent danger, as he is being **led away to death**. Excuses will always be at hand as to why we should pass over his sad condition. We excuse ourselves by saying, **"But we knew nothing about this."** But the true reason is, as Bishop Sanderson has stated, "We lack charity but abound in self-love. Our defect is seen by our reluctance to carry out our duties to our brethren, while we excel in excusing ourselves." But does not God, who knows the condition of every heart, know your brother's needs, the sorrow of his heart, and the grief that presses down his soul? Does he not view your excuse of ignorance as a cover for selfishness? In vain do you plead ignorance before the all-seeing God.

What should we say about such apathy? How do we respond to such sayings as, "We have no right to judge," "Am I my brother's keeper?" or "It is no concern of mine"? Would not many souls have started to move away from ruin if they had known about the danger they were in before it became too late? Other people may expect us to look after the bodies of our fellow creatures, but God commits their souls to our care.

13-14. Honey is the choice product of Canaan, eaten by its inhabitants and even by its children. It is **sweet to your taste**. "So when the spiritual senses are exercised, you will find the knowledge of wisdom unimaginably delightful to your soul" (Bishop Hall). The knowledge of Christ, without which we are helpless, makes us supremely happy.

15-16. The wise man breaks off his affectionate counsel to the children of God with a solemn warning to the wicked man. Should we exclude him from the circle of instruction? If he is left unconverted, it is his own guilt.

But if he is not warned, not instructed, we will be accused of neglecting to help him.

Hatred toward **the righteous** is deeply rooted in **wicked** men. They imagine, especially if they are in power, that they can tyrannize them with impunity. But remember that anyone who touches any of God's followers touches the apple of God's eye (Zechariah 2:8). So, poor, afflicted soul, take courage. Look your enemy in the face, and sing that although you may fall you will rise again. Many trials cannot overwhelm **the righteous**. But one trial is enough to sweep away **the wicked**. He is **brought down by calamity**. And he does not recover. He lies where he falls, and he perishes where he lies. Yet, sinner, whatever your wickedness is, the Lord can save you from the millstone of condemnation for the persecuting of God's saints.

The just man rising again from his fall is wrongly applied to the perseverance of the saints. The word "fall" often appears in the Book of Proverbs, but always in reference to trouble, not to sin (11:5 [KJV], 14; 13:17; 17:20; 26:27). The antithesis obviously fixes the meaning. "There are plain texts enough to prove every scriptural doctrine. But pressing texts into any particular service, contrary to their plain meaning, not only serves to deceive the inconsiderate but to rivet the prejudices and confirm the suspicions of those who oppose the teaching. Just as bringing forward a few witnesses of suspicious character would cause all those, however deserving of credit, who should be examined in the same cause to be suspected also and create a prejudice against them in the middle of the court and of all present" (Scott).

17-18. Do not gloat when your enemy falls; when he stumbles, do not let your heart rejoice, or the LORD will see and disapprove and turn his wrath away from him. But did not God's chosen people rejoice with divine exultation when their enemies fell at the Red Sea? No; this joy was due to the triumph of the righteous. It adored heaven at the manifestation of God's glory. But how different this sublime sympathy is in the triumph of the church from the malignant joy of private revenge! A secret, if not an avowed, pleasure in the fall of an **enemy** is natural. But what has grace done for us if it has not overcome nature by a holier and happier principle?

19-20. This fretting must be a deep-rooted disease to need such repeated discipline (verse 1; 23:17). One moment's recollection of our mercies might show how little reason there is for it. Mercies infinitely more than we discover might be sufficient to sweep the clouds from our sky and make us ashamed of our despondency.

We are reminded that **the evil man has no future hope**. Leave him to his judge. His **lamp**, despite all his efforts to keep it burning, **will be snuffed out**. Sometimes people are bold enough to snuff out their own candle. "I give," said the godless Hobbes, "my body to the dust, and my soul to the Great Perhaps. I am going to take a leap in the dark." Alas, was it not a leap into darkness forever?

Take then the balance of eternity. Learn neither to overvalue the fancied sunshine of the wicked, nor to undervalue our own real happiness. **Do not . . . be envious of the wicked.** "His candle burns, his prosperity flourishes, until it has kindled hellfire, and then it is extinguished; whereas the lamp of the godly is put out here to shine as a star in heaven" (Jermin).

21-22. We have here another affectionate exhortation to **fear the LORD** (see 23:17). And no wonder! Is this not the substance of our holiness and our happiness? Oh, reverence his majesty. Acknowledge your dependence on him. Be as careful in walking before him in your secret thoughts as in your outward behavior.

The link between the fear of **the LORD** and **the king** is not accidental. Our Lord and his apostles have thus linked together the throne of his supremacy in heaven and the throne of his majesty on earth (Matthew 22:21; 1 Peter 2:17). The one principle indeed is the spring of the other. Disloyalty has often been a libel on godliness. But the Christian is loyal because he is godly. Yet there is no doubt about which is the primary obligation. Solomon "puts God before the king, because God is to be served in the first place, and our obedience is to be given to the king only in subordination to God, and not in those things that are contrary to the will of God" (Poole).

Man's independence, however, naturally kicks against submission. Men love change for the sake of change. To become leaders of a party, they disturb the public peace by proposing changes, without any promise of solid advantage. "He who goes about," says our judicious Hooker, "to persuade men that they are not so well governed as they ought to be shall never lack attention and favorable hearers." Beware of the destruction that **the LORD and the king** may inflict on those who despise their authority.

23-26. Here we have a solemn exhortation to the people, words of **the wise.** It is important that truth, not favor, be considered. To do otherwise is an evil in the church as much as in the state. No responsibility is more momentous in our sacred high places than to do nothing from **partiality.** "Reverence and awe unto the prelates, whom Christ has placed in seats of higher authority over me" suggests that "the ancient canon be especially remembered, which forbids a bishop to be led by human affection in bestowing the things of God" (Hooker). Man, corrupt as he is, often abhors unrighteous judgment. A bad magistrate deprives us of the blessing of good laws.

On the other hand, there is no greater national blessing than a government that rebukes the wicked. But we are not rulers. Yet are not many of us in authority, as parents, heads of families, teachers, and guardians of the young? Uprightness and consistency alone can maintain that influence so essential to usefulness. For a spiritual ruler's saying that **the guilty** are **innocent** is a cruel deceit to immortal souls. It hides the ruin that God is bound to reveal. It acts the part of a minister of Satan under the cover of a minister of Christ. Even the people who hate both his Master and his message will kiss the lips of a person who gives **an honest answer**, a reluctant but honorable witness to his faithfulness.

27. Finish your outdoor work and get your fields ready; after that, build your house. This prudent rule applies to all worldly matters. Religion, so far from forbidding, inculcates care and forethought. Much inconvenience and suffering flow from its neglect. Acting on this useful direction, the wise builder first finishes his **outdoor work**. He collects his materials and then shapes them and so builds his **house**. Preparations for Solomon's magnificent temple were made before his house was built. The spiritual house is similarly made of materials that have been prepared and fitted and so grow into a holy temple in the Lord (Ephesians 2:21-22).

But ponder well the care with which the great work should be finished. Lay deep foundations on the Rock. Pray all the time for divine strength. Avoid that outward display that brings shame on the thoughtless builder, who starts to build without making adequate preparations. Build your spiritual house so that it honors God and is of service to his church.

28-29. The welfare of society may sometimes constrain a witness to **testify against** his **neighbor**, but this must never be **without cause**. Yet when compelled to this unpleasant duty, whatever the temptation or consequence is, do not **use your lips to deceive**. Speak plainly, truthfully, the whole truth.

Profit is the bait to the thief, lust to the adulterer, revenge to the murderer. But it is difficult to say what advantage the witness gains from testifying against his **neighbor**. The allurement of this sin is the same as Satan himself feels—that is, the love of sin for its own sake.

As for indulging in personal resentment, it is natural to say, **"I'll do to him as he has done to me; I'll pay that man back for what he did."** But do we dare to take the sword from God's hands and place ourselves on his tribunal? Vengeance belongs to the Lord. "Let wisdom and grace be set to work to extinguish the fire from hell, before it gets ahead" (Matthew Henry). Far sweeter will be the recollection of injuries forgotten than those we have taken revenge for. But grace alone can enable us to forgive from the heart. "The excellency of the duty laid down in Matthew 18:35 is sufficiently proclaimed by the difficulty of the practice. For how hard is it, when the passions are high, and the sense of injury strong, and the way of revenge possible, for a man to deny himself in that luscious morsel of revenge! To do violence to himself instead of doing it to his enemy!" (South). And yet too often the exercise of this duty is so feebly cherished that natural feelings gain the ascendancy. But the wise man sets out in this Book of Proverbs the true rule, which is enforced by the divine example. Humility and tenderness mark the self-knowing Christian, who forgives himself little, his neighbor much.

30-34. Everything around us is a useful lesson to an observant eye.

Every particle of creation may be taxed to furnish its quota to our store of knowledge. We can extract good even from evil and gather grapes from thornbushes. Solomon describes with his usual descriptive style a sight that we have all seen: **the field of the sluggard . . . thorns had come up everywhere, the ground was covered with weeds, and the stone wall was in ruins.** Instead of turning away, Solomon **applied** his **heart to what** he **observed and learned a lesson from what** he **saw.** In the solemn contemplation of this picture of desolation, he could not but turn his thoughts to the wretched owner. He imagined him in his house, stretched out on his bed, and crying out under the noonday sun, **A little sleep, a little slumber, a little folding of the hands to rest.** Stimulated by this effusion of the torpid animal, the response almost unconsciously forced itself: **and poverty will come on you like a bandit and scarcity like an armed man.**

And yet by some strange delusion **the sluggard** thinks of himself as being wise (26:16)! But let us look at the spiritual **sluggard.** If a neglected field is a melancholy sight, what is a neglected soul! Such a soul, when it is left to its own barrenness, instead of being sown with the seeds of grace becomes overgrown with **thorns** and nettles. Time, talents, and opportunities have been given. But the soul sleeps on and shuts both eyes and ears to everything that may disturb his slumber. Everything ends up in devastation and ruin.

Christian, is there no danger of this evil creeping into our religion? No habit is so ruinous. It enervates, and at length stops, the voice of prayer. It hinders the active energy of meditation. It weakens the influence of watchfulness. The way to heaven is steep, rough, hard to climb, immeasurably long, full of toil. Such a false apprehension checks every step of progress. So, instead of the soul being a well-watered garden, it relapses into its former wilderness state. It is laid open to every temptation and all too often is ultimately a prey to sensual appetites.

Look forward, not backwards. Do not complain, but make decisions. Do not only pray, but work. Always link privilege with practice. Prove the principles of moral character as well.

Proverbs
Chapter 25

1. These are more proverbs of Solomon, copied by the men of Hezekiah king of Judah. This seems to be a third division of this sacred book. The selection was probably made from the 3,000 proverbs that Solomon spoke (1 Kings 4:32). The New Testament fully authenticates this section of the book as a part of the inspired canon (compare verses 6-7 with Luke 14:7-10; verses 21-22 with Romans 12:20; 26:11 with 2 Peter 2:22; 27:1 with James 4:14). We are not reading, therefore, the maxims of the wisest of men; the voice from heaven proclaims that these are the true sayings of God.

The Holy Spirit mentions not only the author, but the men who **copied** these proverbs. Often good service has been done to the church not only by original writers, but by those who have **copied** and brought their writings into wider circulation. The world usually honors only the grand instruments and casts the humbler agencies into the shade. But God honors not only the primary but the subordinate instruments—not only the five, but the two talents, faithfully laid out for him. The blessing is not promised on account of their number, but on account of how they are used.

2-3. The great King of heaven and the puny **kings** of earth are here contrasted. **The glory** of each is compared. **It is the glory of God to conceal a matter; to search out a matter is the glory of kings.**

What **glory** indeed belongs to a God whose name and ways and works are open to the view and within the comprehension of worms of the earth. What he has brought to light only shows how much he has concealed. We adore the glorious concealment of his great work of forgiveness, of which Dr. Owen most truly remarks, "Were it not somewhat beyond what men could imagine, no flesh could be saved." This is so far from our sight that no human can comprehend the extent of this vast work.

God educates his children in mystery so that he may exercise them in the life of faith (John 13:7). We are to act and live on incomprehensible objects. We are to come to God's revelation without any mind or will of

225

our own. But is not this shade of mystery our highest joy, as the dwelling-place of our adorable God and Savior? Are not the clouds of his conceal-ment the effulgence of his glory as the most simple, yet the most incomprehensible Being, whom the mightiest intellect can never totally understand? "As there is," says Bishop Hall, "a foolish wisdom, so there is a wise ignorance. I would fain know all that I need, and all that I may. I leave God's secrets to himself. It is happy for me that God makes me of his court, though not of his council. O Lord, let me be blessed with the knowledge of what you have revealed. Let me content myself to adore your divine wisdom in what you have not revealed."

4-5. This is political wisdom in scriptural principles. If righteousness exalts a nation, the open acknowledgment of it is the sure path to national prosperity. And will not the **throne** of our great King **be established** by the complete and eternal removal of **the wicked**? In the great day of trial and decision, shall I be found reprobate or purified silver? *Lord, let me, under the Refiner's hand, be purified, that I may offer to the Lord an offering in righteousness.*

6-7. Our Lord applies this proverb more generally (Luke 14:8-11). Who does not need this caution against ambition? Loving to be preeminent is the bane of godliness in the church. Let each of us set about the work of throwing down our high tower of conceit. We must cultivate a deep sense of our own unworthiness. Think of Christ who made himself the most humble of men.

8-10. Dissension under any circumstances is a serious evil. The consid-erate Christian will concede his rights rather than insist on them to the detriment of his own soul and to the injury of the church (1 Corinthians 6:1-7). Many unholy arguments would be restrained by the practice of these rules of wisdom and love. Obviously the person most at fault should give way. But if, as is usually the case, he is too unreasonable to do so, let us by a generous and self-forgetting kindness deny ourselves the pleasure of a triumph instead of standing on punctilious forms or waiting for an acknowledgment from the offender. And if we find it easier to talk about our neighbor's faults to others than wisely and prayerfully to tell him about them alone, we must ask for self-discipline and for the mind of Christ (Colossians 3:15).

11-12. This alludes to special baskets in which fruit was displayed and served. The beauty of the basket sets off the fruit with additional charm. In the same way a lovely medium enhances the attractiveness of truth.

In our everyday meetings with people, much depends not only on the **word . . . spoken,** but on the occasion and spirit in which it is said. We must not only do good, but do good at the most appropriate moment. In times of affliction **a word aptly spoken** might be like the coming of our gracious Lord to the soul, which is like rain on mown grass. The plow enters most effectually when the earth is softened. The **apples of gold** in their beautiful **settings** evidently imply good sense and good taste for good things.

13. Like the coolness of snow at harvest time is a trustworthy messenger to those who send him; he refreshes the spirit of his masters. We know that **snow** is unseasonable **at harvest time.** But **the coolness of snow** would be most refreshing to the parched and fainting reapers. It is in this sense that **a trustworthy messenger refreshes the spirit of his masters.** Eliezer did this when "he returned with a true account and speedy dispatch of the important affair committed to him" (Poole). The apostle Paul often acknowledged this refreshment to his anxious spirit when he was burdened with all the care of the churches (1 Corinthians 16:17-18; Philippians 2:25-30; 1 Thessalonians 3:1-7). And may we not with reverence mark even God himself condescending to receive refreshment through the agency of his faithful messengers?

14. Like clouds and wind without rain is a man who boasts of gifts he does not give. The previous proverb described an invaluable blessing. This proverb notes a destructive curse. Imagine a drought, as in the days of Elijah, that threatens to make the land desolate; and then a heavy cloud, apparently full of fruitful blessings, passes overhead, but it produces no **rain.** This is an accurate picture of a man who **boasts.** He is rich in promises but performs nothing. If it is bad to promise and deceive, it is far worse to promise with the intention to deceive. This was the very character of the Great Deceiver. Did he not, with a presumption that hell itself might almost be ashamed of, boast about **gifts he** did **not give** when he offered the world to his own Maker as a temptation to the vilest blasphemy (Matthew 4:8-10)?

How sad to find this character in those who stand in the place of God. The church has always been chastened by the presence of false teachers who minister delusion instead of instruction. Oh, let those who bear the Lord's message take heed that they do not corrupt the Word of God but speak of Christ, as in God's sight.

15. Through patience a ruler can be persuaded, and a gentle tongue can break a bone. The wise man had previously given a general rule for gentleness (15:1). Here he takes an extreme case and shows its power with **a ruler,** whose unrestrained anger may rise to immediate revenge. Yet submission and **patience** are strong and persuasive.

The general principle is most instructive. The **gentle tongue** breaking **a bone** might seem to be a paradox. But it is a fine illustration of the power of gentleness above hardness and irritation. Apply it to those who are set against truth. Gentleness is full of power and energy. Indeed, "among all the graces that adorn the Christian soul like so many jewels of various colors and lusters against the day of her espousals to the Lamb of God, there is not one more brilliant than that of patience" (Bishop Horne).

16. If you find honey, eat just enough—too much of it, and you will

vomit. Solomon had previously invited us to **eat honey** (24:13). Here, however, he imposes a restraint. The old proverb about "too much of a good thing" applies. **Eat just enough.** Then it is sweet. Beyond that it is nauseating. Cultivate in all things the wisdom of moderation, a thankful but temperate enjoyment of our earthly blessings (1 Timothy 4:4).

Remember that our affections can never safely flow out to any object unless they are primarily fixed on God. "Then we may be sure not to offend, either in the object or measure. No man can in God love whom he should not; nor immediately love whom he would. This holy respect does both direct and limit him and shuts up his delights in the conscience of a lawful fruition" (Bishop Hall). In earthly pleasure, however, we can never forget how slight the boundary line is between the lawful and the forbidden path. Sin and danger begin on the extremity of virtue. For does not the legitimate indulgence of appetite to its utmost point bring us to the brink and often hurry us to the allowance of gluttony?

But in eating the real **honey** of the Gospel there is no danger of excess. Never shall we know satiety in this delight. The increasing desire will be fully satisfied only in eternity. "O God, let me but taste and see how sweet the Lord Jesus is in all his gracious promises; in all his merciful and real performances. I shall desire no more to make me happy. This is not the honey whereof I am bidden not to eat too much. No, Lord, I can never eat enough of this heavenly honey. Here I cannot surfeit; if I could, this surfeit would be my health" (Bishop Hall).

17. Seldom set foot in your neighbor's house—too much of you, and he will hate you. No code of laws enters, as the Bible does, into minute regulations about the courtesies of life. Yet surely we do not mar the sanctity of religion by spreading it over the face of human society. Daily life is evangelized by the pervading influence of Christian religion's wholesome principles. This rule illustrates one of our own proverbs: "Familiarity breeds contempt." It is safer to err on the side of reserve than to incur contempt by the opposite mistake.

Blessed be God, there is no need of this caution and reserve in our approach to him. Once acquainted with the way of access, there is no wall of separation. Our earthly friend may be pressed too far; kindness may be worn out by frequent use. But never can we come to our heavenly Friend unseasonably.

18. Like a club or a sword or a sharp arrow is the man who gives false testimony against his neighbor. We know that **false testimony** is universally condemned. But where except in the Word of God are its true character and deep aggravation of guilt adequately set forth? What a picture there is here of cruelty and malice. The tongue becomes the weapon of death. Open perjury, like **a sword or a sharp arrow**, pierces the fountain of life. And little better are those calumnies and unkind insinuations, all breaches of love, uttered so freely in common conversation. "Consider, you who indulge in such conversation, whether you care about those you gossip about. Do you think that you act as Jael did with Sisera, or Joab did with Abner? Would you shrink with horror at the thought of beating out your neighbor's brains with a hammer, or of killing a person with a sword or a sharp arrow? Why then do you indulge in a similar barbarity? Why do you seek to destroy others' reputation, which is as dear to men as their life, and so wound all their best interests by mangling their character?" (Lawson).

19. Like a bad tooth or a lame foot is reliance on the unfaithful in times of trouble. We know that **a bad tooth** and **a lame foot** are not only useless for their respective offices but are sources of pain and uneasiness. So are **the unfaithful in times of trouble.** The world abounds with instances of this disappointment. But though many may be **unfaithful,** God is true. Who ever trusted in him and was confounded?

20. Like one who takes away a garment on a cold day, or like vinegar poured on soda, is one who sings songs to a heavy heart. What could be more inhuman than to take away **a garment on a cold day** from a poor man? Such an act of cruelty was forbidden by the God of the poor (Deuteronomy 24:12, 17). Again, what could be more inappropriate than to pour **vinegar on soda?** All that would happen is that it would dissolve it. The **soda** of Scripture is not the salt that commonly goes by the name, but a **soda** or mineral alkali (the Roman *natrum*) that strongly ferments with all acids. Dr. Blayney remarks on Jeremiah 2:22, the only other example of the word, "In many parts of Asia it is called soap-earth, because it is dissolved in water and used like soap in washing." It would be just as inappropriate to sing **songs to a heavy heart.** Though no unkindness is intended, inconsiderate levity or even excessive cheerfulness is like a sword in the bones. The tenderness that shows a brother's tears, knows how to weep with those who weep, and directs the mourner to the mourner's friend and God—this is Christian sympathy, a precious balm for the broken heart.

21-22. In which heathen code of morals would we find this perfection of love? Every system gives way to selfishness. None of them go beyond loving those who love us, to which the true Lawgiver asks, "What reward will you get?" (Matthew 5:46-47). The corrupt Jewish teachers did not rise to this sublime standard. "They did not, it seems, perceive anything to be disapproved in hatred, more than in goodwill. And according to their system of morals, 'our enemy' was the proper natural object of one of these passions, as 'our neighbor' was of the other" (Bishop Butler). They could not come up to the law, and therefore, perverting the rule of justice to authorize private revenge, they brought the law down to their own level.

The agreement between Old Testament and New Testament teaching is complete. Both were given by the same Holy Spirit. Each stamps the other with divine authority. "The law of love is not expounded more spiritually in any single precept, either of Christ or his apostles, than in this exhortation" (Scott). We need not, therefore, disparage one system in order to exalt the other.

We are not bound to trust our enemies, but we are bound to forgive them. And yet too often our love for them only stops us from quarreling with them. "Love is of too substantial a nature to be made up of mere negatives, and withal too operative to terminate in bare desires" (South). If we do not **give him food to eat**, and **if he is thirsty**, but we do not **give him water to drink**, our claim to love our neighbor is mere self-delusion. No man ever conquered his enemy's heart by revenge, but many have by love.

23. As a north wind brings rain, so a sly tongue brings angry looks. The **tongue** wounds four people at one stroke. The person harms himself, the object of his attack, anyone who listens to his words, and the name of God. Flee from this deadly disease. Keep your ears as well as your mouth from this poison.

24. Better to live on a corner of the roof than share a house with a quarrelsome wife. This proverb has been given before (21:9). Scriptural repetitions show the deep importance of the matter laid out. Christian woman, do not think these proverbs are unworthy of your attention. Be sure you do not fit the description of this dreadful picture. And surely the repeated exhibition strongly inculcates the cultivation of the opposite graces, the absence of which clouds the female character in painful deformity.

25. Like cold water to a weary soul is good news from a distant land. Solomon had previously spoken about the refreshment that the messenger brings; here he speaks of the message, the **good news**. Reader, if your light, vain heart has ever leaped within you at the news of some earthly advantage, have you heard and welcomed the Gospel as **good news from a distant land**? Do you know your need, that you are in danger of perishing? Then what refreshment can compare with the good news brought from heaven that to you a Savior was born?

26. Like a muddied spring or a polluted well is a righteous man who gives way to the wicked. Eastern springs and wells, where the rains were only seasonal, were greatly valued. The **well** is, therefore, a blessing or a curse, depending on the purity or the impurity of the waters.

When a minister of Christ apostatizes from the faith, and mournfully frequent have been such spectacles, or compromises his principles from the fear of men, the **well** of truth is **polluted**. In this way Satan uses God's people more effectively than he does his own followers. The gross wickedness of the ungodly passes in silence. But Satan makes the neighborhood ring with the failings of those who profess to be Christians.

27. It is not good to eat too much honey, nor is it honorable to seek one's own honor. We know **honey** is good, in moderation (24:13). **It is not good to eat too much honey** (compare 25:16). A man's own name and reputation is **honey** to him. Let him preserve it carefully. Yet there is danger in seeking fame and even the good name of one's church rather than godliness. Few ministers have not been severely exercised in this. They are tempted to cherish the desire for public approbation rather than to be content with unnoticed fruitfulness. It is most welcome to recall that what men esteem highly is detested in God's sight (Luke 16:15).

28. Like a city whose walls are broken down is a man who lacks self-control. A previous proverb declared, **Better a patient man than a warrior, a man who controls his temper than one who takes a city** (16:32). Certainly the noblest conquests are gained or lost over ourselves. The first outbreak of anger resulted in murder. A king's lack of watchfulness about lust resulted in adultery.

Many examples of this moral weakness are less shameful and yet scarcely less harmful to the soul. Every sign of irritation, every spark of pride burning in the heart, long before it shows itself in the countenance or on the tongue, must be firmly resisted. A man may talk about **self-control** as if the reins are in his own hands. But he who has been born of the Spirit and who has been taught about the plague that is in his own heart knows that effective **self-control** is a divine grace, and not a natural power.

So what should we do? Upon the first assault fortify the walls by prayer. Do not place your trust in the strength of the citadel. Have not repeated defeats taught us the need to call on better strength than our own? How could we enter into the conflict, much less win the fight, but for the promise that sin will not rule us (Romans 6:14). Oh, for the simple faith to draw out from this mighty source energy, perseverance, and triumphant victory!

Proverbs
Chapter 26

1. Like snow in summer or rain in harvest, honor is not fitting for a fool. The richest blessings lose their value when bestowed unsuitably. **Snow** is a beautiful wintry covering of the earth, preserving the seed from the killing cold. But **in summer** it is out of season. **Rain** in its season is a fruitful blessing. But **in harvest** it is an unsuitable interruption to the reaper's work, and often a public calamity. Just so, **honor** unsuitably bestowed on **a fool . . . is not fitting.** "He neither deserves it, nor knows how to use it" (Poole).

We must learn then to adorn our Christian profession with consistency. We must seek that heavenly wisdom that will make us worthy of any honor that may be given to us. For he who is faithful in very little can be trusted with a great deal (Luke 16:10).

2. Like a fluttering sparrow or a darting swallow, an undeserved curse does not come to rest. Groundless fears are real evils and often press heavily on weak minds. An unprovoked and **undeserved curse** flies out of an angry mouth. "What if it should come to pass?" But we need no more fear the **undeserved curse** than the birds flying over our heads. The **darting swallow** flies up and down but never alights on us. It is like that with **an undeserved curse.**

But if the **curse** is deserved, it will **come.** And, reader, if you are an unconverted, unbelieving sinner, without love for your Savior, you are rightly cursed. So take refuge in him while you have time.

3. A whip for the horse, a halter for the donkey, and a rod for the backs of fools! This proverb turns our ideas upside-down. We would have said, "a halter for the horse, a whip for the donkey." But the Eastern donkeys are a very superior race, both in beauty and spirit, and are valued by their owners. The **halter** is needed to curb and guide them, while **the horse,** perhaps badly broken in, may need **a whip.** Every creature subdued for the service of man needs his appropriate discipline. The Lord guides his children with his eye. But let them cultivate a pliable spirit. However, the fool does not hear the voice or see the directing eye. He will be ruled neither by reason nor persuasion.

Discipline is the most probing test. What is its fruit? In the child submission and tenderness. In the fool hardness and rebellion. It is indeed sad that the child sometimes needs the **rod** that is intended for **the backs of fools**. Yet never does his loving Father use it until gentle means have been tried in vain. *Oh, my God, use your own wise means to save me from my own waywardness, folly, and ruin.*

4-5. We are forbidden, and yet commanded, to **answer a fool**. We are told to **answer** him, and we are told to **not answer** him. The following explanation resolves this apparent contradiction. Both pieces of advice are wise methods of dealing with fools, which differ according to character, time, or circumstance. If someone is taking delight in scoffing at religion with witty and profane attacks or with specious arguments against the Word of God, it would be best to follow Hezekiah's words concerning Rabshakeh's blasphemy and not to answer him.

But what may be at one time our duty to restrain, at another time and under different circumstances it may be no less our duty to do. Silence may sometimes be mistaken for defeat. Unanswered words may be deemed unanswerable. An answer may, therefore, be called for, not *in* folly, but *to* folly—"not in his foolish manner, but in the manner that his foolishness required" (Fuller). The answer would not be merely **according to his folly,** but according to your own wisdom. Such words would be sharp as rods. The fool's back needs them.

Oh, for wisdom to govern the tongue, to discover the right time to speak and the right time to stay silent. How instructive is the pattern of our great Master! His silence and his answers were equally worthy of himself. The former always conveyed a dignified rebuke. The latter responded to the confusion of his contentious enemies. Will not a prayerful meditative study communicate to us a large measure of his divine wisdom?

6-9. Surely this diversified exhibition of the foolishness of folly is an incentive to study heavenly wisdom. **Like cutting off one's feet or drinking violence is the sending of a message by the hand of a fool.** The fool makes so many mistakes, is careless, or deliberately sets out to do wrong that trusting him with **a message** is like asking him to run an errand for you when you have cut off his **feet**! Fools are either not qualified to undertake the mission they are entrusted with, or they will only look after their own interests.

Like a lame man's legs that hang limp is a proverb in the mouth of a fool. "A wise saying does as ill become a fool as dancing does a cripple" (Bishop Patrick). A proverb in his mouth becomes a joke.

Like tying a stone in a sling is the giving of honor to a fool. The **sling** makes the **stone** tied in it an instrument of death. The **honor** given to a

fool makes him a curse to his fellow creatures. The prime favorite of a despot, had not God restrained him, would have been the murderer of the chosen nation (Esther 3:1-5). It is dangerous indeed to place unqualified people in places of authority. "It is like putting a sword or a loaded pistol into a madman's hand" (Scott).

Like a thornbush in a drunkard's hand is a proverb in the mouth of a fool. "It is no more fit for a fool to meddle with a wise speech than for a drunken man to handle a thornbush" (Bishop Hall). When a thorn goes into his hand, a drunkard only makes the wound worse. Such is the **fool.** May he be rebuked and restrained.

10. The great God that formed all things both rewardeth the fool, and rewardeth transgressors [KJV]. It is difficult to fix with certainty the interpretation of this proverb. Our venerable translators have filled in with some doubtfulness the meaning of the principal term. The word in the original may mean either **the Great God** or the great man. Nor does the construction clearly determine either meaning. All, however, expound from it the divine government, direct or permissive.

11. As a dog returns to its vomit, so a fool repeats his folly. Is this a picture of a man who has been made a little lower than the angels, even in the likeness of God? The most vile comparisons are made to show man's loathsomeness in the sight of God. "Do any feel disgusted at the allusion? Let them remember that the emblem is far less filthy than the thing denoted by it. Let them remember that the whole race of animals does not afford anything so debasing as not to be far outdone by the excesses of libertines, drunkards, and gluttons" (Scott). We naturally turn away from this sight. Would that we had the same disgust at the sin that it so graphically portrays. If only we abhorred in ourselves that which God infinitely abhors in us!

12. Do you see a man wise in his own eyes? There is more hope for a fool than for him. Regarding **do you see a man . . . ?** God means to point at him. There is something to be learned from him. He struts around in his own conceit. He is **wise in his own eyes.** The false persuasion that he has gained wisdom utterly precludes him from gaining it. He thinks himself to be **wise** because he does not know what it is to be **wise.**

Lord, preserve me from this hopeless delusion. Pull down all my pride and imagined wisdom. Take the blindness from my eyes, that I may know what I am in your sight. Clothe me with humility from the sole of my foot to my head.

13-16. The counterpart to these illustrations may be seen in the man dozing away his life in guilty idleness. But let us look at the pictures of **the sluggard** as they meet our eye in the church. The gradation shows the almost incredible increase of this evil. And it is not resisted.

The lazy man is totally reluctant to work. When therefore his indolence is disturbed, he is ingenious in inventing excuses and imagines dangers that do not really exist. "He who has no mind to work never lacks pretenses for idleness" (Bishop Patrick). His insincerity lulls his conscience to sleep in his false excuses. Were it as easy to be spiritual as to wish to be so, who would not be a Christian? But to see no end of the toil, duty on duty, trouble following trouble, no time to catch one's breath, is an appalling hindrance. And so **"the lion in the road, a fierce lion roaming the streets"** is all such a person needs to excuse himself.

Laziness is presented in many striking ways in this book. Do I not think about it too lightly? Let me consider carefully to what respect I am influenced by laziness bodily, mentally, or spiritually. Does it ever follow me throughout my work, when I am on my knees, in my Bible reading? Do I not excuse myself from work when great exertion is required? May God enable me to resist this paralysis in every shape!

17. Like one who seizes a dog by the ears is a passer-by who meddles in a quarrel not his own. If we want to honor God in our Christian walk, we must take time at every step for prayer and for the exercise of sound judgment. Or else we will rush in, uninvited, to our own loss. To seize a **dog by the ears** will bring good reason to repent of our folly. To meddle **in a quarrel that is not [our] own** will surely bring trouble.

There is a world of difference between suffering as a Christian and suffering as a busybody. Even with Christian intentions, many of us are too fond of meddling in other peoples' affairs. Uninvited interference seldom avails with the contending parties. The true peacemaker, while he deplores quarrels, knows that interference at the moment of irritation will kindle rather than extinguish the fire. So his self-control is not indifference. He commits the matter to him whose wisdom he so greatly needs. He will take the first appropriate moment for favorable remonstrance.

18-19. Like a madman shooting firebrands or deadly arrows is a man who deceives his neighbor and says, "I was only joking!" How little does the thoughtless man consider the misery that his wantonness occasions to others. He bears no malice. He indulges only the pure love of mischief. He carries on a scheme of imposition as harmless play. His companions compliment him on his adroitness and join in the laugh of triumph over the victim of his cruel jest. What are sometimes called "practical jokes" come under this awful charge. "There is little difference in this case between fraud and fury. He who deliberately deceives his neighbor, under the pretext of a joke, is no less prejudicial to him than a lunatic who does wrong out of frenzy and distemper" (Bishop Hall). **A man who deceives** is accountable to God and his fellow creatures. "He who sins in jest, must repent in earnest; or his sin will be his ruin" (Henry). "What has a Christian," says Bernard, "to do with jesting?"

20-22. The busy tongue makes work where it does not find it. Such is the despicable trade of the **gossip**. He spends his time prying into other people's business, ferreting out secrets, diving into family histories, meddling with their concerns. Thus in every way where he can please himself, "man is naturally his own grand idol. He would be esteemed and honored by any means; and to magnify that idol self, he kills the name and esteem of others in sacrifice to it" (Leighton). Real virtue runs from this base selfishness.

Are we closely watching against these sins? Do we carefully squelch the rising flame of a desire to incite quarrels? Do we resist the temptation to speak needlessly about the faults of other people? Do we dread the character of a polished, well-educated, amusing slanderer? We may feel indignant at being accused of being **a gossip.** Yet it requires no ordinary exercise of Christian discipline to maintain the silence of love and to regulate both the tongue and the ear within its well-advised limits.

23-27. Like a coating of glaze over earthenware are fervent lips with an evil heart. A malicious man disguises himself with his lips, but in his heart he harbors deceit. Though his speech is charming, do not believe him, for seven abominations fill his heart. His malice may be concealed by deception, but his wickedness will be exposed in the assembly. If a man digs a pit, he will fall into it; if a man rolls a stone, it will roll back on him. The sin described here is a disgrace to society. Yet it is often **concealed** with flattering clothes, just as a worthless pot is painted with a thin coat of silver. "Hypocrisy is spun often of a very fine thread; and the heart of man, abounding with so much hypocrisy as it does, is the most deceitful thing, yes, and the most easy to deceive too, actively and passively both, of anything in the world" (Bishop Sanderson).

Christian prudence will guard against credulity, which is in fact the harmlessness of the dove without the wisdom of the snake. This weakness cost Gedaliah his life. A sounder spirit saved Nehemiah from the snare of his malignant adversaries. The source of this **wickedness** gives good reason for distrust. The **seven abominations** speak of a great variety of **abominations.** And here lies the root of the disease: "A guileful heart makes guileful tongue and lips. It is the workhouse, where is the forge of deceit and slander; and the tongue is only the outer shop, where they are mended; and the lips its door. So only the goods that are made inside can be sold outside. For evil thoughts, evil words, come from a deceitful heart that is lined with rottenness" (Leighton). Oh, let this despicable character be a beacon to us to shun all approaches to false dealings. Better to risk giving offense by faithfulness, though let this, so far as conscience allows, be avoided, rather than conceal our hatred by flattering words.

28. A lying tongue hates those it hurts, and a flattering mouth works ruin. Rarely do we see a solitary sin. One sin breeds another. **Lying** and malice are linked together here. But again and again watch out for **a flattering mouth.** Alas, where is this type of man not welcomed as a friend? From some favorable position he presents an attractive face. But a closer view reveals him to be a subtle, murderous enemy who **works ruin.**

So how should we deal with a flatterer? Homer puts it into his hero's heart to regard him as a fiend of hell. Our safety, then, is in flight, or at least in frowning resistance. We should be "as much troubled," said a godly man, "by unjust praises as by unjust slanderers" (Philip Henry). We must show clearly that those who praise us most please us least. Pray for wisdom to discover the snare, for gracious principles to raise us up above vain praises, for self-denial, for the capacity to be content and even thankful without such flatteries. This will be our security.

Proverbs
Chapter 27

1. Do not boast about tomorrow, for you do not know what a day may bring forth. The universe does not present a more affecting sight than an elderly sinner with one foot in the grave, losing all in the world, and infinitely more in eternity. A moment more, and he is gone. Heaven and hell are no trifles. **Tomorrow** presumed upon, today neglected ruins all. Standing on the brink of the precipice, how precious is the moment for prayer, before the door of mercy is closed forever!

Has the child of God reason to **boast about tomorrow**? What a change this may make in your worldly circumstances or Christian experience! Never will you feel more secure than in the realization that you have no security for a single hour. Divide your cares with God. Let disappointment prepare you for your heavenly rest, and submit all your wishes and pleasures to his gracious will. Have you no need of warning? Would earthly pleasures be so highly prized if there were no secret dependence on **tomorrow**? Surely this thought may more than sustain in the loss of them. The shadow only is gone; the body of my happiness remains immovable. Remember that "this world is the grand laboratory for perfecting souls for the next" (Sir M. Hale).

2. Let another praise you, and not your own mouth; someone else, and not your own lips. "Praise," says an old expositor, "is a comely garment. But though you wear it yourself, someone else must put it on you, or else it will never sit well on you. Praise is sweet music, but it never sounds well when it comes from your own mouth. If it comes from another person's mouth, it is a pleasant sound to everyone who hears it. Praise is a rich treasure, but it will never make you rich unless someone else says it" (Jermin). Indeed, unless we have to vindicate our character, or unless our Master's honor is at stake, nothing so degrades a man with his fellowmen as setting out his own praise. **Let another praise you.** We will lose nothing by this self-renouncing spirit. If our **mouth** is silent, **some-**

one else will speak to praise us. Recognizing the fact that we are so far from being really humble is enough to make us deeply humble.

3-4. Jealousy is an implacable passion. **Anger** is stirred up by offense, **jealousy** by godliness, prosperity, or favor. Reason operates rather as the oil to fan the flame than the water to quench it. "Proud men would be admired by all and preferred above all; and if it be not so, a secret enmity invades their spirits and settles itself. Men cannot endure the real or reputed excellency of others. The proud creature would shine alone" (Manton).

The wise man had previously described the curse of envy's deadly poison to the man who indulges it (14:30). Here he shows its subtle and almost irresistible power on its victims. For indeed in contrast to mercy, it curses both its subjects and its object. "Like the star called wormwood, which pollutes all the rivers and springs on which it falls, it poisons all the sources and streams of human enjoyment" (Wardlaw).

But, Christian, remember, although the promise is certain that sin will not have dominion over you, yet the struggle is sharp to the end. Let us probe this corruption deeply. Men will look at grace with an envious eye. They will darken the lives that outshine their own and defame the holiness that they have no heart to follow. But "those who have true worth in themselves can never envy it in others" (Sir Philip Sidney).

5-6. Who is the **friend** who will be a real blessing to my soul? Is it one who will humor my fancies and flatter my vanity? Is it enough that he loves my person and would spend his time and energies in my service? This comes far short of my need. I am a poor, straying sinner with a wayward will and a blinded heart, going wrong at every step. The **friend** for my case is one who will watch over me with **open rebuke**, a reprover when necessary, not a flatterer. The genuineness of friendship without this mark is more than doubtful, its usefulness utterly paralyzed. The **hidden love** that does not dare to risk **wounds from a friend** and spares **rebuke** rather than inflict pain, judged by God's standard, is hatred. It is much better that the wound should be probed than covered. **Rebuke**—kindly, considerately, and prayerfully administered—cements friendship rather than weakens it.

The mark of true godliness is a concern to have our faults pointed out and a thankfulness to those who undertake the self-denying office. Even when given most rashly and unkindly, one of the meekest of men could say, "I was thankful to God for admonishing me, and my gratitude to the man was, I think, unfeigned" (H. Martyn). In Martyn's journal, the reprover's name was found specially remembered in prayer. "A faithful reprover is a very great help in our Christian course. He is to be valued above the greatest treasure. He who wants to be safe," says one of the ancients, "must have a faithful friend or a bitter enemy, that he may flee from vice by the admonitions of the one or the invective of the other" (Bishop Kidder).

Who would not choose this **faithful** wound, however painful at the moment of infliction, rather than the multiple **kisses** of **an enemy**? The kiss of the apostate was a bitter ingredient in the Savior's cup of suffering. His foreknowledge of the treachery in no degree weakened those exquisite sensibilities, which from their intimate union with the Godhead rendered him susceptible to suffering beyond all comprehension.

Philip Henry beautifully describes the proper offices and uses of Christian reproof. "To reprove a brother is like as, when he is fallen, to help him up again; when he is wounded, to help to cure him; when he has broken a bone, to help set it; when he is out of the way, to put him in it; when he is fallen into the fire, to pluck him out; when he has contracted defilement, to help cleanse."

7. He who is full loathes honey, but to the hungry even what is bitter tastes sweet. This is true about the enjoyments of this life. Abundance, instead of increasing the happiness of the possessor, deprives him of that which often comes with a more scanty portion. The person whose appetite is overfed with indulgence turns with disgust from the sweetest dainties, while every **bitter** and distasteful thing is keenly relished by **the hungry,** perhaps barely saved from starvation. May not satiety be as great a curse as famine? Is it not fearfully written on many a professing Christian, **he who is full loathes honey**?

Far more enviable is the **hungry** soul, feeding on unpalatable truths—yes, welcoming even **bitter** dispensations as medicine for the soul's health. And is not the **sweet** taste of the Gospel known by its bitterness? Does not this bitterness make Christ **sweet** to the soul? A sinner in all his guilt, a Savior in his perfect merit and love—well does the one answer the other. Every view of Christ embitters sin. Every view of sin endears the Savior.

8. Like a bird that strays from its nest is a man who strays from his home. Instinct teaches **a bird** that **its nest** is the only place of safety or rest. There God has provided her with special protection (Deuteronomy 22:6-7). Nothing, therefore, but danger awaits her if she **strays from . . . home.** She is safe and happy only while she keeps her **nest.**

Not less senseless and dangerous is it lightly to leave the place, society, or calling that divine providence has marked out for us. Here man is "in God's precincts, and so under God's protection" (Swinnock). And if he will be content to remain in **his home,** God will bless him with the rich gain of godly contentment. But the **man who strays from his home** is "the rolling stone that gathers no moss." "He is always restless, as if he had a windmill in his head. Every new crotchet [opinion or preference] puts him into a new course" (Bishop Sanderson). His lack of fixed principles and employment exposes him to perpetual temptation. Always wanting to be something or somewhere different to what and where he is, he only changes imaginary for real troubles. To be full of wisdom is to know and to keep our place. The soul, the body, the family, society—all have a claim on us.

9. Perfume and incense bring joy to the heart, and the pleasantness of one's friend springs from his earnest counsel. We know that **perfume and incense** are most refreshing to the senses. Not less so is the medicine of friendship to the soul. Who does not feel the need of a brother's or sister's heart?

The pleasantness of one's friend springs from his earnest counsel. Here **his earnest counsel** constitutes its excellence. It is not merely official or intelligent. It is the **counsel** of his soul. He puts himself in our case and counsels as he would wish to be counseled himself. The real unction and blessing of this **earnest counsel** will be in proportion as we are living in communion with our Lord.

10. Do not forsake your friend and the friend of your father, and do not go to your brother's house when disaster strikes you—better a neighbor nearby than a brother far away. Man without principle is the creature of caprice. His friendships have no warranted stability. Solomon exemplified his own rule by cultivating friendly links with Hiram, the friend of his father (1 Kings 5:1-10). The unprincipled contempt of this rule cost Solomon's foolish son his kingdom (1 Kings 12:6-19). Though other things are better when new, an old and tried friend is better.

"But if it be an indecency and uncomeliness and a very unfit thing—that is, contrary to the precept of studying whatsoever is lovely and thinking of these things—to forsake my friend and the friend of my father, how much more horrid must it be to forsake my God, and my father's God. 'My father's God shall not be my God'" (Howe).

11. Be wise, my son, and bring joy to my heart; then I can answer anyone who treats me with contempt. Christian parents take their full share of the minister's greatest joy—to see their children walk in truth (2 John 4; 3 John 4). Their hearts are full of **joy** because of their children's godly wisdom. We are strengthened by what flows from their wisdom and their holy prayers. And truly will we put our seal to the example of a parent thus honored and blessed. "I had rather have my house filled with my children's prayers than filled with gold."

12. The prudent see danger and take refuge, but the simple keep going and suffer for it. Even animal instinct is the exercise of prudence (Jeremiah 8:7). Every intelligent man acts on it. It is natural to see the evil when it comes or is close to our door. But the **prudent** man *foresees* evil coming. God is still the same unchangeable God of holiness and justice. Sin is the same abomination to him as ever. **The prudent** man sees the effect in the cause, the consequent in the antecedent. He will, therefore, provide himself with a shelter. We often see the Christian's patience, security, and hope. Here is his prudence, securing a **refuge**.

But the simple, the deliberately foolish, let things take their course. God is so merciful. All will be well at the end. But they refuse to be warned. The fooleries of the world engage their heart. All besides is forgotten. But they **suffer for it. The prudent** hide themselves in God. **The simple** rush blindfolded into hell. The ox has to be driven to destruction, but the sinner plunges into it in spite of every effort to restrain him.

13. Take the garment of one who puts up security for a stranger; hold it in pledge if he does it for a wayward woman. This proverb we have had before (20:16). "What conduces [leads] to the happiness of life it is needful to inculcate again and again, to fix it deep in the mind" (Lavater). It is the perfection of Christian graces that they do not entrench on one another. Kindness loses the name of virtue when shown at the expense of prudence.

14. If a man loudly blesses his neighbor early in the morning, it will be taken as a curse. Is it a sin to bless our **neighbor?** Our Lord openly acknowledged the love of his friends. And yet **a man** who **loudly blesses** and extravagantly praises brings sincerity into question. When a man exceeds all bounds of truth and decency, affecting pompous words and hyperbolical expressions, we cannot but suspect some sinister motive. Real friendship needs no such assurance. One act of love is more than many loud blessings. "There is no wise man but would rather have one promise than a thousand fair words, and one performance than ten thousand promises. For what charge is it to spend a little breath for a man to give one his word, who never intends to give him anything else?" (South).

The rule toward our friend is not to love in word but in deed and truth. The rule for ourselves is to walk before God and not before men. Let worldly things and worldly men be little in your eyes. Man's days will soon pass away. Eternity in all its substance and glory is at hand.

15-16. The figure of **dripping** has been given before. The time is added here, **on a rainy day,** shutting us up at home. There is rain inside and outside, and both are troublesome. The one stops us from going out with comfort, the other from staying at home in peace. The storm within, however, is much more pitiless. Shelter may be found from the other. But there is no shelter to be found from this **dripping.** The other wets only the skin; this gets through to our bones. Prudence and prayer, not blind affection, give the only security of happiness and peace.

17. As iron sharpens iron, so one man sharpens another. Man was framed not for solitude, but for society. It is only as a social being that his powers and affections are fully expanded. **Iron sharpens iron.** Steel, whetted against a knife, sharpens the edge. So in the collision of different minds each whets the edge of the other. We owe some of the most valuable discoveries of science to this active reciprocity. In the sympathies of friendship, when the mind is dull and the countenance overcast, a word from a friend renews blunted energy and exhilarates the countenance.

"The communion of saints" is an article in our Creed. But is it practically acknowledged in its high responsibility and Christian privilege? Gladly let us take up the bond of brotherhood. If a brother seems to walk alone, sharpen his **iron** by godly communication. Walk together in mutual concern for each other's infirmities, trials, and temptations.

18. He who tends a fig tree will eat its fruit, and he who looks after his master will be honored. Here is an encouragement to be diligent in our calling. The **fig tree** was a valuable product of Judea. Its cultivation was probably a profitable labor and therefore illustrated the general reward of faithfulness.

In the service of our divine Master, our happiness is in receiving his Word and studying his will. Our honor is secured by his promises.

19. As water reflects a face, so a man's heart reflects the man. This proverb does not confound all in one indiscriminate mass, as if all were alike. We cannot see infancy and the maturity of age as identical. But with two persons in the same circumstances and on the same level, the parallel is most remarkable and instructive. **As water reflects a face,** so in another **heart** we see our own reflection. Human nature has suffered no change since the Fall. The picture of man's corruption is man as we see and know him now.

From this we learn to be sympathetic with the members of Christ. We share their joys and sorrows, their confidence and temptations. Self-knowledge also instructs us thus to know human nature, and to deal wisely and profitably with our fellow sinners. The practical lesson of humility and forbearance is also deeply taught.

20. Death and Destruction are never satisfied, and neither are the eyes of man. Here is a striking picture of the two great devourers, **Death and Destruction. Death,** ever since Adam's sin, has been insatiable. It has opened its mouth to receive countless millions, and still it yawns, craving for more.

Man is always seeking for what he cannot find, satisfaction in earthly things. He toils after his object, and when he has grasped it, he continues to toil. The one who possesses abundance does not possess happiness. His best efforts only bring him a meager enjoyment not worthy of the name. The summit of ambition, when reached, is not his resting-place, but only the point from where he moves on to something higher. All the affections of fallen man are filled with unquenched thirst.

Now let me ask, have I seen God as that which alone is sufficient for my soul? Have I made the important discovery that all my uneasy cravings from morning to night arise from not seeking him as my only satisfaction? To delight in anything but him is as if we throw him from his throne. All is then misery and delusion. But delighting in him brings us heavenly comfort. Eternity will be an eternity of joy.

21. The crucible for silver and the furnace for gold, but man is tested by the praise he receives. The most searching **furnace** is shown here. He who is praised is not only much *approved*, but much *proved*. The courting of **the praise** of our fellow creatures has to do with the world within.

Praise is a sharper trial of the strength of principle than is reproach. "If a man be vain and light, he will be puffed up with it. If he be wise and solid, he will be not one whit moved therewith" (Bishop Hall). Forwardness to give our opinion, and offense if it is not taken—this is the dross brought out of the furnace. Know your need of purifying, and let the great Refiner do his perfect work.

Fearful often is the trial to a minister of Christ. When he becomes the object of popular applause, his people's idol, when men of strong impulse and weak judgment put the servant in the Master's place, then he is in the **furnace.** "We should feel," said the venerable Mr. Simeon in his own way, "as if our ears were stung with blasphemy when we discover any attempt to transfer the crown of glory from the head of the Redeemer to that of any of his servants." Henry Martyn continually expresses his sensitive conscience on this besetting temptation. Dr. Payson, a careful self-observer, mentions among his trials, "well-meant, but injudicious, commendations!" When praised, "God, humble me" was the prayer of one marvelously preserved in the fearful **furnace.**

Two rules strongly present themselves. *Be careful in giving praise.* Even the children of the world can discover the deadly tenacity of pride in our nature. "Do you know," remarked Madame de Steal on her deathbed, "what is the last thing to die in man? It is self-love." We cannot, therefore, do our brother greater harm than by supplying fuel for pride by unlawful praise. Therefore, until the appointed day for manifestation, it is well to judge each other, whether for good or evil, with becoming moderation. Is it merciful to expose a weak fellow sinner to the frown of a jealous God by stirring up the innate corruption of his heart?

"I do not know," said Neff, "that I ought to thank you so very warmly for what I have too much reason to fear the old man will be ready to take advantage of; his life being, you know, principally supported by praise." "Everyone here," writes Dr. Payson to his mother, "whether friends or enemies, are conspiring to ruin me. Satan, and my own heart, of course will lend a hand; and if you join too, I fear all the cold water that Christ can throw on my pride will not prevent it from breaking out into a destructive flame. As certainly as anybody flatters and caresses me, my Father has to scourge me for it, and an unspeakable mercy it is that he condescends to do it."

Be not less careful in receiving praise. While we may be repelled by extravagant flattery, yet we are apt to think it kindly meant, and it is very rare not to take unconsciously a drop of the poison. And the praise of the church is by far the most insidious poison, being so refined, so luscious. Especially when we feel it to be lawfully obtained, how hard it is to receive it with self-renouncing consecration to God. "Christian, you know that you carry gunpowder around with you. Desire those that carry fire to keep their distance. It is a dangerous crisis when a proud heart meets with flattering lips" (Flavel). Delight mainly in those works that are only under the eye of God. Value only his approbation. Always think of the love of human praise as the most deadly bane of a Christian profession, to be resisted with intense energy and perseverance.

22. Though you grind a fool in a mortar, grinding him like grain with a pestle, you will not remove his folly from him. The allusion is to the Eastern way of beating off the husk from the corn by **grinding** it **with a pestle.** Yet the husk sticks not so close to the grain as foolishness to the fool. The grinding of the **mortar** may separate the one. The other **will not remove his folly** despite repeated strokes. What can correction do for **a fool** who despises it?

Examples of this incurable hardness abound. The belief in the necessary working of affliction for our saving good is a fatal delusion. Never did it of itself bring one soul to God. In all cases it is only what God is pleased to make it. The blows may be so mighty as to make the most stupefied soul quiver with intense feeling. Still if the rock is broken, the broken pieces will retain all their natural hardness. The man may be crushed, but not humbled. He will still cling to his foolishness and ignore Christ and heaven. Was it not so, Christian, with you until omnipotent love awakened what chastisement alone could never have stirred—the cry of unreserved submission?

23-27. Be sure you know the condition of your flocks, give careful attention to your herds; for riches do not endure forever, and a crown is not secure for all generations. When the hay is removed and new growth appears and the grass from the hills is gathered in, the lambs will provide you with clothing, and the goats with the price of a field. You will have plenty of goats' milk to feed you and your family and to nourish your servant girls. "This declares the great goodness of God toward man, and the diligence that he requires from him for the preservation of his gifts" (*Reformers' Notes*). This is a lively picture of the occupations, advantages, and responsibilities of rural life in olden days. It teaches that every man ought to have a business and rebukes the neglect of practical everyday duties.

This picture also exhibits the fruits of industry, far preferable to those of ambition. The comparison with those whose station places them beyond the need of labor affords no matter for envy, but much for thankfulness. The various produce of the field is all the overflowing bounty of our gracious God. How excellent is the loving-kindness of our loving Lord!

Proverbs
Chapter 28

1. The wicked man flees though no one pursues, but the righteous are as bold as a lion. We know that **the wicked** may appear **bold** in facing danger, so long as they drown reflection and stupefy conscience. But when conscience is roused, guilt is the parent of fear. Adam knew no fear until he become a guilty creature.

But if guilt brings fear, the removal of guilt gives confidence. **The wicked man flees . . . the righteous are as bold as a lion.** Fearless as the king of the forest, **the righteous** dare to do anything but offend their God. "This noble animal is the most perfect model of boldness and courage. He never flees from the hunters, nor is frightened by their onset. If their number forces him to yield, he retires slowly, step by step, frequently turning on his pursuers. He has been known to attack a whole caravan, and when forced to retreat, he always retreats fighting, and with his face to his enemy" (Paxton).

When God intends us to do great things, he makes us feel that without him we can do nothing. Thus pride receives its deathblow, and God receives all the glory to himself. Bishop Hall has finely worked out this contrast. "The wicked is a coward and is afraid of everything; of God, because he is his enemy; of Satan, because he is his tormentor; of God's creatures, because they, joining with their Maker, fight against him; of himself, because he bears about with him his own accuser and executioner. The godly man contrarily is afraid of nothing; not of God, because he knows him to be his best friend and will not hurt him; not of Satan, because he cannot hurt him; not of afflictions, because he knows they come from a loving God and end in his good; not of the creatures, since the very stones in the field are in league with him; not of himself, since his conscience is at peace."

2. When a country is rebellious, it has many rulers, but a man of understanding and knowledge maintains order. Is God concerned about the falling of a sparrow? Surely, then, he is much more concerned about the control of kingdoms. If we realized more deeply our national dependence, we would see the clouds of anarchy and confusion working his wise, mysterious, and gracious purposes. Would that the nation had learned from her own records of bygone days the sound and practical lessons of repentance with all its blessed fruits.

But no less must we acknowledge the divine hand in **a man of understanding and knowledge [who] maintains order**. By a man of such high character Egypt was saved from famine. The long and prosperous reigns of the godly kings of Judah contrast strongly with the records of Israel after the revolt.

3. A poor man that oppresseth the poor is like a sweeping rain which leaveth no food [KJV]. Unrestrained power is often an engine of oppression, and never more so than when in the grasp of the **poor**. Put an unprincipled spendthrift in power, and he will be like a destructive flood.

It is a cheering contrast to remember Christ, who was once poor due to his voluntary abasement, but who is now raised to honor and glory. But he has compassion on his poor brethren and is not ashamed of them.

4. Those who forsake the law praise the wicked, but those who keep the law resist them. How potent is the influence of our Christian profession, acting on everyone around us for evil or for good. Those who love sin naturally take pleasure in doing it. **The wicked** may possess some praiseworthy qualities (Luke 16:8). But to praise them for their wickedness identifies us with them. "It is fearful to sin; more fearful to delight in sin; yet more to defend it" (Bishop Hall).

5. Evil men do not understand justice, but those who seek the LORD understand it fully. Ignorance and knowledge are here contrasted, and each is traced to its source. The apostle Paul drew the same contrast when he said that the person without the Spirit does not accept the things that come from the Spirit, but that the spiritual person makes judgments about everything. This unity found in the Old Testament and the New Testament is beautiful and instructive. "The two Testaments, like our two eyes, mutually enlighten us and assist each other" (Serle).

Evil men do not understand justice. They do not know the true standard of right and wrong, the true way to God, or the end of God's dealings with them. Their ignorance is deliberate. The most distinguished scholar is a fool in understanding about **justice**. Unless he is humbled in the consciousness of his ignorance and seeks light from above, he will perish in gross darkness. What a curse are learning and intellect without a humble heart!

Pride fastens on every faculty of man, and the source of light is despised. So there is no understanding because nobody seeks after God (Psalm 14:2-3; Romans 3:11). "Wickedness," Bishop Taylor justly observes, "corrupts a man's reasoning and gives him false principles and an evil measuring of things." "I regard it as a fundamental error in the study of divinity," remarks Professor Franke, "for anyone to persuade himself that he can study divinity properly without the Holy Spirit. As long as he remains in this error, all labor is lost on him." "A grain of true faith is more estimable than a mass of mere historical knowledge" (Professor Franke). "A man may as soon read the letter of Scripture without eyes as properly understand their mysteries without grace" (Bishop Beveridge). Those who seek the Lord, even though they are but babes in intellect and ignorant in worldly things, will **understand justice . . . fully**, in a way that an unspiritual person will never be able to.

Many things, dark to human reason, are simplified by humility. The harmony of the divine attributes staggers reason and can only be understood by humble faith. A reclaimed unbeliever, the French poet and philosopher De La Harpe, describes his own conflict: "In thinking about the justice of the deity, man is at first ready to doubt God's compassion. But the Gospel answers him by the voice of an apostle: 'God so loved the world that he spared not his own Son, but delivered him up for us all.' It is then that the penitent sinner apprehends this ineffable mystery. His proud and blind reason had rejected it. But his humble and contrite heart profoundly feels it. He believes because he loves; he is graceful because he sees all the goodness of the Creator proportioned to the miseries of the creature. Oh, my God, all your mysteries are mysteries of love, and therefore they are indeed divine."

6. Better a poor man whose walk is blameless than a rich man whose ways are perverse. This proverb is repeated (see 19:1) for its valuable instruction. One part of the comparison, implied before, is here expressed—**than a rich man.** Previously he was described as **a fool whose lips are perverse.** A deeper trait of character is given here: His **ways are perverse.** This is one of those paradoxes that sometimes make the feet even of God's children to stumble. A man may walk in a **blameless** way and yet be **poor.** An evil man may be **perverse** and yet be **rich.** And yet the **poor man,** with all his external disadvantages, is more honorable, more useful, and more happy than the **rich man** with all his earthly splendor. This point is illustrated in the following fine passage from Cicero:

"A contented mind is as good as an estate. Frugality is itself a revenue. To be satisfied with one's lot is to be really and infallibly rich. If landed possessions are most highly valued by shrewd judges of human affairs, as a property that is least liable to injury, how inestimably precious must be true virtue, which cannot be snatched from us by force or fraud, which cannot be damaged by shipwreck or by fire, which no tempests or political disturbances can change. They alone who are endowed with this treasure can be said to be truly rich. They alone possess what is fruitful and durable. What is allotted to them they deem sufficient. They covet nothing. They really want nothing. They require nothing. The wicked and the avaricious, on the contrary, so far from being rich, are in reality miserably poor, inasmuch as they have no certain treasure and are always impatient for some addition to their stores, never satisfied with their present possessions" (*Paradox*, vi. 3).

Outward superiority only affects our state before God as increasing proportionably our responsibilities. Many will wish that they had lived and died in obscure poverty rather than having been entrusted with riches, which only made them boldly sin with a high hand against God and their own souls.

7. He who keeps the law is a discerning son, but a companion of gluttons disgraces his father. Keep[ing] the law is the way of wisdom and honor. Invaluable is the training that leads young people, under the Lord's blessing, to this happy personal choice. Such are manifestly taught by God and are guided by his Spirit into true wisdom.

Young people, meet the enticements of your former companions with a decided protest: "Depart from me, you who do evil. As for me, I will keep God's commandments." Here is honor to your father, happiness to yourself, usefulness to the church, and preparation for heaven.

Parents, do we shrink from this overwhelming disgrace? Let us more diligently and more prayerfully cultivate that wise and holy training of our children that is God's appointed ordinance and that, however long or severely he may try our faith, he will not fail to honor in his time (22:6).

8. He who increases his wealth by exorbitant interest amasses it for another, who will be kind to the poor. What a deadly curse it is to be under the spell of covetousness! No laws can bind it. God had fenced in the rights of his poor people with solemn and plain obligations. And he will not allow their rights to be lightly regarded. A man labors for himself, but his harvest falls into better hands "through God's secret providence" (Diodati). Why should we seek to increase our **wealth by exorbitant interest** when we have our Father's promise that all things will be given to us (Matthew 6:33), when his divine power has given to us all things for life and godliness?

9. If anyone turns a deaf ear to the law, even his prayers are detestable. This does not mark the frailty, infirmity, or temptation that too often interrupts listening to **the law.** The case described here is the habitual and obstinate rejection of God that despises his ordinances and refuses the instruction of his ministry. Awful indeed is it that there should be such a rebel. If the subject **turns a deaf ear to the law** of his Sovereign, all **his prayers** that he may present in times of distress, his Lord will regard as **detestable.** Justly is the door closed against the presumptuous hypocrite. "Great reason there is that God will refuse to hear him who refuses to hear God" (Bishop Reynolds). And what if such a man's language now— "Depart from me"—should come from his mouth at the great day as the seal of his everlasting doom!

10. He who leads the upright along an evil path will fall into his own trap, but the blameless will receive a good inheritance. To delight in the enticing of sinners **along an evil path** is the very image and aspect of the tempter. But his chief delight, the main effort, is to make **the upright** go astray. What rejoicing there is when a standard-bearer faints.

The malice of Satan and his emissaries inadvertently demonstrates the faithfulness of the almighty Keeper. Even if they succeed for a while in leading **the upright along an evil path**, recovering mercy is in store for **the upright**. When an **upright** man is brought out of the snare in deep humiliation, he will **receive a good inheritance**. This **good inheritance** can never be fully written about or thought of. It is part of what the eye has not seen and the ear has not heard and the mind has not conceived (1 Corinthians 2:9).

11. A rich man may be wise in his own eyes, but a poor man who has discernment sees through him. To be truly wise and to **be wise in [our] own eyes** are often confused, though they are essentially opposite. Although riches do not always bring wisdom, the **rich man** often pretends to have it and ascribes his success to his own sagacity, though he may be manifestly simple and foolish. Yet the universe does not possess a more dignified character than the **poor man who has discernment**. Did not the incarnate Lord honor this station supremely by taking it on himself? To walk in his footsteps, in his spirit, is wisdom, honor, and happiness infinitely beyond what this poor world of vanity can afford.

12. When the righteous triumph, there is great elation; but when the wicked rise to power, men go into hiding. When **the righteous** are honored, **there is great elation**. The whole kingdom feels more or less the influence of this national blessing. Godliness is countenanced. People are allowed to practice their religion freely.

But when the wicked rise to power, how this **elation** is eclipsed. The people of God are removed into corners, are silenced, and **go into hiding**. The light of more than a hundred prophets, and even Elijah himself, was hidden for a while under the tyranny of Ahab. Yet it was hidden only from the eye of sense. Regarding those who wander about in sheepskins and goatskins, **hiding** in deserts and caves, what greater glory could we give than the divine inscription stamped on them: "The world was not worthy of them" (Hebrews 11:38)?

13. He who conceals his sins does not prosper, but whoever confesses and renounces them finds mercy. God and man each conceal sin—God in free unbounded grace, man in shame and hypocrisy. The proud sinner naturally wants to be thought better than he is. His sin he must conceal. Cicero sees confession of wickedness as disgraceful and dangerous. Thus heathen morality develops the pride of depraved nature.

Confession of sins to God is the first act of the penitent. But it should also be the daily habit of the saint. The further we advance, the deeper will be the tone of confession. The moment sin is seen to be sin, let it be laid on the Surety's head. Every moment of unconfessed sin adds to its burden and guilt. The thought of a nature estranged from God, a heart full of corruption, sins of youth and age, before and after conversion, sins against light and conviction, knowledge and love, the sins of our very confession, their defilement, coldness, and too often self-righteous tendency—all supply abundant material for abasing acknowledgment. See the greatness, not the smallness, of our sin. Never deem any sin so trifling as not to need the immediate attention of the blood of atonement. Genuine conviction gives no rest, until by the believing apprehension of this remedy the peace of God is firmly fixed in the conscience. As Bunyan so accurately pictured, not at the wicket-gate but at the sign of the cross did Christian find the grave of sin. Here it is lost, forgotten, never to be found.

14. Blessed is the man who always fears the LORD, but he who hardens his heart falls into trouble. This proverb continues on from the last one. After confession comes godly fear.

We may here profitably glance at some Christian paradoxes. *How is happiness to be found in constant fear?* Is fear to be the atmosphere of the spirit of a child of God? Godly fear preserves the sunshine and seals our special acceptance. We walk with our Father in holy watchfulness and peace. Faith without fear is self-confidence and self-delusion. "If there is truth in the Christian's assurance, sin itself cannot disappoint him, it is true. But it is no less true that if he does not fear sin, there is no truth in his assurance" (Leighton). Instead of being afraid to mix faith and fear, dread their separation.

The second paradox may be stated like this: *Should a forgiven Christian have any sense of sin?* A deep sensibility of sin is a special mercy. Consider carefully what sin is, what it may be; if the Lord restrain it not, it will end in apostasy. Dare we trifle with it? Do not forget, professing Christian, that we may only be strong in confidence in ourselves because we are sleeping in delusion or hardened in insensibility. From all the mischief of self-ignorance and hardness of heart, Good Lord, deliver us.

15-16. A godly ruler is to a land the clear sunshine of an unclouded morning, the fruitfulness of the springing grass after the rain. But what a curse is **a wicked man ruling**. His arbitrary despotism takes the place of right. We might as well live among the savage wild beasts of the forest. The **lion . . . roaring** for the prey and the **bear** raging in hunger, terrors to their weaker race, are apt emblems of this tyrant **over a helpless people**. "No sentiment of pity softens his heart. No principle of justice regulates his conduct. Complaint only provokes further exactions. Resistance kindles his unfeeling heart into savage fury. Helpless and miserable indeed are the people whom divine anger has placed under his misrule" (Paxton).

Thus indeed injustice is allowed to reign on a wide scale. A whole nation is afflicted by the ruthless tyranny of one man. How much rulers need to seek good **judgment**, that they may rule as the fathers of their people. And what cause we have to bless God for our mild and happy government, preserved as we are from **tyrannical** despots who would not stop at any tyranny that might subserve their selfish purpose. Of Tyndale's celebrated work, "The Obedience of a Christian Man," Henry VIII declared, "This book is for me and for all kings to read." He probably only gave attention to those parts he could use to accredit his own selfish rapacity. Well would it have been had he pondered such important instruction as, "The king is but a servant to execute the law of God, and not to rule after his own imagination." Or, he is brought to the throne "to minister unto and to serve his brethren and must not think that his subjects were made to minister to his selfish desires."

17. A man tormented by the guilt of murder will be a fugitive till death; let no one support him. The first law against the murderer must not be forgotten. Like the law of the Sabbath, it was in force from the beginning. "It was enacted and published before him out of whose loins the whole world after the Flood was to be repeopled, to show that it was not meant for a national or temporary ordinance, but for a universal and perpetual law" (Bishop Sanderson). The reason given for the command confirms its universal obligation. To destroy the image of God must be high treason against God himself. Where blood defiles the land, only the murderer's blood can cleanse it. The death, therefore, of the murderer is an imperative obligation. Protests against all capital punishment is misnamed philanthropy. Shall man pretend to be more merciful than God? Pity is misplaced here. The murderer, therefore, of his brother is his own murderer. Let God's law take its course.

Yet we must not cast out his soul. Visiting the condemned cell is a special exercise of mercy. While we bow to the stern justice of the great Lawgiver, joyous indeed it is to bring to the sinner under the sentence of the law the free forgiveness of the Gospel; not as annulling his sin, but showing the over-abounding of grace beyond the abounding of sin (Romans 5:20).

18. He whose walk is blameless is kept safe, but he whose ways are perverse will suddenly fall. This contrast had been drawn a little earlier as well (verse 6). Indeed the proverb itself in substance has been given. The **blameless** walk will show itself in extreme carefulness—in all doubtful points keeping to the safer side; not venturing on a precipice when we can walk on even ground. This is indeed Christian perfection or maturity, walking before God. We do not need Jacob's vision in order to realize God's presence. Faith sees what is invisible.

19. He who works his land will have abundant food, but the one who chases fantasies will have his fill of poverty. This proverb has also been given before (12:11). Such memories and hearts as ours need line upon line in the enforcement of practical obligation (see Isaiah 28:13). If we are not to be lazy in business but fervent in spirit, in this world and in all its concerns, how much more we need to be like this in the momentous concerns of eternity!

20. A faithful man will be richly blessed, but one eager to get rich will not go unpunished. A study of the contrast shows the definite meaning of the terms. **A faithful man** is contrasted here not with the rich but, mark this carefully, with **one eager to get rich.** A man may be rich by the blessing of God. But he who is **eager to get rich** will be **rich** by his own covetousness.

It is hard not to be overcome with this great temptation. "Yet how does the Scripture combat the vice of covetousness? Not by asserting that gold is only earth, exhibiting itself under a particular modification, and therefore not worth seeking; but by telling us that covetousness is idolatry, that the love of money is the root of all evil, and that some have shipwrecked their lives in seeking this abomination" (Cowper). Even if no criminal means are resorted to, yet the immoderate desire, the perseverance in every track of Mammon, the laboring night and day for the grand object, and the delight and confidence in the acquisition all prove the idolatrous heart and will not go unpunished.

21. To show partiality is not good—yet a man will do wrong for a piece of bread. This proverb has been repeated more than once (see 18:5; 24:23). The act of **partiality** itself **is not good.** The principle is worse—sordid selfishness. Here is perhaps **a man,** not of slavish or naturally degraded mind, but, such is the debasing influence of evil desire, **a man** of weight and influence who abuses his power for his own ends.

Yet a man will do wrong for a piece of bread. Cato used to say of Coelius the Tribune that "he might be hired for a piece of bread to speak or to hold his peace." Are Christians wholly guiltless in this matter? Is not conduct sometimes ruled by the fear of man rather than by trust in God? Let the temptation be resisted at the first step, manfully, prayerfully, in the Lord's strength, and the victory is gained.

22. A stingy man is eager to get rich and is unaware that poverty awaits him. Here is another word of warning. Take heed and beware of covetousness. Abraham was rich without being **eager to get rich.** Remember that it is not the person who knows most, but the person who most loves the things of heaven who will be most deadened to the riches of earth. Inasmuch as you love the earth, so you lose heaven. Is it not your shame that if heaven is your possession, you should have so much interest there and yet so few thoughts, so little love? Keep down most carefully your anxiety to rise in the world. For in its highest glory there is nothing worthy of your heart here. Keep heaven next to your heart as your treasure, your love, your rest, your crown. You will be happy if you have the mind of the holy Paulinus, Bishop of Nola in the fifth century, who when he heard of the ruin of all his property by the plunder of the Goths looked up and prayed, "You know where my treasure has long been!"

23. He who rebukes a man will in the end gain more favor than he who has a flattering tongue. Too often the flatterer finds more favor than the reprover. "Few people have the wisdom to like reproofs that would do them good better than praises that do them harm" (Dr. South). And yet a candid man, notwithstanding the momentary struggle of wounded pride, will **in the end** appreciate the purity of the motive and the value of the discovery. "He who cries out against his surgeon for hurting him when he is searching his wound will yet pay him well, and thank him too, when he has cured it" (Henry).

The flatterer is viewed with disgust, the reprover, **in the end**, with acceptance. Alas, the example of godly Asa presents an exception to the rule (2 Chronicles 16:7-10). When Bernard Gilpin publicly rebuked church abuses before his diocesan bishop, instead of being displeased, the bishop treated him with marked favor. "Mr. Gilpin," said the bishop, "I acknowledge you are fitter to be bishop of Durham than I am to be the parson of your church." When the philosopher Plutarch asked Alexander the reason for his dismissal, "either," replied the monarch, "you have not marked my error, which is a proof of your ignorance, or you have held your peace, which is a proof of your unfaithfulness."

Let us study the spirit of our gracious Master, whose gentleness always poured balm into the wound that his faithful love had opened. A rebuke in this spirit is more like the support of a friend than the punishment of a rod.

24. He who robs his father or mother and says, "It's not wrong"—he is partner to him who destroys. The aggravation of sin is proportionate to the obligation of duty. A murderer is a heinous transgressor; how much more a parricide! To rob a stranger, a neighbor, a friend is evil; how much more a **father or mother**! The filial obligation of cherishing care is broken. Ingratitude is added to injustice. What length of wickedness will such a hardened sinner stop at!

Young people, as you value your soul, your conscience, your happiness, ponder the wide extent of filial obligation; the honor, deference, and consideration included in it; the clear stamp of God's authority on it; the mark of his reprobation in despising it; the certain seal of his blessing on its practical and self-denying acknowledgment.

25. A greedy man stirs up dissension, but he who trusts in the LORD will prosper. The contrast between the **greedy man** and the one **who trusts in the LORD** is very remarkable. It shows that pride is the root of unbelief. The man, having cast off God, expects nothing and fears nothing from him. He lives as if there is no God. His proud heart is large—not like the wise man's, in fullness of capacity, but in ambitious grasp and insatiable appetite. He is never content within his own bounds.

Christian, dread any occasions of stirring up **dissension**, the cancer of vital godliness. Keep near to your Lord. It was when the disciples were talking together by the way, instead of walking in close communion with their Master, that strife was stirred up (Mark 9:33-34).

26. He who trusts in himself is a fool, but he who walks in wisdom is kept safe. Contrast the sound and faithful confidence mentioned in the previous verse with man's natural trust. Our confidence determines our state (Matthew 7:24-27). To trust an impostor who has deceived us a hundred times or a traitor who has proved himself false to our most important interests is surely to deserve the name of **fool**. This name, therefore, the Scriptures, using great plainness of speech, give to the person **who trusts in himself**. Well does Bishop Hall call the **fool** "the great impostor." Has self-trust not been deceiving us from our first moment of consciousness? Truly the traitor finds his home in our own heart, prompting, in concert with our deadly enemy, the most elaborate efforts for self-destruction.

Truly, as good Bishop Wilson remarks, "there is no sin that a man ought not to fear or to think himself incapable of committing, since we have in our corrupt will the seeds of every sin." None of us can safely presume that his heart may not hurry him into abominations that he can now contemplate only with horror. The best of men, when left to themselves, are mournful spectacles of weakness and instability.

Blessed be our God, for our standing is not based on the uncertainty of man's best purpose. It rests on the faithful promise, the unchangeable will, the free grace, and the almighty power of God. It does not rest on ourselves, but on the Rock, on which the church is immovably built. We value, then, a deep knowledge of our indwelling weakness and corruption. Painful and humbling as it is, it establishes our faith. This study of the heart strengthens the principle of holy fear, which enables us to walk **in wisdom** and thus keeps us **safe** from the evils of a self-confident state.

27. He who gives to the poor will lack nothing, but he who closes his eyes to them receives many curses. "There is none who wants to be in need or desires to be poor. And therefore the worldly-minded, to save themselves from it, carefully gather together and enclose as much wealth as they can by any means possible; and they think that by such means they will lack nothing. And indeed in man's judgment, that is the best way a man can take. But the Holy Spirit teaches us another way, which is totally opposite to natural reason. 'He who gives to the poor will lack nothing.' This is against reason, which says that we must gather and hold fast to avoid poverty. She looks not to what God can and will do. She is blind in the works of the Lord, and chiefly in those in whom he works according to his free promise" (Cope).

However close we may hold our material possessions, who can give security against coming into desperate need? But this promise gives a security that no earthly abundance can afford. Covetousness indeed combines with reason to contradict the Word of God. Yet the promise is given by him who has full power to make it good, who has a thousand ways of repaying what is done or sacrificed at his command. The fruit is absolutely certain, "as the best preventive against poverty, putting money into the bank of heaven, which can never forfeit credit" (Lawson). The best securities on earth will not stop riches from taking wing and flying away. But when have the promises of heaven ever proved to be untrue?

We must not neglect to look at people in distress, and we certainly must not turn away from them. Ponder this well, so that prudence and discrimination do not check the glow of love and prove to be a cloak for selfishness and obscure the light of Christian benevolence and compassion, which should shine before men from God's true servants.

28. When the wicked rise to power, people go into hiding; but when the wicked perish, the righteous thrive. The substance of this proverb was given in verse 12. **When the wicked rise to power** is indeed a national judgment, greatly to be deprecated as the engine of cruel malice against the church of God. But what a tremendous weight of guilt and punishment is involved in fighting against God in this way (Acts 9:4)!

The **power** of **the wicked** even here, however, is but for a moment. When they **perish**, as they will, **the righteous thrive**. In the early ages of the Christian church, after the death of the persecuting Herod, the Word of God grew and multiplied. The cross is an enriching blessing to the church and to every individual member of it.

Proverbs
Chapter 29

1. **A man who remains stiff-necked after many rebukes will suddenly be destroyed—without remedy.** The intractable ox becomes **stiff-necked** as a result of the yoke being put on him. But being **stiff-necked** is an apt picture of the stubborn sinner casting off the restraints of God.

Such instances are frequent among the children of godly parents or the hearers of a faithful minister, when every means of grace is a solemn but despised rebuke. Aggravated sin makes the judgment of a righteous God more manifest. The more enlightened the conscience, the more **stiff-necked** the person becomes.

An alarming illness, a dangerous accident, or the death of a companion in wickedness is the rod and reproof that is intended to give wisdom (verse 15). But if the fool continues to despise all of God's **rebukes**, his destruction will be sudden and **without remedy.**

2. **When the righteous thrive, the people rejoice; when the wicked rule, the people groan.** "The robes of honor to the righteous are the garments of gladness to the people. The scepter of authority to the godly is the staff of comfort to the people. On the other hand, the vestments of dignity to the wicked are the weeds that make the people groan. The throne of command to the one is the dungeon of misery to the other. The titles of honor given to the one are sighs and sorrows wrung from the other" (Jermin). What but righteousness can truly bless either an individual, a family, or a nation? "It is no peculiar conceit but a matter of sound consequence that all duties are so much the better performed by how much the men are more religious, from whose abilities the same proceed. For if the course of political affairs cannot in any good sort go forward without fit instruments, let polity acknowledge itself indebted to religion, godliness being the chiefest, top, and wellspring of all true virtue, even as God is of all good things." Thus admirably does our great Hooker insist that "religion, unfeignedly loved, perfects man's abilities to all kinds of virtuous services in the commonwealth."

What need we have to thank God that our guilty country, with so much to humble us in shame, should have been so long spared from the curse of **the wicked** ruler. The tyrant rules for his own sinful ends, the Christian sovereign for the good of the people.

3. A man who loves wisdom brings joy to his father, but a companion of prostitutes squanders his wealth. The substance of this proverb has been given before (10:1; 15:20; 23:15, 24-25; 27:11; 28:7). Yet the variations are instructive. The **wisdom** is here more distinctly described as **lov[ing]** wisdom. For "he is wise not only who has arrived at a complete habit of wisdom, but who does love it or desire it and listen to it" (Basil). Let this be manifestly our great object, not as a good thing but the best, the principal thing.

4. By justice a king gives a country stability, but one who is greedy for bribes tears it down. The best laws are of little use when they are badly administered. Partiality and injustice make them null and void. And yet it requires great integrity and moral courage to withstand the temptations of worldly policy and self-interest. The article in our Magna Charta, "We will sell justice to none," is but too plain evidence of the recklessness of all social principles before the great standard was erected among us. Let men of God be in our high places, and righteousness will then exalt our nation, and our church will be the joy and praise of the whole earth.

5. Whoever flatters his neighbor is spreading a net for his feet. Most wisely were Bunyan's pilgrims warned, "Beware of the flatterer." Yet, "forgetting to read the note of directions about the way," they fell into his **net** and, even though delivered, were justly punished for their folly. The doctrine of man's goodness, strength, or freedom; innocent infirmities; venial offenses; softening down the statements of man's total corruption; a general gospel without application; its promises and privileges without the balance of its trials and obligations—all this is frightful flattery. Unwary souls are misled.

Religious flattery is a common snare for the Christian. It may be natural, perhaps well-intentioned, to be willing to profit by more advanced experience and to inquire of a brother by what means he has been able to rise above the ordinary level and, indeed, to even express our envy at his superior knowledge, faith, or love. But all this tends to cherish self-complacency, the bane to that self-renouncing confidence in his Savior that is the clear characteristic of the faithful follower of his Lord. "Surely it is enough for us to have foes within and without to contend with, without having snares for our feet laid by our fellow pilgrims. Oh, it is a cruel thing to flatter. The soul is often more exhausted and injured by disentangling itself from these nets than by the hottest contest with principalities and powers. Those who have once known the torture the believer undergoes while this poison is pervading his soul, the bitter, lowering medicines he must take as antidotes, the frightful oblivion of lessons of humility that he has been studying for years, will, I think (unless much under the influence of the enemy of souls), not administer the noxious potion a second time" (Helen Plumptre).

6. An evil man is snared by his own sin, but a righteous one can sing and be glad. There is always a snare in the ways of **sin**, always a song in the ways of God. Sinner, think for a moment. What are the pleasures of **sin** compared to the pleasures of paradise? Remember, **sin** and ruin are bound together, and who can separate them?

Is it not worth pursuing this dishonorable evil to its sources, whether remote or close to hand? Are we incapacitated or only disinclined to **sing**? Seek a clearer exercise of faith, to rouse from indolence and to remove mistaken apprehensions. And in the active energy of faith, repent, return, watch and pray, mortify besetting sins. Inquire seriously: Are the materials for our song passed away? Are not the countless mercies yet remaining enough to swallow up the most bitter circumstances? Let faith be used in putting them together and in counting them. Surely under the deepest gloom that could ever rest on the soul, the harp would be taken down from the willows, and the **righteous** would **sing and be glad**. To some Christians of a morbid temperament, Bernard's advice may be important: "Let us mingle honey with wormwood, that the wholesome bitter may give health when it is drunk tempered with a mixture of sweetness. While you think humbly of yourselves, think also of the goodness of the Lord." "Always there are evil days in the world, always there are good days in the Lord" (Augustine).

7. The righteous care about justice for the poor, but the wicked have no such concern. To respect **the poor** is as important as to honor a mighty person. The man of God will follow the example of the great King of righteousness. "Let him have the conscience first," says Bishop Sanderson, "and then the patience too (and if he has the conscience, certainly he will have the patience), to search into the truth of things and not be dainty of his pains herein, though matters be intricate, and the labor like to be long and irksome."

Selfishness, however, not truth, **justice**, or mercy, is the standard of **the wicked**. But fearful is it to sit in the place of God as his representative, only to pervert his judgment for selfish aggrandizement. For "he who rejects the complaint of the poor and beats them off with big words and terror in his looks, either out of the hardness of his heart or the love of ease, when he might have leisure to give them audience if he were so minded and to take notice of their grievances cannot justly excuse himself by pleading, 'Behold, we knew it not'" (Bishop Sanderson).

Most striking was Bishop Ridley's concern for **the poor**, imploring the queen in his last moments at the stake on behalf of certain poor men's leases in his bishopric likely to become void by his death. In the same noble spirit was the remembrance of the dying Scott to his son of the arrival of the season when he would plant a root for the supply of the poor.

8. Mockers stir up a city, but wise men turn away anger. The comparison here is between proud, haughty scorners (in the Hebrew, "men of scorn") and **wise men**. The one involves public injury, the other public blessing. The one raises a tumult; the other quells it. The man who scorns being bound by common restraint will **stir up a city** by his presumption or set it on fire by bringing the fire of divine **anger** upon it. Happily, **wise men** are scattered through the land, and their energy and prudence turns away divine wrath. "Proud and foolish men kindle the fire that wise and good men must extinguish" (Henry).

9. If a wise man goes to court with a fool, the fool rages and scoffs, and there is no peace. It would generally be far better not to meddle with such **a fool** as is here described. We can only deal with him on very disadvantageous terms, and with little prospect of a good result. But what if I am appointed to contend with such fools? Can I return their unreasonable provocation with tenderness and compassion? Yes, when as the most effective means for their benefit I commend them to the almighty and sovereign grace of God. Can I forget that if this grace has healed my deep-rooted stubbornness, it is no less rich, no less free, no less sufficient for them?

10. Bloodthirsty men hate a man of integrity and seek to kill the upright. The noble army of martyrs stands before us. See the intensity of malice in the contrivance of the variety of their torture. **Bloodthirsty men hate a man of integrity.** The innocency of God's saints is the only ground for hatred. On the threatened apprehension of any outbreak of evil, the cry of the **bloodthirsty** was, "The Christians to the lions!"

And yet God is not unmindful of the troubles that threaten his servants. Saul sought to murder David, but Jonathan protected him. Jeremiah's enemies plotted against him, but Ebed-melech saved his life. Herod sought to kill Peter, but the church shielded him with her prayers.

11. A fool gives full vent to his anger, but a wise man keeps himself under control. Indeed the words of the **fool**, as an old expositor remarks, "are at the very door, so to speak, of his mind, which being always open, they readily fly abroad. But the words of the wise are buried in the inner recess of his mind, whence the coming out is more difficult" (Cartwright). This is wisdom to be valued and cultivated.

12. If a ruler listens to lies, all his officials become wicked. The influence of the ruler's personal character on his people involves a fearful responsibility. A wicked prince makes a wicked people. In his more immediate sphere, **if a ruler listens to lies** that are contrary to the laws of God and of love, he will never lack those about him who are ready to minister to his folly. "Lies will be told to those who are ready to listen to them" (Henry).

All in authority must learn the lesson of responsibility. Let Christian ministers especially not only hold the truth in its full integrity and take heed that their character will bear the strictest scrutiny, but let them turn away from the fawning flattery of those of whose uprightness there is at best but doubtful proof.

13. The poor man and the oppressor have this in common: The LORD gives sight to the eyes of both. The teaching of this proverb, as of one similar to it (22:2), seems to be the real equality of the divine dispensations under apparent inequalities. While these two categories of people are so different, they **have this in common:** They are on the same level before God. However much men may differ—one may oppress and despise, another may complain about the oppressive ways of his rich neighbor—**the LORD gives sight to the eyes of both.** God is no respecter of persons. Both classes partake in his providential blessings. Both are the subjects of his divine grace, "members of the same body, animated by the same spirit, appointed for the same inheritance, partakers of the same great and precious promises. There was not one prize for the soul of the poor, and another for the rich. There was not one table for the meaner guests, and another for the greater" (Bishop Reynolds). The beggar Lazarus and the rich tax collector Matthew have met together in one common home. Both are the undeserved monuments of wondrous, everlasting mercy. The eyes of both are enlightened spiritually, eternally.

14. If a king judges the poor with fairness, his throne will always be secure. This maxim has often been repeated in substance (verses 4, 7; 20:28). The writer of this book was a king. He was naturally led to write for his own benefit, even while the divine Spirit guided his pen for the use of rulers to the end of time. May every king and ruler place this picture of a godly ruler constantly before his eyes.

15. The rod of correction imparts wisdom, but a child left to himself disgraces his mother. Discipline is the order of God's government. Parents are his dispensers of it to their children. Let **correction** be first tried, and if it succeeds, let **the rod** be spared. If not, let **the rod** do its work. "Take this for certain," says Bishop Hopkins, "that as many deserved stripes as you spare from your children, you do but lay on your own back. And those whom you refuse to chastise, God will make severer scourges to chastise you."

Without a wise and firm control, the parent is miserable, and the child is ruined. "I earnestly entreat you," writes the wise and experienced Josiah Pratt to his sons and daughters, "to subdue the wills of your children most tenderly if you can. But if not, your duty and your love require measures that shall enforce obedience. A very young child puts forth perhaps his first approaches to sin in acts of cunning and rebellion. Rely with unshaken confidence on that divine maxim, 'Train up a child in the way he should go, and when he is old, he will not depart from it.'"

16. When the wicked thrive, so does sin, but the righteous will see their downfall. "Let not the righteous," said good Bishop Patrick, "be discouraged; for the wickeder men are, the shorter is their reign." The faithful Christian minister, conscious of his inability to stem the ever-flowing torrent of iniquity, would sink in despair but for the assured confidence that he is on the conquering side, that his cause, being the cause of his Lord, must eventually prevail.

17. Discipline your son, and he will give you peace; he will bring delight to your soul. Once more the wise man returns to the subject of discipline. These repeated inculcations (verse 15; 13:24; 19:18; 22:15; 23:13-14) strongly show its importance. The command is positive—**discipline your son.** This Book of Proverbs is not out-of-date. Like every other part of the sacred volume, it is the book for every age, given by the inspiration of God. To try, therefore, more self-pleasing rules is to set up our will in opposition to God's, and to place reason or feeling where faith should stand. It is making ourselves wise above that which is written. Put his Word to the test. The simplicity and perseverance of faith will be richly honored in God's own best time and way.

18. Where there is no revelation, the people cast off restraint [KJV: where there is no vision, the people perish]; but blessed is he who keeps the law. The **revelation** here, as appears from the contrast, is divine instruction. The Christian ministry is the appointed ordinance to communicate this blessing and is therefore the main instrumentality of conversion and subsequent Christian perfection. And yet this most fruitful organ of divine agency (preaching), which our blessed Lord honored as the grand medium of his own teaching (Psalm 40:9-10; Isaiah 61:1-2), is now depreciated as the mark of "a church only in a weak and a languishing state, and an instrument that Scripture, to say the least, has never much recommended" (*Tracts for the Times*). Far more orthodox is the sentiment from one of our venerable reformers: "Thus we may learn the necessity of preaching, and what inconvenience follows when it is not used. 'Where preaching falls,' says Solomon, 'there people perish.' Therefore, let everyone keep himself in God's schoolhouse and learn his lesson diligently. For as the body is nourished with meat, so is the soul with the Word of God" (Bishop Pilkington). "The meanest village," Luther was apt to say, "with a Christian pastor and flock is a palace of ebony."

No greater calamity, therefore, can there be than the removal of the **revelation.** For "when there is none that can edify and exhort and comfort the people by the Word of God, they must needs perish. They become thralls and captives to Satan. Their heart is bound up. Their eyes are shut up; they can see nothing. Their ears are stopped up; they can hear nothing. They are carried away as a prey into hell, because they have not the knowledge of God" (Bishop Jewell). Where **revelation** is withdrawn from a church, the people perish in ignorance and delusion. For as our Protestant Cranmer nobly testified, "I know how Antichrist both obscured the glory of God and the true knowledge of his Word: overcasting the same with mists and clouds of error and ignorance through their false glosses and interpretations. It pitieth me," he adds, "to see the simple and hungry flock of Christ led into corrupt pastures, to be carried blind-fold they know not whither."

But blessed is he who keeps the law. Truly to be interested in God's promises, to be an inheritor of everlasting glory, to be the present posses-sor of divine favor, to be secured from the peril of everything that is against him and assured of the supply of all things that will work for his good—this is the **blessed** portion of the practical disciple. Who, then, can justly cast a cloud of gloom over the ways of God? Let the Pentecostal Christians witness to their joy (Acts 2:46-47). Let every servant of his Lord invite his fellow sinners to the enjoyment of his privileges by the manifestation of their holiness and joy.

19. A servant cannot be corrected by mere words; though he under-stands, he will not respond. Discipline must be carried not only into the family (verses 15, 17) but throughout the whole household in order to pre-serve God's authority and order. An important hint is here given about the management of servants. The Scripture fully sets out the duties of servants (Titus 2:9; Ephesians 6:7). Sullen resistance to reproof is most inconsistent with the profession of a Christian. And if the offender escapes the correc-tion of an earthly master, he will be visited with the rod of his angry Lord, as a self-deceiver or backslider withdrawing from his high obligation.

20. Do you see a man who speaks in haste? There is more hope for a fool than for him. We have just been warned against sullen silence. This next warning is directed against hasty words. When a person flows on in his words, evidently without time for consideration, when he gives his opinion as if there were no time to take counsel or to take notice of the judgment of others, this is the **fool** speaking. It is very difficult to deal effectively with him. Until the stronghold of his own conceit is shaken, argument and instruction are lost on him.

21. If a man pampers his servant from youth, he will bring grief in the end. We have here another valuable rule for domestic discipline, directing masters to a wise treatment of their servants. It is a grievous error to convince ourselves or to induce another to step out of the path that a God of order has marked for us.

22. An angry man stirs up dissension, and a hot-tempered one com-mits many sins. Anger is not necessarily a sinful passion. But in a fallen nature, to preserve its purity is a rare and most difficult matter. It must be confined to points where God's honor is concerned, and even here the sun must not go down on our anger.

But let us not be satisfied with the outward constraint on passion. God condemns the deep-rooted principle that gives it birth—the wretched heart filled with soul-destroying corruption. Oh, for the mystery and teaching of the cross, to mold our temper into a genuine godly spirit and influence.

23. A man's pride brings him low, but a man of lowly spirit gains honor. This proverb, Bishop Hall remarks in his own style, "is like unto Shushan: in the streets whereof honor is proclaimed to the humble Mordecai; in the palace whereof is erected an engine of death to a proud Haman." It shows the spirit of our Lord's oft-repeated declaration expounded by his daily providences that whoever exalts himself will be abased, and whoever humbles himself will be exalted. The speech of Artabanus to Xerxes before his invasion of Greece is a striking testimony from a heathen. "God delights to depress whatever is too highly exalted. Thus a large army is often defeated by a small one. When God in his jealousy throws them into a panic or thunders against them, they miserably perish. For God suffers no mortal to think magnificently" (Herodotus). The real value of man in himself is so small that the psalmist is at a loss where to find it (Psalm 8:3-4).

The world counts nothing great without display. But note the substantial honor that comes from God only. Humility is indeed true greatness. It is "the crown," as Mr. Howels remarks, "of finite beings, made and jeweled by the hand of God himself. Supremacy is the glory of God; humility is the ornament of his child."

It is with us as with our Lord—**honor** comes out of humiliation. "You are not only our Savior but our pattern too. If we can go down the steps of your humiliation, we shall rise up the stairs of your glory" (Bishop Hall).

24. The accomplice of a thief is his own enemy; he is put under oath and dare not testify. This is a warning under the eighth commandment. The law makes no distinction between the **thief** and **the accomplice.** Consenting to sin, receiving the stolen goods, involves us in the guilt and punishment. **The accomplice** may be less practiced in sin. He may be only commencing his course. But even the first step is the way to death. One step naturally leads to another.

Oh, how frightful is the history of thousands whose fellowship with sinners has drawn them into fellowship with sin, and ultimately to take the lead in sin. And of these thousands, how few, it is to be feared, retrace their steps and become, like Onesimus, true followers of Christ and faithful servants to man!

25. Fear of man will prove to be a snare, but whoever trusts in the LORD is kept safe. We know that **a snare** brings a man into difficult straits. He is not master of himself. Here Satan spreads **a snare,** and the **fear of man** drives people into it. And a fearful **snare** it is, and always has been, to thousands. Many, once entangled, have never escaped. It besets every step of the pathway to heaven.

What, especially among the young, makes so many ashamed to be found on their knees, to be known as readers of their Bibles, to cast in their lot decidedly among the saints of God? For them the **fear of man** is **a snare.** And therefore they do not ask, "What should I do?" but "What will my friends think of me?" They cannot brave the finger of scorn. And if they seem for a while to be in earnest, "they have slavish fears" (as Bunyan well describes the case) "that do overmaster them. . . . They betake themselves to second thoughts, namely, that it is good to be wise and not to run . . . the hazard of losing all, or at least of bringing themselves into unavoidable and unnecessary troubles." (This is a conversation between Hopeful and Christian, from *Pilgrim's Progress*.) They prefer to writhe under their convictions rather than to suffer reproach for the sake of Christ.

How different is this servile principle from the godly fear of sin, which the wise man had earlier noted as the substance of happiness (28:14). "By the fear of the Lord men depart from evil; by the fear of man they run themselves into evil" (Flavel). The one is the pathway to heaven (19:23). The other, involving the denial of the Savior, plunges its wretched slave into the lake of fire.

But even apart from this tragic end, observe the weighty hindrance to Christian integrity. Indeed, as Mr. Scott most truly observes, obeying God and not fearing man is, often at least, "the last victory the Christian gains. He will master, by that grace which is given by God, his own lusts and passions and all manner of inward and outward temptations. He will be dead to the pleasures of the world long before he has mastered this fear of man. This kind of spirit is not cast out but by a very spiritual and devout course of life." Oh, for deliverance from this principle of bondage.

26. Many seek an audience with a ruler, but it is from the LORD that man gets justice. We must, in the light of this proverb, seek God to be our Friend. Here is solid ground for faith. Begin with God; all judgment is in his hands. Let him choose and dispose your lot. Consider everything that happens as coming from him. As Thomas à Kempis put it, "As you will, what you will, when you will." This is the shortest and the surest way of peace. Only believe!

27. The righteous detest the dishonest; the wicked detest the upright. Here is the oldest, the most rooted, the most universal quarrel in the world. It was the first fruit of the Fall (Genesis 3:15). It has continued ever since and will last to the end of the world.

The soul is wearied with the unceasing struggles with the enemies of truth. How can we not want to fly away on the wings of a dove and be at rest? And how can we fight in this contest but for the blessed hope God has given us? *O Lord, may the time come quickly when the woman's conquering seed will bruise the serpent's head and the head of all his descendants finally and forever, and then reign as King and Savior over his redeemed people.*

Proverbs
Chapter 30

1. The sayings of Agur son of Jakeh—an oracle: This man declared to Ithiel, to Ithiel and to Ucal. We now come to **the sayings of Agur son of Jakeh.** The two concluding chapters of this book are an appendix to the proverbs of Solomon. Nothing definite is known about the writers, and it is vain to speculate where God is silent. It is much better to give our full attention to the teaching than to indulge in unprofitable speculation about the writers. Our ignorance about the writers of many of the Psalms in no way stops them from being useful to us. We know their Author, though the penmen are hidden. It is enough for us to be assured that they were holy men who were moved to write by the Holy Spirit.

Agur was doubtless one of the wise men found in many ages of the Old Testament church. His words were **an oracle**—that is, divine instruction. This teaching was given to **Ithiel and to Ucal,** but especially to **Ithiel.** These were probably two pupils of **Agur.** We know nothing further about them.

2-3. "I am the most ignorant of men; I do not have a man's understanding. I have not learned wisdom, nor have I knowledge of the Holy One." Stronger language could scarcely have been used. He confesses to be **the most ignorant of men.** Whoever knows his own heart knows that of himself and can hardly conceive of anyone else being as degraded as himself.

The following remarks of a profound divine will illustrate this subject: "He that has much grace apprehends much more than others that great height to which his love ought to ascend; and he sees better than others how little a way he has risen toward that height. And therefore, estimating his love by the whole height of his duty, hence it appears astonishingly low and little in his eyes. True grace is of that nature that the more a person has of it, with remaining corruption, the less does his goodness and holiness appear, in proportion, not only to his past but to his present deformity, in the sin that now appears in his heart and in the abominable defects of his highest and best affections" (J. Edwards).

The nearer our contemplation of God, the closer our communion with him, the deeper will be our self-abasement before him. Unless a man stoops, he can never enter the door. He must become a fool, that he may be wise. There is a fine ray of wisdom in that consciousness of ignorance that led Socrates to confess, "I only know one thing, that I know nothing." And when a person is humbled in his shame, then he can see the house of his God in its breadth and length (Ezekiel 44:5), enjoying clearer and panting still for clearer manifestations of the incomprehensible God.

4. "Who has gone up to heaven and come down? Who has gathered up the wind in the hollow of his hands? Who has wrapped up the waters in his cloak? Who has established all the ends of the earth? What is his name, and the name of his son? Tell me if you know!" Can we wonder that Agur acknowledged his brutishness now that he was contemplating the majesty of God, so amazing in his deeds, so incomprehensible in his nature? The eye is blinded by the dazzling blaze of the sun. **"Who has established all the ends of the earth?"** There can be no doubt. The challenge is thrown out as a demonstration that it was God alone. "Show me the man who can or dares arrogate this power to himself" (Bishop Hall).

"What is his name, and the name of his son? Tell me if you know!" Many are so bewitched by their own thinking that they conceive themselves to understand this **name**. They think far higher of their wisdom than Agur did and are at no loss at all to explain the complete meaning of the inscrutable subject. But the genuine disciple acknowledges the nature of the Son to be as incomprehensible as that of the Father.

Yet what revelation has brought up to us from these untraceable depths are pearls of great price. Let us reverently gather them for the enriching of our souls. So far as our divine Teacher leads us by the hand, let us diligently follow him. May we have a holy eagerness to be wiser continually in that which is written. "Curiously to inquire is rashness; to believe is piety; to know indeed is life eternal" (Bernard).

5-6. Nothing is learned solidly by abstract speculation. Go to the Book. Here all is light and purity. While the secret things belong to the Lord our God, yet the things that are revealed are our holy directory. Everything is intended to influence the heart and conduct (Deuteronomy 29:29).

"Every word of God is flawless." Of what other book in the world can this be said? Where else is the gold found without alloy? The Word has been tried, and it has stood the trial, and no dross has been found in it. "Having God as its Author, it has truth without any mixture of error for its matter" (Locke).

"He is a shield to those who take refuge in him." Nothing honors God like turning to him in every time of need. Here there is rest, peaceful confidence, safekeeping. And where else can this be found? Despondency meets the poor, deluded sinner who looks for some other support. And even the child of God traces his frequent lack of protection to his feeble and uncertain use of his divine **shield**.

"**Do not add to his words, or he will rebuke you and prove you a liar.**" The Word of God is not only pure and unable to deceive. It is also sufficient, and therefore, like tried gold, it needs no addition for its perfection. Hence to **add to his words**, stamped as they are with his divine authority, will expose us to his tremendous **rebuke** and cover us with shame. The Jewish church virtually added their oral law and written traditions (Mark 7:7-13). The attempt in our own day to bring tradition to a near, if not to an equal, level with the sacred testimony is a fearful approach to this sinful presumption. A new rule of faith is thus introduced, adding to the divine rule and creating coordinate authority. Never indeed was it so important to clear from all question the momentous controversy of what is and what is not the Word of God.

7-9. Although Agur has confessed his brutishness before his God, yet his prayers (the most accurate test of a man of God) prove him to possess deep spiritual understanding. Agur's heart must have been taught by God, for he directs his prayers by a primary regard for his best interests and by a spiritual discernment of what would probably be harmful and what would be beneficial to those interests.

"**Two things I ask of you, O LORD; do not refuse me before I die.**" His prayers are short but comprehensive. Although little is said, that little is full of meaning. Spiritual blessings occupy the first place; temporal blessings are secondary and subservient to them.

"**Keep falsehood and lies far from me.**" Is not this the atmosphere of the world? **Falsehood** is its character, **lies** its delusion, promising happiness, only to disappoint its weary and restless victims. Everything deadens the heart and eclipses the glory of the Savior. A soul that knows its dangers and its besetting temptations will live in the spirit of this prayer of the godly Agur.

"**Give me neither poverty nor riches, but give me only my daily bread.**" "If Agur be the master of a family, then that is his competency which is sufficient to maintain his wife, children, and household. If Agur is a public person, a ruler of the people, then that is Agur's sufficiency which will conveniently maintain him in that condition" (Mede). Let us seek God's grace to glorify him in either state. Or, if it seems right to pray for a change in our condition, let us not forget to pray for a single eye to his glory, that his will, not ours, may be done in us. "Whatever God gives," said the pious Bishop Hall, "I am both thankful and indifferent; so as, while I am rich in estate, I may be poor in spirit; and while I am poor in estate, I may be rich in grace."

10. "**Do not slander a servant to his master, or he will curse you, and**

you will pay for it." Do not allow this proverb to be a shelter for unfaithfulness. We owe it alike to master and to servant not to wink at sin. But beware of the busy wantonness of the talebearer (Leviticus 19:16). Never cause trouble over trifles or **slander a servant** when he may not have the full freedom and power to defend himself. When conscience does not constrain us to speak, the law of love always supplies a reason for silence. The Jewish servants were normally slaves, most of whom were crushed by their master's oppression. Cruel, therefore, would it be without good reason to heap degradation on a lowly fellow creature, for whom the Mosaic law prescribed kindness and protection (Deuteronomy 23:15).

11-14. Agur here gives in artificial order (as in some of the Psalms) his observations, probably in answer to his disciples' inquiries. He describes four different groups of people. These different types of people have always existed, and always will, to the end of time.

"There are those who curse their fathers and do not bless their mothers." What a disgrace to human nature this first group is! They **curse** their parents. Solon, when asked why he had made no law against parricide, replied that he could not conceive of anyone so impious and cruel. The divine Lawgiver knew man better, recognizing that his heart was capable of wickedness beyond conception (Jeremiah 17:9). Many are the forms in which this proud abomination shows itself: resistance to a parent's authority, contempt of his reproof, shamelessly defiling his name, needlessly exposing his sin, coveting his substance, denying his obligation. Every village bears sad testimony to this crying sin that brings many a parent with sorrow to the grave and spreads anarchy throughout the whole land.

In what church do we not find the next group of people? **"Those who are pure in their own eyes and yet are not cleansed of their filth."** We often see this self-deceiver in the spiritual church, exhibiting a full and clean profession to his fellowmen, while himself living at an infinite distance from God.

The next group of people provokes our sorrowful amazement. **"Those whose eyes are ever so haughty, whose glances are so disdainful."** Such intolerable arrogance! What greater anomaly does the conscience afford than that of a proud sinner? Their **eyes are ever so haughty**, instead of being cast down to the ground. Such is his self-confidence even in the presence of God (Luke 18:11-12).

The last group of people appears before us as monsters of iniquity. We can scarcely draw the picture in its full colors. **"Those whose teeth are swords and whose jaws are set with knives to devour the poor from the earth, the needy from among mankind."** Imagine brutes with iron **teeth**, a wild beast opening his mouth and displaying, instead of **teeth, swords** and **knives,** sharpened and ready for their murderous work. Yet withal, these cruel oppressors are marked by pitiful cowardice. They vent their wantonness only where there is little or no power of resistance as they **devour the poor.** God thus shows us a picture of man left to himself. When the reins are loosened or given up, is there any length of wickedness to which he will not proceed?

Indeed these four groups of people teach us a lesson that is most valuable, yet most humbling thoroughly to know. So depraved is man that he does not understand his own depravity. Nothing is as hidden from him as himself. He keeps a good opinion of himself by keeping the light out of his heart and conscience.

Adored indeed be the grace of God if we are not among these groups of people! However, let us remember that we used to be like them, but we have been washed from our filthiness. So it is most profitable to reflect from what we have been raised, and to whom we owe all that we have and are for God's service.

15-16. "The leech has two daughters. 'Give! Give!' they cry. There are three things that are never satisfied, four that never say, 'Enough!': **the grave, the barren womb, land, which is never satisfied with water, and fire, which never says, 'Enough!'"** Agur describes in an artificial expression (see verses 21, 24, 29; compare 6:16), but with forcible imagery, the cravings of human evil desires. If viewed with reference to the last group of people in the previous verse, they make an admirably finished picture of the merciless and avaricious tyrant.

Every indulgence provokes the appetite. "'The leech has two daughters.' But we have," says Bishop Sanderson, "I know not how many craving lusts, no less importunately clamorous than they, till they be served, incessantly crying 'Give! Give!' but much more unsatisfied than they. For they will be filled in time, and when they are filled, they tumble off, and there is an end. But our lusts will never be satisfied. Like Pharaoh's cattle when they have eaten up all the fat ones, they are still as hungry and as whining as they were before."

How blessed, then, is the state to which the Gospel brings us. Having food and clothes, let us be content.

17. "The eye that mocks a father, that scorns obedience to a mother, will be pecked out by the ravens of the valley, will be eaten by the vultures." Agur here returns to the first group of people he had described in verse 11. He had previously described their character. Now he links it with the punishment. Observe the guilt of even a scornful look or the mocking eye, with perhaps not a word spoken. Certainly if the fifth commandment is the first with promise (Ephesians 6:2), it is also the first with judgment. No breached commandment is visited with more tremendous threatenings. What a picture of infamy!

18-20. "There are three things that are too amazing for me, four that I do not understand: the way of an eagle in the sky, the way of a snake on a rock, the way of a ship on the high seas, and the way of a

man with a maiden. This is the way of an adulteress: She eats and wipes her mouth and says, 'I've done nothing wrong.'" The kingdom of nature is full of wonder, and these wonders are full of instruction. Where the philosopher cannot give a reason, the humble disciple may learn a lesson. The depths of nature are figures of the depths of sin, of the unsearchable, deceitful heart.

Eminently practiced is the seducer in the depths of Satan, and a thousand arts does he use to allure the affections of his unwary victim. And it is often as difficult to penetrate his designs and to escape his snares as to trace **the way of an eagle, the way of a snake,** or **the way of a ship.** Let this be a warning to young and inexperienced females not to trust their own purity or the strength of their own resolutions or to place themselves in unprotected situations.

Equally unfathomable are the devices of the **adulteress.** "**She eats and wipes her mouth and says, 'I've done nothing wrong.'**" Solomon too described the picture with striking and minute accuracy (chapter 7; 5:3-6). Such a course of abomination, wickedness, and hypocrisy is scarcely to be conceived—indulging her sin as a sweet morsel under her tongue, feasting greedily on her stolen waters and secret bread, yet keeping up the appearance of innocence and purity. **She ... wipes her mouth** to prevent all suspicion, allowing no sign of the action to remain. A woman must be advanced very far in the way of sin before she can present such an unblushing front. Let, then, the first step be shunned, and the most distant path that may lead to temptation. When shame ceases, the ruin of the victim is accomplished. Abundant warning is given—solemn instruction, many beacons in the path to show the certain end of this flowery road.

21-23. "Under three things the earth trembles, under four it cannot bear up: a servant who becomes king, a fool who is full of food, an unloved woman who is married, and a maidservant who displaces her mistress." Next to things that are unsearchable, Agur now mentions some things that are intolerable, things under which **the earth trembles,** which bring confusion wherever they are found. Who does not naturally condemn things out of place as unsuitable and unseemly? The law of the works of God are in the world no less than in the church, and any breach of order is to be deprecated. **Four** such evils are here mentioned—two connected with men, two with women.

The first evil mentioned is **"a servant who becomes king."** This is a serious evil in the family, whether it arises from the mismanagement of the master or from the servant's own intrigue. He is obviously out of place; ruling where he ought to serve, he will certainly bring disorder.

Then look at the **fool** (not an idiot, but a willful sinner) **who is full of food.** Can we wonder that he causes trouble and is a curse, since he gives full rein to his appetite and becomes even more devoid of understanding than before?

Look again into the inner room of the family. We are told about **an unloved woman who is [becomes] married.** Some wed out of desire and not love; marriage is then the ordinance of lust and not of godliness.

The last evil noticed is a frequent source of family trouble—**a maidservant who displaces her mistress.** Lack of discipline or integrity leads to waywardness and self-indulgence. So the house, instead of being under wholesome rule, becomes prey to envy and strife. Our own history presents sad illustrations of this intolerable evil. Anne Boleyn and Jane Seymour were maidservants who unhappily displaced their respective mistresses while living in the affections of the sovereign. The royal example of selfishness and lust was a national grievance, in which the maidservants were not wholly guiltless.

How necessary it is to be consistent in every part of our Christian lives. Oh, let us be careful that no lack of wisdom, godly contentment, or self-denial brings reproach on that worthy name by which we are called.

24-28. "**Four things on earth are small, yet they are extremely wise: Ants are creatures of little strength, yet they store up their food in the summer; coneys are creatures of little power, yet they make their home in the crags; locusts have no king, yet they advance together in ranks; a lizard can be caught with the hand, yet it is found in kings' palaces.**" The mind of man spreads over the length and breadth of creation and draws instruction from every part of the universe presented to his senses. Everywhere God teaches us by his works as well as by his Word. The stupid beasts reprove our ingratitude (Isaiah 1:3). The birds of the air rebuke our inattention (Jeremiah 8:7) and our unbelieving anxieties (Matthew 6:26), and lilies rebuke our anxious fears (Matthew 6:29-31).

Agur had before mentioned four things that seemed to be great but were really despicable. Here he produces **four things on earth** that **are small, yet they are extremely wise.** Therefore, do not despise them because of their size, but admire the wonder-working hand that has made these little creatures with such sufficient means of provision, defense, and safety. As has been beautifully remarked, "God reigns in a community of ants and ichneumons [flies] as visibly as among living men or mighty seraphim" (McCheyne). Truly nothing was made for no purpose. The world of instinct shows that which will put to shame our higher world of reason. Yes, these four remarkable instances of almighty skill, the natures and habits of these four little animals, teach many useful and important lessons, to which the greatest philosopher might attend with profit.

"Industry is commended to us by all sorts of examples, deserving our regard and imitation. All nature is a copy thereof, and the whole world a glass [mirror], wherein we may behold this duty represented to us. Every creature about us is incessantly working toward the ends for which it was designed, indefatigably exercising the powers with which it is endued, diligently observing the laws of its creation" (Barrow). The **ants** have already brought the lesson before us (6:6-8). They indeed have **little strength.** Thousands are crushed by one tread of the foot; **yet they store up their food in the summer.** A quickening sermon do these little insects preach to us as they prepare for the coming winter. What must be the thoughtlessness of men who make no provision for the coming eternity!

"Coneys are creatures of little power, yet they make their home in the crags." Although they have **little power, coneys** secure themselves from impending danger by making **their home in the crags,** holes in inaccessible rocks. Thus what they lack in strength, they make up in wisdom. Is not our refuge, like theirs, in the "mountain fortress" (Isaiah 33:16)? And are we, like them, making our **home** there?

Observe again the instinct of the **locusts.** Some insects, like the bee, are under monarchical government. But **locusts have no king.** Yet how wonderful is their order as **they advance together in ranks,** like an army under the strictest discipline. Do not these little insects give us a lesson on the importance of unity and unanimous movement?

The **lizard is found in kings' palaces** as well as in the cottages of the poor, as if God would instruct even the great ones of the earth by its pattern of diligence.

The general lesson to learn from these diminutive teachers is the importance of acting wisely according to the principles of their nature as the best means to secure the greatest amount of happiness of which they are capable. God has provided for every creature and for its own happiness. How many of us stand condemned by the sermons of these little insects! Let us not be too proud to learn or too careless to attend to the humbling but most valuable lessons taught in this school of instruction. **Let the wise listen and add to their learning** (1:5).

29-31. "There are three things that are stately in their stride, four that move with stately bearing: a lion, mighty among beasts, who retreats before nothing; a strutting rooster, a he-goat, and a king with his army around him. Agur naturally lingers on this vast field of natural wonders. They are such a splendid exhibition of divine perfections. They are the source of so much light to the world, before the book of revelation was fully opened (Job 12:7-10). After mentioning some striking instances of wisdom, he now singles out a few objects that appeared to him marvelous for their **stately bearing: a lion . . . a rooster, a he-goat, and a king.**

Let us take note not only about the various duties of the Christian life, but also about the manner and spirit of their performance. Cultivate not only the *integrity* but the *beauty* of Christian character. Christians should be attractive and engaging by the courtesy of their general demeanor. Any obvious lack of such beauty repels the world from the Gospel of Christ. "If we desire to reign in heaven, we must present ourselves there with this beautiful crown, from whence radiate all kinds of virtue and praise" (Daille).

32-33. **"If you have played the fool and exalted yourself, or if you have planned evil, clap your hand over your mouth! For as churning the milk produces butter, and as twisting the nose produces blood, so stirring up anger produces strife."** A humble heart will repress the sparks of this unholy fire. A spirit sorrowing for the evil of our thoughts is an essential part of the cure (Ecclesiastes 7:4). We should not readily indulge the sin for which we have been truly humbled before our God. When we lack this genuine spirit, how reluctant we are to acknowledge our offense toward each other! How difficult it is for us with our proud tempers to be the first to put a hand over our mouths! We are quicker to open our mouths in self-justification than in self-abasement. Oh, hasten the blessed time when the church will be fully transformed into the image of her divine Lord, when it will be a church of perfect love in a world of love.

Proverbs
Chapter 31

1-2. The sayings of King Lemuel—an oracle his mother taught him: "O my son, O son of my womb, O son of my vows." We know no more about **King Lemuel** than we do about the prophet **Agur** in the last chapter. Both Agur and Lemuel have been identified with Solomon, although there is no historical evidence. It seems unlikely that Solomon, having given his own name more than once in this book (1:1; 10:1), should give two mystical names at the end, without any distinct personal application. Nor is there any scriptural testimony in favor of Bathsheba that would lead us to stamp her with this peculiar honor as one of the writers of God's Word (**an oracle his mother taught him**). "The admonitory verses composed for King Lemuel by his mother, when in the flower of youth and high expectation, are an inimitable production, as well in respect to their actual materials as to the delicacy with which they are selected. Instead of attempting to lay down rules concerning matters of state and political government, the illustrious writer confines herself, with the nicest and most becoming art, to a recommendation of the gentler virtues of temperance, benevolence, and mercy and a minute and unparalleled delineation of the female character, which might bid fairest to promote the happiness of her son in married life" (Dr. Good).

All we know is that King Lemuel was endowed, like many of God's people, with the invaluable blessing of a godly mother who, like Deborah of old (Judges 5:1), was honored by God to be the author of a chapter of the sacred volume.

What an animating burst from the yearning of a mother's heart! **"O my son, O son of my womb, O son of my vows."** Like Samuel, King Lemuel was the subject of many of his mother's prayers. If there were more Hannahs, would there not be more Samuels? If you want, Christian mother, your child to be a Samuel or an Augustine, you must yourself be a Hannah or a Monica. The child of your prayers, of your **vows**, of your

279

tears will be in the Lord's best time the child of your praises, your rejoicings, your richest consolation. Yet your faith will not end with the dedication of your child. For King Lemuel's **mother taught him**. And such is the practical habit of godliness that faith in vowing quickens diligence in teaching.

3-7. Solomon has given us his father's wise counsels (4:4). Lemuel gives us his mother's. Both have an equal claim to reverence (1:8). Filled with deep anxiety, impassioned tenderness bursts out in this godly mother, as if some besetting enticements were imminent, perhaps already working poison in her beloved son.

"Do not spend your strength on women." What a beacon Solomon had set up earlier (chapters 2, 5, 7). These forbidden gratifications **ruin kings**. Such was the judgment on David. His kingly authority was shaken. And Solomon's sin destroyed his kingdom. The fruit of this sin is shame. The end of it, without repentance, is death.

The anxious mother of Lemuel next warns against another sin—intemperance. The vice that degrades a man and makes him into a beast is shameful to everyone, especially **kings**. They are cities set on a hill. Men look, or ought to look, to them for guidance and example. How sad it is **for kings to drink wine** and **for rulers to crave beer** if they then become drunk **and forget what the law decrees and deprive all the oppressed of their rights**. Priest and prophet err through strong drink (Isaiah 28:7; 56:12). A wise veto is set for the rulers of the church, that they should not be given to drunkenness (1 Timothy 3:3; Titus 1:7).

Yet the abuse of God's blessing does not destroy its use. **Wine** is the gift of God. It make a man's heart glad. It restores and refreshes. **Give beer to those who are perishing, wine to those who are in anguish.** The Samaritan did just this to the wounded traveler, and Paul prescribed it for the illness of his beloved son in the faith (1 Timothy 5:23). The rule, therefore, of love and self-denial is as follows: Instead of wasting **beer** and **wine** on yourself and merely indulging your own appetite, share your luxuries with those who really need them, such as the **perishing** and **those who are in anguish**.

8-9. Very soundly does the wise mother inculcate mercy in her royal son. This is one of the pillars of the king's throne (20:28 [KJV]). He must be the father of his people, using all his authority to protect those who cannot protect themselves. No case of distress, when coming to his knowledge, should be refused his attention. Thus our law makes the judge the counsel for the prisoner who is unable to plead for himself. **"Speak up for those who cannot speak for themselves."**

10. A wife of noble character who can find? She is worth far more than rubies. We now come to the principal part of the chapter. The wise mother of Lemuel had warned her royal son against the seduction of evil women and accompanying temptations and had given him wholesome rules by which to govern. She now sets before him the full-length portrait of **a wife of noble character**. This choicest gift is emphatically said to be from the Lord (19:14).

The elegant power of these twenty-two verses, like Psalm 119, is artificially constructed, each verse beginning with one of the successive letters of the Hebrew alphabet. "All mothers should teach female pupils under their care to read and learn it by heart" (Bishop Horne). The more deeply this passage is studied, provided that it is studied in a practical way, the more its beauty will be understood and felt. No treasure can be compared to the woman described in these verses.

11-12. The different features of this wife are now given. The first lines of the portrait describe her character as a wife. Her faithfulness, oneness of heart, and affectionate attention to duty make **her husband** have **full confidence in her**. Such was Luther's description of his wife: "The greatest gift of God is a pious amiable spouse who fears God and loves his house, and with whom one can live in perfect confidence." Isaac Walton's account of Bishop Sanderson's wife followed Solomon's pattern: "A wife who made his life happy, by being always content when he was cheerful; who was always cheerful when he was content; who divided her joys with him and abated his sorrow by bearing a part of that burden; a wife who demonstrated her affection by a cheerful obedience to all his desires during the whole course of his life."

The husband feels his wife's comfort as his burdens are relieved and his mind is spared many annoying problems. A faithful wife and a confiding husband thus mutually bless each other. With such a jewel for his wife, the husband has no misgivings. His home is the home of his heart. He does not need to look into the matters entrusted to her with suspicious eyes. We often hear about prudent management, but without the fear of God. But in this picture **she brings him good, not harm**.

Her husband's comfort is her interest and her rest. To live for him is her highest happiness. Even if all the detailed attention she gives to this object are not always noticed, she does not accuse her husband of indifference or unkindness. Nor does she pay back imagined neglect with sullenness.

13-27. She selects wool and flax and works with eager hands. She is like the merchant ships, bringing her food from afar. She gets up while it is still dark; she provides food for her family and portions for her servant girls. She considers a field and buys it; out of her earnings she plants a vineyard. She sets about her work vigorously; her arms are strong for her tasks. She sees that her trading is profitable, and her lamp does not go out at night. In her hand she holds the distaff and grasps the spindle with her fingers. She opens her arms to the poor and extends her hands to the needy. When it snows, she has no fear for her household; for all of them are clothed in scarlet. She makes coverings for her bed; she is clothed in fine linen and purple. Her husband is respected at the city gate, where he takes his seat among the elders of the land. She makes linen garments and sells them, and supplies the merchants with sashes. She is clothed with strength and dignity; she can laugh at the days to come. She speaks with wisdom, and faithful instruction is on her tongue. She watches over the affairs of her household and does not eat the bread of idleness.

This lovely character is drawn according to the ways of ancient times, although the general principles have universal application. It describes not only the wife of a man of rank, but a wise, useful, and godly woman in her domestic responsibilities. She is a Mary no less than a Martha. "It may be necessary to retouch the lines of the picture that have been obscured by length of years; in plain terms: to explain some parts of the description that relate to ancient manners and customs, and to show how they may be usefully applied to those of our own age and country" (Bishop Horne).

One thing, however, is most remarkable. The standard of godliness shown here is not that of a religious recluse shut up from active obligations under the pretense of greater consecration to God. Here are none of those habits of monastic asceticism that are now extolled as the highest point of Christian perfection. One half at least of the picture of this **wife of noble character** is taken up with her personal and domestic industry. What a rebuke this is to self-indulgent inactivity!

But let us look in detail at the features of the portrait in front of us. *Her personal habits are full of energy.* Manual labor, even menial service, in olden times was the work of women in the highest ranks. Self-denial is here a main principle. The woman of **noble character** goes before her servants in diligence no less than in dignity. Instead of being idle herself while they are working, she is not ashamed to work **the spindle with her fingers** (verse 19). Always alert for her husband's interests, **she considers a field and buys it** (verse 16) if it is a good buy.

We note again her behavior as mistress of her household. She builds her house with industry, self-denial, and heartiness. **She gets up while it is still dark,** not for the sake of being admired and talked about, but as one who **provides food for her family and portions for her servant girls** (verse 15). Nothing is neglected that belongs to order, sobriety, economy, or general management. She fully understands the exact work of each person in her care and their different abilities—when they need to be directed and when they may be left to their own responsibility.

Nor is her provident care limited to her own dependents. Her **spindle and distaff** are used not for herself or for her household only, but for **the poor** and **the needy** (verse 20). This godly woman does not only have the law of love in her heart, but **she speaks with wisdom** (verse 26). "She says nothing that is foolish, nothing that is ill-natured" (Bishop Horne). Hooker probably had this portrait in his mind when in his exquisite funeral sermon for his "virtuous gentlewoman" he enumerated "among so many virtues hearty devotion toward God; toward poverty, tender compassion; motherly affection toward servants; toward friends serviceable kindness; mild behavior and harmless meaning toward all." Bishop Taylor's finely drawn portrait of Lady Carbery is similar: "If we look on her as a wife, she was chaste and loving, discreet and humble. If we remember her as a mother, she was kind and severe [strict, scrupulous], careful and prudent, very tender; a greater lover of her children's souls than of their bodies. Her servants found her prudent and fit to govern, and yet openhanded and apt to reward, a great rewarder of their diligence." Mrs. Godolphin's biographer mentions her "employing herself in working for poor people, cutting out and making waistcoats and other necessary coverings, which she constantly distributed among them, like another Dorcas, spending much of her time, and no little money, in relieving, visiting, and inquiring after them."

This wife of noble character is indeed the **crown** of her husband (12:4). **Her husband is respected at the city gate, where he takes his seat among the elders of the land** (verse 23). Her husband is blessed with no ordinary treasures of happiness, "as indebted perhaps for his promotion to the wealth acquired by her management at home and, it may be, for the preservation and establishment of his virtue as to the encouragement furnished by her example and conversation" (Bishop Horne).

28-31. Her children arise and call her blessed; her husband also, and he praises her: "Many women do noble things, but you surpass them all." Charm is deceptive, and beauty is fleeting; but a woman who fears the LORD is to be praised. Give her the reward she has earned, and let her works bring her praise at the city gate. This wife of **noble character** is obviously subserving her own interest. For what greater earthly happiness could she know than that **her children arise and call her blessed** and that **her husband . . . praises her** (verse 28)? Her husband's attachment to her is well founded—not on deceitful and vain charms of beauty, but on one **who fears the LORD.** She is therefore in his eyes to the end, a support in his declining years. She soothes his cares, and she comforts him in sorrow. Both **her children** and **her husband** combine in grateful acknowledgment: **"Many women do noble things, but you surpass them all"** (verse 29).

If she has no herald to sound her praise, all will say, **Give her the reward she has earned, and let her works bring her praise at the city gate** (verse 31). "Let everyone," says Bishop Patrick, "extol her virtue. Let her not lack the just commendation of her pious labors. But while some are magnified for the nobleness of the stock from whence they sprung, others for their fortune, others for their beauty, others for other things, let the good deeds that she herself has done be publicly praised in the greatest assemblies, where, if all men should be silent, her own works will declare her excellent worth." All will see in her the light and luster of a sound and practical way of life, noting that the promises of godliness are the richest gain, the grace of God the best portion, and his favor the highest honor.

In conclusion, "if women," says pious Bishop Pilkington, "want to learn what God wants them to do and be occupied with, although they be of the best sort, let them read the last chapter of Proverbs. It is enough to note it and point it out to them who will learn." "That which is to be done," concludes Jermin, "is to mark it well, and let every woman strive to make it agree to herself as much as she can. Let every man be ashamed that any woman shall excel him in virtue and godliness."

"Thus," says pious Matthew Henry in his quaint style, "is shut up this looking-glass for ladies, which they are desired to open and dress themselves by; and if they do so, their adorning will be found to bring praise and honor and glory at the appearing of Jesus Christ."

Conclusion

We would conclude with a brief summary of a few prominent points involved in the study of this most instructive book.

Let us observe the connection between inward principle and outward conduct. Never let it be forgotten that the exercises here described or inculcated suppose an internal source. It is the light within that shines without. The hidden life is manifested in this way. Religion, grounded in the heart, will regulate the outward conduct and put everything in its proper place and proportion.

Let us mark also the flow of true happiness throughout the whole sphere of godliness. Often has the wise man painted this connection with the most glowing interest (3:13-18; 4:4-13; 8:17-21, 32-36). It is most important to leave the impression on everybody's mind, especially on young readers, that religion is a joyful thing. With the world it is a matter to be endured, not to be enjoyed. But no reality is more certain than this: Holiness is happiness. This happiness is not the mirth of the fool, but it is the only thing that deserves the name of happiness. It is the only permanent principle of enjoyment.

"Happy the believer," as the eloquent preacher Saurin forcibly puts it, "who in his warfare with the enemies of his salvation is able to oppose pleasure to pleasure, delight to delight; the pleasures of prayer and meditation to the pleasures of the world; the delights of silence and retirement to those of parties of dissipation or of public amusement. Such a man is steady and unmoved in the performance of his duties; and because he is a man, and man cannot help loving what opens to him sources of joy, such a man is attached to religion by motives like those that lead men of the world to attach themselves to the objects of their passions, because they procure him unspeakable pleasure." In fact, the world's contracted vision little qualifies them to pass judgment on what they have never understood. They see our infirmities, not our graces; our cross, not our crown; our affliction, not the joy of the Holy Spirit, which compensates and pays infinitely more than all that we can endure.

It is of great importance to note the wise man's estimate of real good.

Every particle of the chief good he centers on God. To find him is life (8:35). To fear him is wisdom (1:7). To trust him is happiness (16:20). To love him is substantial treasure (8:18-21). To neglect him is certain ruin (8:36). Man is naturally an idolater. He himself is the center, his object, his end. Instead of submitting to guidance, he guides himself. He disputes the sovereignty with God. He wants to change the laws of the great Lawgiver. But our true good is knowing God and being at peace with him. This privilege is worth ten thousand worlds. It satisfies us throughout eternity.

Let us study Christian completeness and consistency. The elements of this character will be brought out by a diligent and prayerful study of this important Book of Proverbs. We want religion to be to the soul what the soul is to the body—the animating principle. The soul operates in every part of the body. It sees in the eye, hears in the ear, speaks in the tongue, and animates the whole body with ease and uniformity, without ostentation or effort. Thus should religion direct and regulate every thought, word, and action. Never admit the maxims or habits of this world. Guard against everything that dampens vital spirituality, lowers the high scriptural standard, or slackens the energy of unremitting Christian watchfulness. Let our path be steadily balanced between compromising concession and needless singularity. Let the Christian only walk with God in the way of the Gospel. We must no more indulge an uncharitable spirit than a course of profligacy. An angry tone, glowering look, sharp retort, or disparaging word will cause grief to the conscience and will be visited by its rebuke as severely as those gross outbursts that disgrace our character before men. Walking before God in this way, not before men, is the path to Christian perfection (Genesis 17:1). God's eye is our restraint, his judgment our rule, his will our delight.

"Who is sufficient?" Child of God, let the trembling of insufficiency in yourself be stayed by the recollection of all-sufficiency in your God (2 Corinthians 2:16; 3:5; 12:9). What he demands from you, he works in you. His covenant secures your holiness no less than your acceptance— your holiness, not, as some would have it, as the *ground* but as the *fruit* of your acceptance. Let the one be primarily sought, and the other will assuredly follow.

"I will put my law in their minds and write it on their hearts. . . . For I will forgive their wickedness and will remember their sins no more" (Jeremiah 31:33-34).

led by the Spirit — Luke 4: mens 4

RAA RAA RAA RAA · Devil · Judas

+ 2x2 ↑ 40 Days · Acts 2 · The clash · Acts 5, Acts 6 · Act 15

Problem

Prov 28:9
mens 9:
Acts 15
mens 5:17
Rom

66 BOOKS
70% = one nation
Israel

The spirit of Jezebel
is Real.

Ps 68:6

If Life is flesh
and Blood - chain
Reaction.

2 Cor 5:17

Eph 5:37
wrinkle
spot

How
does
He Bible sees
me - As New
Creation —